The L

Medieval English Romances

Part One

General Editor A. V. C. Schmidt

Medieval English Romances

Part One

Medieval English Romances

Part One

Edited by A. V. C. Schmidt
Fellow of Balliol College, Oxford

and

Nicolas Jacobs
Fellow of Jesus College, Oxford

HODDER AND STOUGHTON
LONDON SYDNEY AUCKLAND TORONTO

In Memory of James Maxwell

Medieval English romances. – (London Medieval
    and Renaissance series).
    Part 1
    1. Romances, English   2. English poetry
    – Middle English, 1100–1500
    I.   Schmidt, Aubrey Vincent Carlyle
    II. Jacobs, Nicolas   III. Series 821'. 1'08   PR2064

ISBN 0 340 20031 6
ISBN 0 340 20032 4   Pbk.

First published in this edition 1980

Printed and bound in Great Britain for
Hodder and Stoughton Educational,
a division of Hodder and Stoughton Ltd,
Mill Road, Dunton Green, Sevenoaks, Kent,
by Hazell Watson & Viney Ltd,
Aylesbury, Bucks

Contents

Acknowledgments

We wish to express our thanks for permission to publish material in their possession, and in some cases for use of the library and for the provision of photographs, to the Master and Fellows of Gonville and Caius College, Cambridge; the Trustees of the National Library of Scotland; the Dean and Chapter of Lincoln Cathedral; the Feoffees of Chetham's Library, Manchester; the British Library Board; and the Bodleian Library, Oxford. We are most grateful to Mrs A. Merriman for typing part of the lexical notes and to Mrs M. Bügge for typing the Introduction, some of the lexical notes and the Commentary; to Mrs J. V. Schmidt for checking the drafts and helping with the correction of the proofs; and to the Winston Churchill Birthday Foundation for help towards expenses.

A.V.C.S.
N.J.

Oxford, 1977

Abbreviations

ME	Middle English
OE	Old English
OF	Old French
ON	Old Norse

These standard abbreviations are used for well-known learned journals and works of reference:

EETS	*Early English Text Society*
EGS	*English and Germanic Studies*
HMSO	Her Majesty's Stationery Office
MÆ	*Medium Ævum*
MED	*Middle English Dictionary*
MLN	*Modern Language Notes*
MP	*Modern Philology*
N & Q	*Notes and Queries*
OED	*Oxford English Dictionary*
PL	*Patrologia Latina*
PMLA	*Publications of the Modern Language Association of America*
RES	*Review of English Studies*
SP	*Studies in Philology*
Spec.	*Speculum*

Abbreviations used in the Commentary

AMA	*Alliterative Morte Arthure*
Ath.	*Athelston*
Fer.	*Sir Ferumbras*
Hav.	*Havelok*
Horn	*King Horn*
Ipom.	*Ipomadon*
MA	*Mort Artu*
PP	*Piers Plowman*
SD	*Sir Degarré*
SGGK	*Sir Gawain and the Green Knight*
SMA	*Stanzaic Morte Arthur*
SO	*Sir Orfeo*
YG	*Ywain and Gawain*
Yv.	*Yvain*

Introduction

Romance

The medieval English romances are stories in verse which deal with the adventures of noble men and women and which end happily. If the definition is vague, it goes as far as the evidence permits. It is hardly possible to 'characterise'[1] the romances more precisely, so miscellaneous is their character, and while they can be 'classified' according to their narrative material, length, verse-form or other prominent feature,[2] they exhibit so much variety that some critics have questioned whether it is possible to speak of a romance genre at all.[3] It cannot be maintained that 'fighting' or 'the marvellous', which are certainly common in romances, are universal and therefore defining features: the first is lacking in *Floris and Blancheflour* and *Athelston*, the second in *Ipomadon*. Love, the main theme of the latter work, plays an important part in French but a smaller part in English romance. The 'courtly' tone which makes it possible to distinguish the works of Chrétien de Troyes and his followers as a definite genre, the *roman courtois*, is found in the best single English romance, *Sir Gawain and the Green Knight*, but not in *Havelok*, which is arguably the second best. Indeed, 'tone' generally is not a good criterion for dividing the surviving English works, since most deal with their protagonists in a manner that tells us little that is certain of the audience they were intended for or of the social standing of the author. But if the opening definition is scrutinised closely it will be seen to yield enough information to enable a reader to tell a romance from other medieval narrative types and so to recognise within the great corpus of fictional narrative, which was the leading genre in medieval England, a genuine category to which the surviving specimens, for all their variety of subject, form and tone, may be safely assigned.

Many of the fifteenth-century examples (generally inferior) and all the thirteenth- and fourteenth-century ones are written in verse, prose romances being of negligible importance if we except the works of Malory. All the chief verse-forms of the English Middle Ages, the alliterative long line, the octosyllabic couplet, the tail-rhyme, were used in romances and are represented in this selection. The first two are widely found in other narrative types, such as the saint's legend (*St Erkenwald*, alliterative) and exemplum (*Handlyng Synne*, couplets), and the third, though used sporadically in other genres, was largely con-

Notes on the Introduction will be found between pages 29 and 33.

fined to romances. The special frequency of the octosyllabic (properly 'four-beat') couplet may be due to its being the regular metre of French romances, from which most of the English poems were adapted, but the form is found as early as *The Owl and the Nightingale* (twelfth century) and as late as Gower's *Confessio Amantis* (last decade of the fourteenth), and may be called the staple narrative metre of the age. Although the verse of the romances is often of great interest (see Introduction to *Sir Orfeo*, Part One, pp. 23–4 and to *Ipomadon* and the two *Mortes*, Part Two, pp. 40–49, 20–39), it was presumably taken for granted as the expected medium (the only *literary* prose of much merit before the fifteenth century being the prose of religious instruction). Prose narrative grew up with, though it was not actually begotten by, printing,[4] and there are no early English romances in prose to correspond to the great Vulgate Cycle of Arthurian romances in French. The English romances were inevitably in verse because they were designed in the first instance to be heard, a fact which accounts for many of their beauties as well as their faults.

The romances are almost totally fiction, even if the authors sometimes introduced a surprising amount of local 'realism' into their tales (as with the places and distances in *Athelston* (see stanzas 31–33, C)). 'Romance' seems to have been loosely contrasted with 'chronicle'; yet in the absence of a widespread critical standard for distinguishing fact from legend, the accretion of fictional episodes around a 'historical' core must have been an easy process, as can be seen if we compare the *Morte Arthure* with Laȝamon's *Brut*, one of its likely sources. 'Invention' consisted not so much in 'making up' incidents as in 'finding' them wherever the author could lay his hands on interesting (not necessarily 'suitable') material. This was the inevitable method of composition, since a medieval romance consisted of a basic plot generally amplified by episodic extension, whether its author was a humble anonymous redactor or a master like Chrétien de Troyes. Early English romances like *King Horn* seem to be pure narrative, story for story's sake; work of this kind is exemplified in *Sir Degarré*, and in many of the tales of Gower. But Chrétien had used his plot and episodes as a vehicle for serious and often subtle moral themes, and the structure of his poems, from his momentous *Erec et Enide* onwards, mediates their significance.[5] Many English romances are totally lacking in thematic significance, but the poems in this volume, mostly of the fourteenth century, demonstrate that Chrétien's approach had been thoroughly absorbed into the world of vernacular storytelling, in the first place through the discipline of translation from French originals. Translation could occasionally be pure rendering, e.g. *Landevale*, from Marie de France's

Lanval (see Part One, p. 22), but this procedure was exceptional, the rule being to *adapt* the original, abbreviating and expanding, sometimes from other sources, and often according to a definite artistic plan. Where the French original is at hand, as with *Ywain and Gawain*, *Le Morte Arthur* and *Ipomadon*, all interpretation must necessarily begin from a comparison of the English poem with its source, a procedure which is highly illuminating. But in these instances, however enterprising the English writer may be, he is not engaged in the same activity as a Chrétien drawing a 'bele conjointure' out of various narrative materials and imbuing it with an ethical 'sen'. In the absence of written sources of *Havelok* and *Sir Orfeo* (not to mention *Sir Gawain*), however, we remain free to see the authors of these poems as doing approximately the same sort of thing as Chrétien, the evidence being the presence in them of narrative threads drawn from several traditions as well as clear design and transparent ethical concerns. *Ywain and Gawain* also reveals considerable independence in the latter respect (see Part Two, p. 12); but its design is wholly Chrétien's and, far from being extended episodically, it is somewhat compressed and reduced.

The main plot of a typical romance, together with the episodes which amplify it, nearly always consists of adventures, the essence of which is not necessarily physical 'action' (though this is generally, even excessively, the case) so much as the occurrence of unexpected and hazardous events. A classic analysis of romantic adventure is provided by Erich Auerbach in *Mimesis*, where he examines the story of Calogrenant's experience at the fountain in *Ywain*.[6] It is hard to know whether the pattern revealed here is also a paradigm. Certainly, a very large number of later romances in French follow it, and these may be modelled on Chrétien's example. What is not clear is whether the pattern was already fully worked out in the 'stories of adventure' to which Chrétien refers at the beginning of *Erec*, a work which has claims to be the first proper romance.[7] If it was, then the element of adventure would seem to be necessary but not sufficient to account for the genre. For in spite of the disagreements that still exist about the meanings of Chrétien's terms 'conjointure' and 'sen', it appears certain that he saw in them a means of transforming a mere narrative of adventure into a work with a design or plan and a meaning or purpose or significance.[8] The 'basic pattern' consists of the attempts by a knight to test his prowess by undertaking feats of arms, not as a member of an army at war, as in the *chansons de geste* or classical epic, but as an individual seeking occasions for martial encounters. At its most unrealistic extreme, such adventure may be a fight with a monster. Examples chosen at random from medieval literature are Beowulf's fight with Grendel or Arthur's with the Giant of St Michael's Mount in the alliterative *Morte*. Neither of these poems is, however, a romance,[9] and it is probably significant that both fights, while they unquestionably test and prove the hero's prowess, are not primarily sought for that purpose but rather as a means to deliver afflicted people from oppression. In an episode such as that of Gawain's encounter with Priamus in the alliterative *Morte*, we see something closely approaching the pure romance-type combat as analysed by Auerbach (but see Part Two, p. 37).

However, it would be a mistake to see adventure-for-adventure's sake as the distinguishing feature of romance; at any rate, it would be a misleading simplification of the matter. Even sophisticated storytellers have been aware of the appeal of pure narrative incident to the simpler members of their audience or, for that matter, to the more sophisticated in certain moods, and Chrétien, though distinguishing his work from that of the *conteurs*, must have recognised that at one level he was appealing to the same tastes as they were. But over and above this secondary, 'tactical' purpose, he had a main, 'strategic' purpose, which was to transform adventure from mere incident into meaningful human action.[10] So far-reaching is this purpose that it goes some way to accounting for the bi-partite structure of *Erec* and *Yvain*.[11] In *Erec*, the adventure of the sparrow-hawk with which the poem begins serves to establish the hero's prowess, while the later series of adventures after his marriage to Enide, culminating in the combat with Mabonagrain (the adventure of the 'Joy of the Court'), serves as a means for Chrétien to bring out the proper relation that should exist for a knight between chivalry and love. *Yvain*, in some ways a re-handling of *Erec*, goes a step further in that it offers a conscious and deliberate revaluation of adventure as such. Not only is the initial adventure of the combat at the fountain told twice (Calogrenant's defeat, Yvain's victory) so as to distinguish two grades of adventure-for-adventure's sake, the second combat being more strongly motivated than the first; the rest of the poem provides us with what is virtually a second hero (the Knight of the Lion) whose adventures consist of acts of altruistic chivalry the effect of which is to question the earlier act, a martial victory with no ethical content.[12] In *Sir Gawain and the Green Knight*, physical action is not eliminated, but its significance is minimised: the adventure still consists in a test of the hero, but since it is a test of his integrity, the inter-dependence of his various virtues, rather than specifically of his prowess, there is no need for physical combat as the inevitable medium of the test. Indeed, the poet goes out of his way to imply that success in physical trial is no kind of guarantee of success in the higher and subtler kinds of testing.[13]

In *Sir Gawain* the stress is on the moral significance of the hero's action, and the poem can be considered a criticism of romance inasmuch as it implies indirectly, through presenting right action as something difficult even for a paragon, that conventional romances are shallow and naive in their assumption of the hero's invincibility and in their assimilation of moral problems to problems of prowess. The test imposed on the hero of *Sir Gawain* is a Gordian one—and it seems clear that an Alexandrian solution (e.g. a purely chivalric second encounter with the Green Knight) could not lead to success. 'Success' for Sir Gawain requires knowledge not only of the chivalric code but also of his own nature and its limitations. Generally speaking, however, romances do not emphasise the limitations of the hero but his strengths: he is invariably 'noble', both in the social sense and in the sense of embodying an ideal of behaviour. It is certainly true that this latter feature necessitates a measure of sameness in the heroes, especially since most of them are knights (though the instances of Havelok and Orfeo reveal the variety possible within the genre). The principal novelty of a romance thus resides in its plot. These are often hackneyed enough in the case of average run-of-the-mill composers such as Thomas Chestre. But the romances of Chrétien show great inventiveness and narrative resource, as does *Sir Gawain*, which is a triumph of suspense as well as tension. Nevertheless, a secondary source of variety is undoubtedly the heroines, whose adventures also form the substance of the narrative and whose attitudes and acts not only determine the progress of the hero but also affect the tone and colouring of the whole work.[14] The diversity of relationships between men and women which the romances make possible is amply illustrated by the poems in these volumes; the extremes are perhaps those of Orfeo and Heurodis on the one hand and Ywain and Alundyne on the other.

The delineation and definition of noble qualities is a pervasive concern in romances,[15] though their authors rarely attempt an analysis as comprehensive and profound as that of the *Gawain*-poet. More often they concentrate on particular aspects of the ideal of nobility, commonly seeking the ethical dimension or justifying moral significance of chivalric prowess. The course of a romance is thus as often an education for the hero as an illustration of already achieved excellence. This pattern is clearest in *Sir Degarré* and in *Ywain and Gawain*. In *Havelok*, nobility of the highest kind—that of a king—is seen to be more than a matter of birth and prowess; it is a recognition that to rule a man must be able to serve. In *Ipomadon* the aspect of nobility under particular scrutiny is courtesy, especially in its sense of refined intercourse between men and women in social life, including what we would have to

call by the inadequate term 'etiquette'. Frequently in romance behaviour in this sense can become the vehicle or occasion for momentous ethical trials, the rationale being the hypothesis that a man's true
nature is manifested in the least of his acts. Whatever the limitations of
this hypothesis from the point of view either of ethics or of novelistic
psychology, its dramatic potential is considerable. The love-looking of
the young hero in *Ipomadon*, trivial as it may seem in itself, serves to
focus the reader's attention on the intense idealism that informed the
chivalric aspiration,[16] an idealism that envisaged as its termini not
success and failure but perfection and shame. Paradoxically, however,
the romances show the chivalric ideal to be *more* flexible in some ways
than mundane pragmatism. For whilst perfection can be lost, shame
can be redeemed: the hero of a romance does not become a hero
through his success or cease to be one through his failure.[17] Unlike a
tragic hero, such as Othello, a hero of romance never ceases to be noble.
His fault may be ostensibly trivial, as in *Ipomadon;* or it may be insult-
ingly gross, as in *Ywain and Gwain*; but the 'noble substance' is not (in
Hamlet's phrase) 'adoubted'. It is because the evil in the hero's soul
is capable of being purged that his story inevitably ends happily.

The achievement of happiness in the romances is attended, almost
invariably, by suffering. If the structure of a romance is comic, it is
comedy in Dante's sense, and the hero generally has to go through a
purgatory of 'loneliness and pain' before reaching the heaven of true
(earthly) happiness. The latter most commonly consists of union or re-
conciliation with the beloved, as in *Ywain* and *Ipomadon* and, in a more
unusual manner, *Orfeo* (unusual in that the hero has not lost the heroine through his own fault). But the endings of *Athelston* and *Havelok*
make it clear that the establishment of justice as well as the union of
loved ones can be a major cause for rejoicing and universal happiness.
The suffering in a romance normally tests the temper of the hero's
spirit, the capacity to face and overcome his weaknesses and imper-
fections in which the true essence of a knight's virtue consists. The
greater the weaknesses, the more far-reaching the evil consequences,
which in the *Morte Arthur* include suffering on a grand scale for the
innocent even more than the guilty. This poem stands at the outermost
boundary of romance, and the happiness won by its hero and heroine
is correspondingly singular: renunciation of erotic fulfilment in recognition of their responsibility for evil. But the work remains, narrowly yet
decisively, a true romance, whereas the alliterative *Morte* is a tragedy.[18]
And it is in the genre of tragedy that we should seek the complementary
form and illuminating antithesis to romance. So valuable is a comparison of the two English poems on the death of Arthur for appreciating

the differences between the two genres that it has seemed worthwhile to discuss the alliterative *Morte* at some length (see Part Two, pp. 29–39), even though the extract from it in this volume is not representative of the whole. In the alliterative *Morte* chivalric heroism is treated in depth from a tragic point of view; similarly, in *Troilus and Criseyde*, we are given a tragic treatment of the hero's love, Chaucer having deliberately chosen *not* 'to write/The armes of this ilke worthy man' (V 1765–6). *Ipomadon*, almost the same length, is perhaps the only English romance of love that can be usefully compared with the *tragedie* of *Troilus*.

Havelok

The Life of Havelok appears, along with a text of *King Horn* in the same hand, in a manuscript in which the two romances are preceded and followed by a number of saints' lives. The naming of the hero as a former king of England would suggest that *Havelok* had been linked with *Horn* as a poem on a subject drawn from English (legendary) history; but the term *Vita* indicates more particularly an attempt (whether that of the author, the scribe or the collector) to link the poem with the Saint's Life, a genre for which the usual name was *Vita*.[19] The Saint's Life or Legend had a twofold purpose, to praise God by showing His marvellous works in the lives of chosen individuals, and to assure the audience that God's omnipresence often took the specific form of intervention in the lives of men, now loving, now vengeful. *Athelston* is pious and exemplary in this way, the outcome of the ordeal serving to vindicate Egelan's innocence and to endorse the Archbishop's authority in one and the same dramatic incident. But the poem could not aptly be titled the *Vita* of Athelston, since it does not concern his life from childhood to death and is exemplary only in a negative and partial sense, whereas *Havelok* gives a positive model of a divinely favoured individual in whose life God intervenes not on one but on several occasions.

If the Latin title is possibly non-scribal in origin, the term *gest*, used twice in the poem, is unquestionably to be attributed to the author, who apparently contrasts it with *romanz* in 2332–4 (see Commentary). *Gest(e)* is a term favoured by writers of long alliterative poems,[20] often of a markedly heroic and even tragic kind, but it is far from clear what, if anything, the *Havelok*-poet might have intended by using it. Nonetheless, even if there is no authority for doing so, it may be useful to apply the term *gest* to poems such as *Havelok* or *Athelston*, which seem at times closer to Old English heroic poetry than to polished courtly romances of the *Ipomadon* type. (Havelok certainly resembles Beowulf in being *manna mildust* 'the kindest of men', though not, admittedly, *lof-geornost* 'most eager for renown'. For, unlike the Old English hero, Havelok has a humility which links him more with the saint-figure, a fact which would explain why the poem might appeal to a clerical collector of Saints' legends.)[21]

The divinity that hedges Havelok's person (and manifests itself most spectacularly in the fiery light that issues from his mouth when he sleeps) superficially resembles what one might call the commonplace marvellous of romance.[22] But the light, and the wonderful birthmark also, are better viewed as *signs* attesting God's active involvement in the affairs of men. Kingship is depicted as sacred not for any abstruse philosophical reason but simply because God really is seen to protect His legitimate representative, when the latter is good and just, even as in *Athelston* He chastises him when he is unjust. Another and more striking point at which *Havelok* seems to diverge from the typical romance is in its treatment of chivalry and courtesy, the dominant concepts in the genre as developed in France. *Havelok* is plainly a 'non-courtly' poem, though this does not necessarily make it 'popular' in the sense intended by Bliss when he remarks that it 'tells its story entirely in terms of the experience and desires of its peasant audience . . . the inarticulate lower classes, whose ideas and aspirations are scarcely represented elsewhere in medieval literature'.[23] These peasants would presumably be the 'Wyves, maydnes, and alle men' addressed in the opening lines. The minstrel-author asking for 'a cuppe of ful good ale' is presumably to be envisaged as delivering his poem in a tavern. This was scarcely the only place where good ale could be had[24] and the lines could indicate equally an aristocratic household after dinner, the poet asking for the evening's entertainment to be opened in the traditional festive manner.[25] The author may well have been a clerk of humble origins, but however much 'lewed folk' might have enjoyed his work,[26] there is little proof that he was writing specifically for them, or even from their standpoint. Clerical authorship, however, would account not only for the earnest tone and pronounced *interest* in the life of the non-courtly classes, but also the lack of emphasis on the courtly-chivalric ethos dominant in romances deriving from French sources.[27]

This is not to deny that the *Havelok*-poet is familiar with the language of courtly love. Thus, he uses the semi-technical *love-drurye* in rhyme with *curtesye* in a passage describing the education Athelwold's barons swear to give his daughter (195–7). But for all his awareness of these courtly qualities, he is not concerned to exemplify them in action.

The description of Grim's daughter Levive is equally laconic: 'Hire semes curteys for to be'. Again, while the happy love between Havelok and Goldeburh is described in conventionally idealistic terms (2966ff.), the reference to their 'sones and douhtres riht fivetene', each of whom becomes a king or queen, is significant because it serves to recapitulate the main theme of the poem, which, as argued below, is kingship.

Lack of direct interest in the courtly conception of love and in the details of feeling and behaviour[28] is paralleled by an absence of detailed descriptions of the courtly scenes and milieux in comparison with the humble ones, a fact which leads Schelp also[29] to call *Havelok* 'popular' rather than 'courtly'. But it is always risky to argue from the *content* of a poem to its audience or its author. The *style* of the poem seemed to Creek to indicate a popular origin, but colloquial features such as the similes, proverbs, curses and interjections he considered[30] can also be found in so thoroughly courtly an author as Chaucer. 'Low' elements, even if these were a mark of popular origin, are totally absent,[31] as are the rough boisterous comedy of works such as *Gamelyn* or *The Tournament of Tottenham*, and the provocative and challenging attitude found in pieces dealing with the encounters between working men and kings such as *Rauf Coilȝear* and *King Edward and the Shepherd*.[32] The outlook of the *Havelok*-poet, by contrast, is one of idealistic aspiration tempered with realistic observation and informed by a passionate moral seriousness.

Chivalry, it is true, figures more prominently in the poem than *courtoisie*. Thus we have the dubbing of a man as knight for his prowess (2314–5). But it is less the presence of knightly practices and customs as such than the total attitude to the conception that is important (see below). Ubbe thinks Havelok worthy to be a knight merely from observing the signs of potential prowess in him. Strength was the prime requisite for prowess, which was itself the prime quality of a knight. But noble birth was also necessary, and it is not till Ubbe has determined the young hero's identity that he actually dubs him knight. (Havelok's prowess, displayed in the highly realistic fight with the brigands, is to be understood as having been inherited from Birkabeyn, 'þe beste knicht' (347), as is that of the young and untrained Degarré from his fairy father; see Part Two, p. 8.) So highly, indeed, is chivalry valued in the poem that Havelok can offer the usurper Godrich an amnesty just because he is 'of [his] bodi so god kniht' (2721). Partly, no doubt, he does this because the value of such a man as a vassal would be far greater than his value as a corpse, but also because to kill a heroic enemy is not so noble as to make him your friend. Godrich's refusal of this offer is not only an error which proves fatal for him; it is, though seemingly heroic in the defiant manner of Germanic epic, fundamentally unknightly. For one important quality of the good knight, a quality both moral and intellectual, was *sagesse*—wisdom or prudence, which enabled a knight to accept defeat from a better man.[33] Godrich's courage proves self-destructive because impelled by pride: he has not only misjudged Havelok's prowess (a perhaps purely tactical error); he has also forgotten that courage without justice is doomed to fail.

That, at any rate, is how events turn out in the world of this romance, which is to some extent an ideal world. Nonetheless, so highly esteemed is the chivalry found in the villain Godrich that even after defeat he is offered proper trial as a knight by his magnanimous captor and is not actually put to shame until found guilty by law. In his life, Godrich serves as a foil to the hero—he is brave and strong, but not true, gentle or just; in his death, he offers a minor but significant contrast to his rival in villainy with the like-sounding name. For Godrich's *end* is far less horrific than that of Godard, whom the poet clearly regards as the greater villain, not only a more wicked criminal, but a coward too. Godrich may be a usurper, but he is not, like Godard, a murderer.

For all the importance attached to chivalric prowess in a knight, it remains the case that the attitude to chivalry differentiates *Havelok* from such works as *Sir Degarré*, *Ipomadon* and the Arthurian poems in this book. Nowhere is the life of knighthood seen as a quest for self-realization through adventure (see Part Two, pp. 9, 15). The typical questing knight of romance lives only in response to challenges that will actively test his innermost quality as a chivalric hero, whether in tournament or joust or any other form in which adventure comes to him. The essence of *aventure*, as the very name seems to imply, is the taking of risks, the exposing of oneself to dangers, hardships and trials, foreseen or unforeseen. Havelok is much less like the Gawain of the alliterative *Morte Arthure* in his encounter with Priamus (see Part Two, pp. 37–8) than he is like Arthur himself in his fight with the Giant. More generally, he recalls the epic hero of a type less 'romantic' even than Beowulf (who, after all, sails to Denmark to *seek* the monster Grendel, of whom he has heard), the type we find preserved in a story such as that of *Waldere*. His fights are dictated by dire necessity, whether that of self-preservation or the recovery of his and his wife's rightful kingdoms. (Even Beowulf, though his cause is a similar one—to restore their just rights to the Danes harassed by a monster—lacks Havelok's practical involvement and personal ground for action and is more like the *héros libérateur* such as Chrétien's Lancelot in the *Chevalier de la Charrette*, if not the hero of *Yvain* in the fountain adventure.) Arguably,

Havelok's freedom from conventional romance motivation makes him more credible and his ideal features more readily acceptable. More certainly, knighthood is seen by his creator as necessary to a king, because in a world such as his hero moves in, knightly courage and skill are essential for survival.

The absence from *Havelok* of concern with courtly-chivalric issues is a negative feature of the poem which is compensated by the poet's very positive preoccupation with the quality of *royalty*, which can be fairly regarded as the theme of the work. The heroes of many romances are the heirs of kings, and such poems often end with a coronation. *Havelok* follows this pattern, but in it the idea of royalty becomes the focus for analysis and illustration, and a support for the whole fabric, not merely an ornamental flourish. *Havelok* opens with a portrait of the just king,[34] notable both for its length and its prominent position, which raises an expectation that the poem is not going to deal with love or with adventure for its own sake, or even primarily with an aspect of the chivalric ethic such as *troupe*, but with the nature, perhaps even the *art*, of being a king. In the case of Havelok's father, the poet does not merely repeat his praise of Athelwold, but he does remind us at a later point in the work, in the dramatic scene of Ubbe's recognition of the hero, that

> ... he was Birkabeynes sone
> Þat was here king, þat was hem wone
> Wel to yeme, and wel were ...

(2155-7)

The allusion to the role of the king as leader and protector of his people, an aspect less strongly emphasised in the lines on Athelwold, is one which is to be authoritatively exemplified in Havelok himself. If justice is to prevail it must be backed by force, and that requires a king who shall be a hero.

The recognition of Havelok's royalty assumes concrete form in the manifestations which, like the outcome of the ordeal in *Athelston*, testify to God's active presence in the world.[35] The supernatural light which Ubbe sees and which leads him and the Danes to acknowledge Havelok as the true heir, also appears on two other important occasions in the poem. In Grim's cottage in Denmark, it saves the young hero's life; in Grim's house in England, it reveals to Goldeburh the royalty of her husband and proves that she has not suffered 'disparagement' by the marriage. The supernatural signs have two functions: they show that Havelok is a king supported by God's authority who will eventually and inevitably triumph, and they affirm that he is a good man (the light) and a true Christian (the cross). The cross on Havelok's shoulder is admittedly interpreted by Ubbe as a symbol of royalty, a point explicitly made by the angel on the previous occasion. But while the cross had been the ancient Germanic emblem of rule, the pagan device had long ceased to have a significance completely separate from its meaning as the *general* symbol of the Christian faith and one *especially* appropriate to Christian rulers consecrated by the Church. There seems therefore little doubt that in the poem Havelok is an idealised embodiment of the 'Davidic' king whose image had first been revived as early as the time of Charlemagne.[36] (Direct divine support of the hero is of course found as early as *Beowulf*; but in the later Middle Ages it is confined to the protagonists of saints' legends until the rise of the Grail theme and the specifically religious conception of a 'spiritual' chivalry in the thirteenth century.)

The secondary themes of the poem are loyalty and treachery, which are generally widespread in romance, especially in the fourteenth century (see pp. 26–8 below). Throughout the action, an important part is played by oaths and promises, and a sharp contrast is drawn between those who keep and those who break their solemnly pledged word. Just as the main focus of the principal theme of kingship is Havelok himself, so the secondary themes are examined mainly in the persons of the important secondary figures. Perhaps partly for this reason, the keeping of *troupe* is not, as in romances where it is the hero's own *troupe* that is at issue, primarily a test of personal integrity. The oath is seen as functional, an invocation of God into the affairs of men so as to seal and ratify the order of human society, rather than an affirmation of a personal commitment. Athelwold and Birkabeyn make their regents solemnly swear to execute their wills and the latter are nominated collectively by the nobles, who believe them to be loyal (*trewe*). To emphasise the depth of their treachery, the poet brands both with the names of the arch-traitors Judas and Sathanas—although the 'Judas' title perhaps applies more aptly to Godard who, like Wymound in *Athelston*, is 'þe kinges oune frende' (375). The poet's intense detestation of *swykes* emerges in his vigorous denunciation of the false Godard (421ff., 447). Like Shakespeare in *King Lear*, the *Havelok*-poet uses a double plot to emphasise a single theme, thereby intensifying the antithesis of loyalty and treachery. But because the action is of the sophisticated parallel rather than the primitive repeating type as in *King Horn*, not only is monotony avoided, suspense of a kind is also maintained.[37] Desire to avoid monotony may also lie behind the discrimination of the two villains' characters, the unusually balanced portrait of Godrich even suggesting, in Judith Weiss's words, 'the insidious corruption by power of an originally good man'.[38]

Whereas a short, concentrated poem like *Athelston* emphasises the treachery of Wymound while leaving the loyalty of the good earl Egelan to be inferred (see below, p. 20), the more expansive *Havelok* affords an opportunity to depict the virtue of loyalty in the characters (principally) of Grim and Ubbe. All the 'trew' characters, as it happens, are Danes: Bernard Brun and the sons of Grim have no parallels among the English, although a good-hearted character like Bertram the cook may have a small part to play. A further contrast between Danes and English appears when the two parallel movements of the story reach their respective climaxes: Havelok on his return to Denmark receives the homage of the Danes enthusiastically and without question, whereas Goldeburh finds that the English (admittedly incited by Godrich's lies) oppose their rightful queen and later have to beg a pardon from her. It is difficult to read any precise significance into this contrast, although one may be reminded of Malory's famous attack on the English for their lack of stability and loyalty.[39] It is hard to discern a directly topical motive in the poem like that now widely recognised in the Old English *Battle of Maldon*.

The author of *Havelok* is an idealist, and his idealism is at the basis of his plot-construction. His use of parallel plots unified by the active endeavour of the hero enables him to contrast the state of England under the good Athelwold with that of Denmark under the evil Godard: in Athelwold's England there are no thieves and robbers, while in Godard's Denmark brigands range at will (cf. the comment on Henry I's reign in the *Peterborough Chronicle* for 1135). To achieve a purely mechanical symmetry, the poet would have needed to show England and Denmark before and after the death of its respective good king. But by avoiding repetition and allowing the two parts of his story to supplement each other, he achieves economy of narrative without loss of thematic significance. The powerful antithesis between a people living in fear and one living in peace and concord is not diluted either by repetition or by episodic amplification.

Whereas the tendency to idealisation in romances often puts a strain on our credulity, the *Havelok*-poet is sober and unsensational in his treatment of the hero and the marvellous manifestations of which he is the almost unwitting focus. The angelic voice and fiery light act more as symbols than pieces of supernatural machinery designed to excite wonder. One might go so far as to say that the prevailing mode of the poem is a realistic one. Even the towering prowess of the hero in the night-fight with the thieves is tempered by a sense of actuality: Havelok is badly hurt, just as in the brief and unextended affray with the doughty Godrich he receives wounds and does not win without effort.

Such details help to humanise Havelok and to enhance our sense of the mysterious numinousness of the divine providence, which would be compromised by the hero's possession of an *invulnerability* such as Degarré, for instance, seems to display. For the *Havelok*-poet *invincibility* is quite enough; his hero's path to greatness, though sure, is beset with obstacles and suffering.

Part of this suffering, of course, is humiliation through poverty, a circumstance which provides the occasion for the poet's most celebrated exercise in realism, the account of Havelok's life as a working man (737ff.). This section is not the less enjoyable for standing in such marked contrast to the numerous descriptions of aristocratic life that stud the French romances and poems adapted from them, especially those of the alliterative tradition. But the realism does not exist as an end in itself; it fulfils a definite function in the poem as a whole, being a highly original variation on the theme of the education of the hero. Whereas in *Sir Degarré* we are given a somewhat unusual preparation of the hero for *knighthood*, in *Havelok* the discipline of kitchen and market-place is a preparation for *kingship*. Havelok learns to serve in order that he might 'yeme' and 'were', for in doing so he comes to know the people and so acquire the humility which will prevent him from ever becoming a tyrant. Whereas in Chrétien's *Perceval* the hero, who is brought up alone by his mother in isolation from courtly civilisation, acts like a boor when confronted with situations demanding tact, Havelok among the servants displays a natural courtesy all the more remarkable for not having been learned. It would be a mistake, however, to assume that this quality is merely a conventional tribute to the hero's royalty of nature: not the least striking feature of the 'kitchen' scenes is the unsupercilious treatment of the common people.

Through combining in himself the attributes of humility,[40] gentleness and strength, Havelok unites the virtues of both Athelwold and Birkabeyn, and so becomes the ideal king. Not that he is lacking in piety, as his prayer at 1363ff. reveals. He rewards his friends, from the Cook to Ubbe, with truly royal generosity and either pardons his adversaries (the English who oppose him and Goldeburh) or punishes them by due process of law (Godrich). Finally he is, as the ideal *rex justus* had to be, a peacemaker. Yet throughout, his engaging humanity prevents him from seeming, like so many romance heroes, a mere type or else too good to be true.

Havelok is written in a lively, energetic style that rarely flags or descends into bathos. If the style is less memorable than the characterisation, the atmosphere, the construction of the plot and the development of the main themes, this may simply be because the poet's purpose is to convey certain moral truths with maximum force and immediacy. He has accordingly used, like the poet of *Athelston*, a language as free from the lavish descriptive vocabulary characteristic of the later alliterative poets as from the ornately figured rhetoric of the near-contemporary *Kyng Alysaunder*.[41] Whether the fact that he was working on traditional oral material rather than a finished literary source has anything to do with the quality of his style remains a matter for conjecture. *Havelok* is surely a 'popular' poem in the sense that anyone could enjoy it.

Athelston

Athelston is a poem characterised by (in Dr F. R. Leavis's famous phrase) 'a marked moral intensity'. 'There are few Middle English tales,' observes Dieter Mehl, 'which are governed by human passions to this extent and are so full of dramatic tension from beginning to end.'[42] This is a sounder judgment than that of its most recent editor, Trounce: 'a highly interesting poem, but an uneven one, which provokes interest rather than satisfies it'.[43] Much of Trounce's interest was aroused by the elements of English custom and history in the poem (which he nonetheless believed to have had a French original)—the ordeal, sworn-brotherhood, and so on.[44] But the importance of these elements for the reader who is primarily interested in *Athelston* as a work of art is the way in which they are skilfully deployed to handle the poem's main themes of justice and truth (with its obverse, 'untruth'). These two concepts are related to the religious and human values in the poem in a way recalling *Havelok*, which Mehl has shrewdly compared with *Athelston*. The historical and literary interest of the work are quite distinct. Perhaps belief in trial by ordeal provokes rather than satisfies a reader's interest; but thematically, the miraculous reward granted to faith in God as the ultimate judge, revealer of secrets and protector of the innocent, must amply satisfy an audience capable of sharing the poet's convictions, or at least of entering into his way of thinking.

The poem's religion is, in fact, remarkably free from grossness and sensationalism, and this makes the miracles easier to accept. The many Biblical echoes also serve to strengthen the moral impact of the story (though Mehl overstates this point in calling *Athelston* 'a homiletic romance', as if teaching a lesson were its *prime* aim).[45] A good example of the force of Biblical suggestiveness[46] is the description of the children in the fire:

> Þanne þe chyldryn stood and lowȝ:
> 'Sere, þe fyr is cold inowȝ'.
> Þorwȝ-out þey wente a-pase.
> Þey weren unblemeschyd, foot and hand;
> Þat sawȝ þe lordys off þe land,
> And þankyd God off his grace.   (57)

The phrase 'unblemished, foot and hand' is used in each of the three trials, and of course means 'uninjured'; but its overtones cannot be missed. The Earl and Countess and their children are uninjured *because* unblemished by the treachery they are accused of. To the innocent, the poet shows, God's elements are not hostile but friendly.[47] The variety with which the fire is presented does credit to the poet: it is 'bright' when the Earl is stripped; 'hydous and red' to the children (though guiltless, they swoon, like the Isaac of the Miracle Plays, through natural weakness, not lack of faith); but for the most important character, the mother of the future St Edmund, the fire is 'fayr and lyȝt'. The imagery of light is deftly used. When the messenger brings Wymound the false news that his male victims are dead and the Countess imprisoned, he says with feigned relish:

> 'Schal sche nevere more out come,
> Ne see neyþer sunne ne mone.'   (67.11f.)

In our enjoyment of the ironic situation in which Wymound has now become the victim—of a higher cunning than his own—we may overlook the image of a deep and solitary dungeon evoked by line 12 and so miss the grim appropriateness of the later lines describing how the *traitor* encounters the fire of the *judicium Dei*, which to Edyff had seemed 'merry and bright':

> ... doun he ffel þe ffyr a-mydde—
> *Hys eyen wolde hym nouȝt lede*   (73.11f.)

The attempt of this 'devyl off helle' (13.12) to destroy the innocent is not only thwarted, it becomes an occasion to manifest the power and love of God. Unobtrusive and quasi-symbolic as its operation is, religion plays a major role in the story.

Against the divine justice which operates through the agency of the Archbishop (it is he who 'involves' God in the action by instigating the ordeal) is set the cruel injustice of the titular hero. For, like Leontes in *The Winter's Tale*, it is Athelston who stands at the centre of this tragi-comedy, with his blind 'affection' (as Shakespeare calls it) whose 'intention stabs the centre' and 'makes possible things not so held' (I.ii.139). From the disclosure of Wymound's *counsayl* to the arrival of the Archbishop halfway through the poem, Athelston is dominated by a mad urge to destroy. Compounded of fear and hatred, it is, of course, as much a basic *donnée* of the poem as the jealousy of Shakespeare's Leontes; but it would be wrong to see the interest of Athelston's 'case' as purely moral and in no way psychological. The actual situation it-self is more like that in *Othello*—for the King has the fatal suggestion put into his mind by a trusty friend who, like Iago, is suffering from wounded pride (as well as having other motives). Yet no more than in the case of Othello can Athelston's evil act be extenuated by Wym-ound's villainy, since the King not only refuses to assume Egelan inno-cent until proof is forthcoming—and he has no more reason to believe Wymound than the latter—he sets out singlemindedly to liquidate him and his family. In Athelston we have the portrait of a tyrant, an unjust king less like Havelok than the villainous Godrich.

The presentation of Athelston betrays a certain ambiguity, however, as is clear from two crucial speeches that reveal the role of Providence in deciding the King's course of action. The first of these is his prayer in the church (39.4–12). The tone of Athelston's words here is not self-evidently *blasphemous*. For though he has only a short while ago brutally killed the child in his wife's womb (without any comment being elicited from the narrator),[48] it would be anachronistic to maintain that a medieval audience *must* have regarded Athelston as a conscious hypocrite. While recognising the King to be in error, they would not necessarily have judged him harshly. Further, they would probably not have thought his treatment of the Queen unjustified if Egelan *had* been guilty and the Queen had been intervening, *however unwittingly*, on a traitor's behalf. Athelston's prayer should perhaps be regarded not as consciously insincere (like that of Claudius in *Hamlet*)[49] but as in the nature of a rhetorical *plea* of self-justification and at the same time a kind of *challenge* to God to prove him wrong. It is less important whether Athelston 'really believes' Wymound's story than that he accepts it and acts upon it. His speech is tragically inviting nemesis, since in his blindness he cannot see that if God's justice is to be shown on 'hem . . ./þat garte hem þere to dwelle' this means not only Wymound but also himself. Nonetheless, Athelston is saved from tragedy, like the tyrant Nebuchadnezzar in Chaucer's *Monk's Tale*,[50] and receives, inasmuch as he acted from folly more than deliberate malice, not only divine justice but divine mercy also. Yet this mercy operates in a wondrously ironic fashion, as the lines quoted above delicately reveal; for while Athelston escapes death himself and only

loses his heir, the consequence is that he will be succeeded by the son
of the man he tried to destroy as a traitor. The evidence that God's
mercy has changed Athelston, and so made him capable of the audience's own indulgence, is that he willingly grants the kingdom to the
child of Egelan the moment the miracle is accomplished (62.10f.),
drawing from the narrator an exclamation which affirms that 'wo' has
turned to 'wele':

Now i-blessyd be þat stounde!

But what is the 'folly' of the King that causes him to destroy? The
second speech (43) reveals the king as 'wroþ' and 'wod'; but the poet is
not attempting to excuse Athelston, who is really no madder than Lear
when he rejects Cordelia. Wrath, the sin of blind, murderous anger, is
what drives him to swear destruction, with pagan oaths 'be sunne and
mone', not envy (however thinly disguised) but a pure evil which is
mysterious and opaque. For while Wymound can claim—with however little justice—'He lovyd hym to mekyl and me to lyte', the King
is given no 'motive' for acting as he does. This is a disquieting but
dramatic force in the poem. We see in Athelston the tyrant the usual
corruption of power—he is only the nephew of a king who died without
issue, not a king's son himself, and, for all his kingly generosity to his
messenger brothers, is revealed by his actions as profoundly insecure.[51]
We had learned in 4.9 that Egelan was 'A man of gret renoun', and
this could provide a cause for Athelston's sudden switch from intimate
affection to unreasoning hatred (the 'cases' of Shakespeare's Othello
and Leontes show what an explosive mixture forms in the psyche when
love and resentment towards a friend co-exist and the conscious ego is
compelled to suppress emotions that do not flatter its idealised conception of itself). Athelston *is* generous towards Egelan, giving him his
own sister 'With gret devocyoun' (4.12). Such prior generosity would of
course account for Athelston's rage on thinking it betrayed, but his
readiness so to think still remains unexplained. (The fact that Egelan's
wife is of the blood royal, however, neatly ensures that when Edmund
is born he will prove an acceptable successor: God's mills grind fine
and Athelston's loss is England's gain.)

An interest in the psychology of characters in a medieval romance is
no mere anachronistic whimsy, provided it is subjected to the guidance
of the text and not some all-embracing theory. The poet's approach
may not be analytical, but he undoubtedly shows psychological insight, the fruit of experience rather than the learning displayed by a
Chaucer, say, in recounting the dreams of Criseyede and of Troilus.[52]
This insight is shown, for instance, in the lines describing Athelston's

reaction to Wymound's news that he has something secret to impart to him:

> Þe kyngys herte þan was ful woo
> Wiþ þat traytour for to goo   (11.7f.)

Are we to take this as meaning that Athelston *knows* Wymound to be a traitor, or that he fears to hear from him what he does in fact hear? Obviously the latter, one would think; but the poet does not settle the matter for us: he does not explain. The poet, for all his intense partisanship, is like the author of *Havelok* in leaving not only the working of Providence but also the genesis of evil in the human heart a mystery. His approach is not rational, like that of Chrétien de Troyes, who dissects and explains the emotions of his characters;[53] in the last resort, he observes effects, he does not analyse causes. A child is destroyed in the womb, another is born in the fire of the divine ordeal, and Athelston's evil, unlike that of Shakespeare's Leontes, is not redeemed through the agency of his *own* child. Divine justice in this poem is severe. Wymound's secret is plucked from him under duress by his own victims, but his 'confession', unquestionably moving to modern ears, does not move the poet, who grimly exults in his horrible and deserved end.

Scarcely less important than the theme of justice in *Athelston* is that of *troupe*, a concept of immense importance in the literature and (it seems fair to assume) the life of fourteenth-century England. As chivalry decayed and the old rigid social bonds dissolved, writers seem increasingly to have shown a close interest in the nature and meaning of the basic value on which feudal society was founded—that loyalty between man and man expressed particularly in fidelity to the pledged word. In Chaucer and the *Gawain*-poet the virtue is examined in its more inward and subjective form, as personal integrity.[54] In *Athelston* we have only the basic objective sense, as in *Havelok*, where both villains break solemn oaths sworn to the dying fathers of the royal infants. Athelston does not appear to feel *guilt* for breaking his pledge to Egelan, and the *troupe*-theme finds expression primarily in the context of treachery to the king. The special heinousness of Wymound's sin may lie, for us, in the fact that Egelan is his 'weddyd broþer dere' (11.12); similarly, we may be revolted by Macbeth's murder of Duncan primarily as the murder of a trusting friend, where for the Elizabethans the prime horror was to kill a good king. But the *Athelston*-poet and his audience must have distinguished between treachery (in the sense of treason) and personal *untroupe*, or else they would have found intolerable the cruel execution of Wymound while Athelston escaped with life and throne. Like much medieval literature, *Athelston* is highly offensive to modern democratic sentiments, and assuredly requires to be read with a sense of history. Seen within its own frame of reference, it is intelligible and acceptable. It does not offer, like *Havelok*, an idealised picture of royalty, but something much more like the reality.

The poem's 'dramatic realism', as Mehl calls it,[55] goes some way towards reducing its homiletic effect, which is less marked than in *Sir Gowþer* and *Emaré*, with which Mehl classes it. But it is still difficult to accept details such as the poet's speaking in 72.10 of 'þe goode kyng Athelston', an expression a modern reader is as likely as not to mistake for irony. What must be remembered here is that medieval people accepted the rights of kingship without question, while knowing from history and experience that that there were far more bad kings than good (this may be one reason why heroes of romances are so often kings: they represent a form of wish-fulfilment!). By the standard of some kings in the real world and by comparison with his own earlier behaviour, Athelston is at this point in the poem 'good', that is, having done evil, he does not persist in it, and so, unlike the tyrants Godrich and Godard, he does not meet a tragic end. At the same time, the poet takes pains to show Wymound's evil as *malice*, persisted in and denied (72.1f.), not *folly* acknowledged and repented. In contrast to Athelston's speech of plea-cum-challenge at 39.4ff. (see above) Wymound's words at 68.1–3 are pure blasphemy:

> þanne þat eerl made hym glade,
> And þankyd God þat lesyng was made:
> 'It haþ gete me þis eerldome!'

The naked diabolism of these words justifies the narrator's earlier exclamation at 13.12 after Wymound had sworn the king to secrecy— 'He was a devyl off helle!' Greed and ambition, as the line about the earldom shows, enter into his motivation as much as or even more than envy.

The 'trewe' Earl of Stane is, when set beside the villain, something of a lay figure. In contrast with the much longer *Havelok*, with its full characterisation of Grim, Ubbe and Bernard Brun, as well as Godrich and Godard, the goodness of the Earl and Countess has to be assumed, while that of the Queen finds expression in one single powerful gesture when she hears of the former's arrest—'Gerlondes off chyryes off sche caste' (24.4).

Enough has perhaps been said to vindicate the poem from the charge of unevenness, but there remains one small inconsistency which is worth attempting to explain. If in contrast to the king, who at least tries to stick to his *troupe* and defend Wymound by concealing his treachery, Wymound himself is a cold and calculating Machiavellian, how seriously are we to take the speech wrung from him by the Earl's children, which cannot fail to win him some sympathy? In the light of the poet's own reaction to Wymound's end, already commented on (see above, p. 16), it is probably best to take this speech, like the final speech of Othello, as the expression of a dramatic pose. In simplifying the truth, Wymound is more than partial to himself: we are left with a more favourable image of the traitor than the sum total of his acts will endorse; so to that extent the speech is a lie. But compared with an Iago, the valedictory eloquence of Wymound is better than Spartan silence, and nothing in his life becomes him like the leaving it. His admission of envy is not repentance, but it is the next best thing for a traitor—honesty (something 'honest' Iago never achieves). Thus, while the portrait of Wymound may not be perfectly consistent, it is undoubtedly memorable. Compared with most of the other romances in this collection—*Havelok* being the exception—*Athelston* is outstanding for the strength and sureness of its characterisation, which is what guarantees its lasting human appeal.

The Breton Lays and Sir Orfeo

The Middle English Breton lays stand in a kind of Platonic relation to their ultimate originals: they are the imitation of an imitation. This is not the place to summarise what evidence exists for defining the genre.[56] Very briefly, the original Breton *lais*, of which no specimens survive, appear to have been songs in the Breton language which were accompanied on the harp and followed by a narrative (*conte*), probably in French, explaining the contents and background of the lyrical *lai*. It was on these *contes* that Marie de France (who was active in the third quarter of the twelfth century, probably in England for a time) based the exquisite short narrative poems which have made the genre famous. Neither of the two lays given here, which have been chosen for representativeness as well as intrinsic merit, is actually based on a *lai* of Marie's, but *Sir Orfeo* at least stands comparison with the best of her work.

Of the nine poems that call themselves, or claim to derive from, Breton lays, two, *Emaré* and *Sir Gowþer*, are really examples of a separate genre, the 'Saint's Legend'. *Emaré*[57] is a version of the popular 'Constance Saga', of which Chaucer's *Man of Law's Tale* is the best known treatment. *Sir Gowþer*,[58] which begins with the begetting of the hero by a demon upon a noble lady, offers what seems at first sight a basic Celtic motif. However, Gowþer's father is emphatically not a mere fairy, but the devil himself, and the whole purpose of the tale is homiletic—to show the miraculous power of God's grace, which can turn even a creature of such unpromising origins into a great saint. A third poem, *The Erle of Tolous*,[59] is a typical chivalric love story; the arbitrariness of its author's claim that it is a Breton lay stands revealed in his very words:

> Yn Rome thys ge*st* cronyculyd ys,
> A lay of Bretayne callyd *ywy*s . . . (1219–21)

The generic terms *gest* and *lay* are not merely juxtaposed with characteristic medieval vagueness, both are said to be 'chronicled'—and since the tale does *not* deal with *mervailles*[60] we are left in doubt as to whether we are being offered fiction or history. In each of these three cases, 'Breton lay' seems to be used to recommend the story to the audience, suggesting that their interest would have been captured thereby as a modern reader's might be by a phrase such as 'a true spy story'.

That the genre was fashionable in the late fourteenth century is indicated by the revival of Breton lays by two named authors. Chaucer's *Franklin's Tale*, an imitation at two removes, is in one respect more authentically Breton than the poems in the Auchinleck MS. which Chaucer seems to have read:[61] its geographical details are strikingly precise. But this highly sophisticated tale merely employs the conventions of the genre (including 'marvellous' elements) as a vehicle for a human drama of great moral complexity. It is no more a typical lay than *The Merchant's Tale* is a straightforward *fabliau*. Thomas Chestre's *Sir Launfal*,[62] while it cannot be called sophisticated by Chaucerian standards, is more elaborately developed than its main source, an English poem of the earlier fourteenth century found in MS. Rawlinson C.86, *Landevale*, which is a fairly close rendering of Marie de France's *Lanval*. Chestre's poem, despite some striking touches, is actually more disfigured by the clichés of minstrel-style (tags, poor rhymes, empty repetitions, stock phrases) than its predecessor, which has benefited by sticking so closely to the chaste, economic manner of the original.

Apart from *Landevale*, the other three early fourteenth-century lays are all in the Auchinleck MS. (dated about 1330).[63] *Sir Orfeo* and *Sir Degarré* here appear in their earliest texts, while *Lai le Freine* is found nowhere else. It is these poems which form the main basis for generalisation about the Middle English Breton lay. All are short, fast-moving narratives; all deal with love; in three (*Freine* is the exception) a fairy (male or female) plays a major part; in two (*Landevale* and *Degarré*) the hero is an adventurous knight. *Landevale* is too unoriginal to have merited inclusion here; but lack of space alone has prevented the reprinting of *Lai le Freine*, the shortest of the four, which is also adapted from one of Marie's *lais*. The following extract must suffice to illustrate the excellence of the writing:

> Þe weder was clere, þe mone was liȝt, —
> So þat hye com bi a forest side;
> sche wax al weri and gan abide.
> Sone after sche gan herk
> cokkes crowe and houndes berk.
> Sche aros and þider wold.
> Ner and nere sche gan bihold.
> Walles and hous fele hye seiȝe,
> A chirche wiþ stepel fair and heiȝhe;
> Þan was þer noither strete no toun,
> Bot an house of religioun, . . . [64]

Here we have the effortlessly simple and pure style which Coleridge in *Christabel* and Keats in *The Eve of St Mark* sought so consciously to recreate and which the Pre-Raphaelites pursued as the authentic manner of early romance.

In spite of its brevity, *Sir Orfeo* ranks high by virtue of its profundity and its excellence of structure and style. In few English romances is there such reality in both the supernatural atmosphere and the human emotions of the characters. Like *Sir Gawain and the Green Knight*, *Sir Orfeo* gives dramatic form to the supreme challenge faced by man— that of his mortality. This is one reason why the poem seems to reach out of its age with an appeal that is timeless and universal. That it is also direct and powerful is largely due to the poet's art, which is seen as much in *Sir Orfeo*'s thematic coherence as in its qualities of language. A. J. Bliss has noted how 'the potency of the magical atmosphere' must be attributed to the poet's 'particular skill'.[65] *Sir Orfeo* is characterised by a deliberate economy and compression, as if the poet were consciously avoiding rhetorical elaboration in the interest of emotional truthfulness and aiming at what might well be called, reversing Yeats's dictum, 'intensity through simplification'.

A good example of the poem's descriptive manner is the lines describing the fairy band as Heurodis first sees it (142–52). They reveal a 'technical brilliance' which, as Bliss reminds us, must not be taken for 'untutored simplicity'.[66] There is a subtlety in the distinction between

the 'snowe-white stedes' and the 'wedes' 'as white as milke' (well-worn
as both phrases were), and conscious art in the evocation of 'gold red'
(150) only to describe what the Fairy King's crown was *not* made of.
The reader may be reminded of the cunning simplicity of Chaucer's
style in the *General Prologue*, which is probably indebted to the native
tradition to which *Sir Orfeo* and the other Breton lays of the Auchinleck
MS. belong.[67] In its reliance on suggestiveness, it produces a very
different effect from the richly detailed miniaturist art of Marie de
France, who shows much less reticence when it comes to describing
supernatural beings.[68] The *Orfeo*-poet's 'particular skill' can be best
brought out by considering in some detail a characteristic passage.
Read closely and pondered with careful attention, lines 237–48 disclose why the poem, despite its brevity, gives a very unusual impression
of density (compare the much longer *Sir Degarré*):

> Þurth wode and over heþ
> Into the wildernes he geþ.
> Noþing he fint þat him is ays,
> Bot ever he liveþ in gret malais.
> He þat hadde y-werd þe fowe and griis,
> And on bed þe purper biis,
> Now on hard heþe he liþ—
> Wiþ leves and gresse he him wriþ.
> He þat hadde had castels and tours,
> Rivers, forest, friþ wiþ flours,
> Now, þei it comenci to snewe and frese,
> Þis king mot make his bed in mese.

Apart from the trisyllables *wildernes* and *comenci* and the disyllabic
malais, *purper*, *castels*, *river* and *forest*, the passage is composed of mono-
syllables that seem to reflect the 'unaccommodated' simplicity of
Orfeo's new life. The bed's royal covering of 'purper biis' has yielded
to 'mese', the raiment of 'fowe and griis' to 'leves and gresse'. After six
neutral repetitions of the pronoun *he*, the poet finally reminds us of the
nullity to which Orfeo's rank has been reduced by retaining until the
last line the phrase 'Þis king'. The implication of all men, whatever
their rank, having to abandon the joys of *life* to 'make their bed in
moss' is real but unobtrusive. The writer's moral purpose works
through poetic suggestion, not didactic statement.

Orfeo does not substitute hardship for luxury as a merely histrionic
gesture. In losing Heurodis, he has lost everything, inwardly and
emotionally, and by his act of self-exile, matches the inner (and more
important) desolation with an outward, material deprivation which is

nonetheless symbolically appropriate. The number of verbs in the passage brings out the active resolve with which Orfeo leaves behind not himself (for, unlike Ywain, he does not go mad)[69] but the world of shared happiness which has now been destroyed. Suffering is actively embraced, not passively endured: he *geþ, fint, liþ, wriþ, make(þ)*. Every word seems chosen with deliberation: in the first two lines, the prepositions—the vaguest words in the language—carry a full semantic load: þurth *wode*, over *heþe*, into *þe wildernes*. The rhythm is carefully controlled so that the pause after *wode* and *heþ* is followed by a sudden precipitated movement of release with *Into þe wildernes* culminating in the verb *geþ*, which bluntly registers Orfeo's final separation from the human world. The fourfold repetition of the 'He that had had . . . Now . . .' formula deftly brings out the antitheses between Orfeo's old and his new life, the active verbal forms preventing the narrative from turning into a static series of oppositions (*make, seþ, digge, wrote*). Against the 'gentle weal' of civilised existence emblematised by the *castels* and *tours* in their tamed landscape is set the desert horror also faced by the hero of *Sir Gawain* in his winter journey through the Wirral.[70] It is expressed in a word which today has associations radically different from those it held for the medieval audience, whose need was not to preserve nature from themselves but to preserve themselves from nature: *wildernes*. The echo of Heurodis' description of the land she saw in her dream (159–60) in the phrases 'castels and tours/River, forest, friþ wiþ flours' reminds us that what Orfeo is abandoning is what his wife has been (unwillingly) carried off to. The poignancy of the contrast is ironically underlined by the exact identity of phrasing.

Orfeo's departure into the *wildernes*, which is to all appearances the adoption of a new (if gratuitously ascetic) mode of life, is really more like a preparation for death. The fact that existence without the 'queen of priis . . . Ful of love and of godenisse' is a kind of death is, of course, what makes the continuance of life in the sense of mere biological survival so pointless to Orfeo after he glimpses Heurodis in the hunting-party of ladies:

> 'Allas!' quaþ he, 'now me is wo!
> Whi nil deþ now me slo?
> Allas, wroche, þat Y no miȝt
> Dye now after þis siȝt!' (331–4).

The *siȝt* appears to seal the permanence of their separation; but in fact it is from this very despair and negation that Orfeo draws the energy to follow her 'tide what bitide'. The worst that can come from his entering the rock *is* death; but because there is little distinction between real death and the life he is living he can say, with a wholly unrhetorical truthfulness:

Of liif no deþ me no reche   (342).

It would be wrong, however, to see *Sir Orfeo* as merely a love-romance, another *Floris and Blancheflour*, with adult married lovers rather than adolescents for protagonists. Authentic as the love between this ideal king and queen is shown to be, its intensity does not strike us as distinctively *erotic*. Much as the abduction of Heurodis is a personal blow to Orfeo—and it must be, to justify his drastic reaction—it seems to symbolise, in a more general way, man's being deprived of what he prizes supremely through an agency profoundly indifferent to the dearest human values. In the true 'comedy' of which this romance is a perfect specimen, the frighteningly alien fairy world must be shown to possess tragic potentialities. The poet's dramatic skill ensures that the Fairy King's eventual acceding to Orfeo's request and adhesion to their bargain have the faintly incredible quality attaching to any relief of acute distress: we are still too much in the grip of apprehension really to believe it has happened. The poem's coda (the incident of the return) thus has a precisely calculated *emotional* function—to enable the audience to make the transition from suffering and tension to the relaxation that follows relief. (Its further, thematic function is discussed below.)

In considering the structure and theme of *Sir Orfeo* it is useful to begin from the analysis given by A. J. Bliss in the introduction to his edition. Bliss sees the 'Prologue' of the poem as extending from lines 1 to 56; but it seems better to confine this term to the part taken over from (or shared with) *Lai le Freine* before the latter's story begins. The whole section dealing with Orfeo's character, ancestry and queen (25–36) should be regarded as the opening of the poem's first section. This extends to line 194 (though there is obviously no *sharp* break between the loss of Heurodis and the departure of Orfeo). Bliss sees the first section as dealing with the abduction of Heurodis and the second as presenting Orfeo's *search*[71] for her. But his stress on the disjunction between the two actions is not justified, because there is no clear break. While Orfeo's self-exile is the direct consequence of his losing Heurodis, it is incorrect to speak of this extreme reaction as a 'search'. It is arguable that the only genuine narrative 'break' occurs at line 477 (which in Bliss's analysis is the beginning of the poem's third section). This is the only point where the *story* could end satisfactorily: Orfeo's return and reinstatement would remain untold, but could be inferred, whereas a break at any earlier point would leave the tale incomplete.

But in point of fact, *Sir Orfeo* is a seamless web, for the poet does not leave the incident of the return as a mere piece of narrative 'rounding off'. Instead, he develops it as a vehicle for part of his thematic purpose.

The theme of loyalty or *trouthe* had been foreshadowed in Orfeo's renunciation of women (expressing the lifelong fidelity he intends to show his wife) and his entrusting of the kingdom to his steward (expressing the fidelity he expects to be shown by his deputy).[72] The theme assumes prominence in the central incident in which Orfeo wins back his wife by relying on the Fairy King's *trouthe*—his fidelity to his pledged word. With the regaining of Heurodis, the theme of Orfeo's fidelity to his wife is consummated. It now becomes the second function of the return-incident (Bliss's third section) to conclude the remaining theme—the fidelity of the deputy to his lord. This incident thus becomes an organic extension of the main story inasmuch as the significance of the latter is only fully unfolded when the story of the faithful steward is completed.

The theme of *trouthe* is brilliantly highlighted in the scene in the underworld already referred to (419–76), where Orfeo obtains from the Fairy King a promise worded in exactly the terms he needs:

> 'Now aske of me *what it be*.
> Largelich Ichil þe pay . . .' (450–1)

The Fairy King's gesture is truly royal (and, we may be sure, the ideal response desired by all minstrel-poets such as the author of *Sir Orfeo*!); but *largesse* is not the only royal virtue that Orfeo, himself a king, is to 'assay'. Nor is it the main one: *that* is *trouthe*. The whole scene, which is pregnant with delicate irony, is handled with a subtlety that exemplifies the writer's 'particular skill' at its height. It is an admirable poetic tact that has made him avoid doing the striking (but obvious) thing— to have Orfeo proclaim his *own* royalty so as to justify his claim to the queen's 'compani'. Thus he makes Orfeo display a third[73] royal virtue as he reminds the Fairy King:

> 'Зete were it a wele fouler þing
> To here a lesing of þi mouþe . . .'   (464–5)

The thematic thread is now drawn in as the poem speeds to its conclusion. Because the classical legend with its tragic issue has been altered, Orfeo does not look back and so lose his wife a second time; instead, we are swiftly conveyed to Winchester, where Orfeo now 'assays' the 'gode wille' of his deputy, whose fidelity fits him to be king after Orfeo:

> His steward was a trewe man
> And loved him as he auȝt to do ... (554–5)

These lines, in their unselfconscious linking of 'truth' and 'love', present a parallel between the steward's relationship with his lord and the king's with his lady. They are worth comparing with two sets of lines which do not appear in the Auchinleck MS. (on which the text in this edition is based) but which have a particular interest in the light of the thematic concerns this discussion has centred upon.[74] In the Harley and Ashmole MSS., after Orfeo's pointed assertion that 'A kingis word most nede be hold' (H 429, B 455), the Fairy King replies, '[Forsoþe], þou art a trew man.' It is a curious remark, since Orfeo, notwithstanding his insistence on the Fairy King's obligation to *his* '*trouthe*', does not appear himself to have *done* anything to merit this particular epithet (the Fairy King does not, of course, know who the minstrel is and a more fitting epithet to describe Orfeo would perhaps have been *sleiȝe* 'clever, cunning'). What is revealing is the way in which the author of these lines—even if he was only an inventive scribe — seems to have wished to underline at this point the Fairy King's acknowledgment of a *trouthe* in Orfeo of which he should strictly speaking be unaware—the fidelity to his wife that brought him into the otherworld as it had made him abandon human society and female solace. A second striking illustration of concern with the *trouthe* theme occurs only in the Ashmole text, which explicitly links the Fairy King's recognition of Orfeo's *trouthe* with his granting of Heurodis to him as a reward (in a manner which anticipates Orfeo's own reward of his faithful steward):

> The ryche kyng spake word*ys* þan
> And seyd: 'Þ*o*u arte a trew man!
> Ther-for j grante þat it be so ...' (B 456–8)

Sir Orfeo is as impressive in the way it develops a theme as in its basic narrative architecture and vivid dramatic style. The three *trouthes* exemplified in the poem—those of Orfeo, the Fairy King and the Steward—reveal the world of this Breton lay as one of lofty idealism and noble conduct. Suffering, far from being excluded, plays a central and indispensable part in the pattern of the work, but human virtue is allowed to prevail over adversity, and 'love' and 'truth' are rewarded in the end. The darkness of the poem's 'wo' yields dramatically to the light of 'joie and mirþe'; it is never clouded over by 'trecherie' and 'gile'.[75]

Notes to the Introduction

1. For an attempt, see Dorothy Everett's well-known essay 'A Characterisation of the Middle English Romances' in *Essays on Middle English Literature* (Oxford, 1955).

2. *Narrative material*: as by W. H. French and C. B. Hale in their collection *Middle English Metrical Romances* (New York, 1930) under 'Matter of England', etc.; *length*: as by Dieter Mehl in ch. 2 of *The Middle English Romances of the Thirteenth and Fourteenth Centuries* (London, 1968); *verse-form*: as by Derek Pearsall, 'The Development of Middle English Romance', *Medieval Studies*, XXVII (1965), 91–117.

3. See Pamela Gradon, *Form and Style in Early English Literature* (London, 1971), ch. 4, 'The Romance Mode'.

4. One thinks of Caxton's translations and, above all, his version of Malory's work. See also a recent essay by Derek Pearsall, 'The English Romance in the Fifteenth Century', *Essays and Studies*, 1976, pp. 56–83.

5. See the classic study by Reto R. Bezzola, *Le sens de l'aventure et de l'amour: Chrétien de Troyes* (Paris, 1947) and more recently Eugène Vinaver, *The Rise of Romance* (Oxford, 1971), ch. II, 'The Discovery of Meaning'.

6. Tr. W. R. Trask (Princeton, 1953); ch. 6, 'The Knight Sets Forth'.

7. *Erec*, ed. W. Foerster (Halle, 1890), lines 13–14: [*Crestiiens de Troies*] . . . *tret d'un conte d'avanture/Une mout bele conjointure*; Claude Luttrell, *The Creation of the First Arthurian Romance: A Quest* (London, 1974), ch. 8, 'Conjointure'.

8. See Vinaver, *op. cit.* pp. 34–7, 47–9 (*conjointure*), 16–17, 21–3 (*sen*); a very valuable discussion.

9. On the epic *chanson* in relation to romance see respectively chapters 5 in Auerbach and 1 in Vinaver (*op. cit.*) and John Finlayson (ed.), *Morte Arthure* (London, 1967), Introduction pp. 5–11, 'Chanson de geste and romance'. The two genres are fully discussed in W. P. Ker, *Epic and Romance* (London, 1897: 2nd edn. repr. New York, 1957).

10. See especially Vinaver, *op. cit.* ch. 2.

11. For a recent discussion of the problem of structure in Chrétien, see Z. P. Zaddy, *Chrétien Studies* (Glasgow, 1973); on bi-partition generally, see W. W. Ryding, *Structure in Medieval Narrative* (The Hague, 1971), especially pp. 83–6, 131–3.

12. This view is fully developed in the discussion of *Ywain and Gawain* in Part Two, pp. 11–19.

13. Lines 715–25, with their dismissive reference to the hero's miscellaneous adventures, of which 'Hit were to tore for to telle of þe tenþe dole'.

14. See especially the discussion of the hero and heroine in *Ipomadon*, Part Two, pp. 47–9.

15. A subject well discussed in ch. 3 of John Stevens' *Medieval Romance: Themes and Approaches* (London, 1973), 'Man and Society: the Romance of the "Gentil" Man'.

16. See the interesting ch. 2, 'Man and Woman: Idealisms of Love', in Stevens, *op. cit.*

17. The paradigm instance is no doubt the hero of Wolfram's *Parzival*; but Sir Gawain in *SGGK* is more problematic, and much recent criticism of the poem has concentrated on Gawain's 'fault'.

18. See the discussion of this question, Part Two, pp. 29ff.

19. See Commentary, Headnote, p. 173.

20. Finlayson (*ed. cit.* p. 7) calls some of these *chansons de geste*; the heroic and tragic poems he discusses contrast sharply with the romances proper. *Hav.* and *Ath.* share something of their tone but possess the basic structural pattern of romance.

21. The appeal of *King Horn* to such a collector is less obvious, though it too presents a young innocent hero protected by Providence. Much in *Horn*—the concern with knighthood, the love-element, the episodic plot with its incremental repetition—relates it closely to conventional romance.

22. See Stevens, 'Man and Supernature: The Marvellous in Romance' (*op. cit.* ch. 5).

23. A. J. Bliss (ed.), *Sir Launfal* (London and Edinburgh, 1960), Introduction, p. 42.

24. To judge from the strictures on adulterated beer in *Piers Plowman* (B, V, 217–23) a tavern was one of the *last* places it could be had!

25. As in *Wynnere and Wastoure* (ed. I. Gollancz, rev. M. Day, London, 1931), a poem which must have been written for a noble household, conceivably even for the royal court.

26. 'For lewed peple loven tales olde' (*Pardoner's Tale, CT*, C, 437).

27. *Hav.* is not directly based on the OF *Lai d'Havelok*, a contemporary analogue, which the poet could have known (see Weiss, *art. cit.* (C on *Hav.* 775 for ref.), p. 257, n.17).

28. As found in *Ipom.*, or in *William of Palerne* (re-ed. W. W. Skeat, EETS, Extra Series 1, 1867), both based on French originals.

29. H. Schelp, *Exemplarische Romanzen im Mittelenglischen* (Göttingen, 1967), p. 33.

30. See Commentary on lines 1–26.

31. An analysis of the abundant colloquial elements in the language of so 'courtly' a poem as *The Book of the Duchess* is instructive in this respect. Again, the 'low' elements in Chaucer's fabliaux can hardly be said to indicate popular origin.

32. All in French and Hale except *Rauf Coilzear* (ed. F. J. Amours, *Scottish Alliterative Poems* (Edinburgh, 1892)).

33. As does Mador de la Porte in the Stanzaic *Morte* (*SMA*) 1598ff.;

cf. also Sir Priamus in the Alliterative *Morte* (*AMA*), 2646.

34. The passage has no parallel in the *Lai d'Havelok*. Schelp mentions similar passages in OE and sees the lines as holding up the good times past as an exemplary criticism of the present (*op. cit.* pp. 49–50).

35. The appearance of the signs is bound to awaken echoes of such New Testament epiphanies as the Transfiguration (Matt. 17, 1–8) and the Baptism of Christ (Matt. 3, 16–17).

36. See J. M. Wallace-Hadrill, *Early Germanic Kingship in England and on the Continent* (Oxford, 1971), pp. 104–5. S. Delany and V. Ishkanian stress the importance of the kingship theme but take a somewhat different view of it in 'Theocratic and Contractual Kingship in Havelok the Dane', *Zeitschrift für Anglistik und Amerikanistik* (1974).

37. Suspense is rare in romances, where the outcome of the hero's fights is rarely in doubt. *SGGK* has genuine suspense, but more usually what we get is *mystery* (as in Chrétien's 'Joie de la Cort' episode at the end of *Erec*) or *tension* (as in the climactic fight in *YG*). Moments of genuine suspense occur in *SMA* (the parley, st. 419) and, exceptionally, throughout *Athelston*. Absence of suspense is inevitable in epic, where the story is known to the audience; in romance, where the story may not always be known, it is the audience's familiarity with the *convention* that predisposes them to expect a happy outcome.

38. *Art. cit.* p. 256 (see (C) on line 775 for ref.).

39. *Works*, ed. E. Vinaver (Oxford, 1967), p. 1229.

40. On the importance of *humilitas* for the office of king, see Gregory's *Moralia* (*PL* 76, esp. 203c, 377a–b); cf. also Augustine's *De Civ. Dei*, V. 24, XIX. 15; see Wallace-Hadrill, *op. cit.* pp. 30–1 for valuable refs.; Isidore's *Sentences*, iii, 49 (*PL* 83, col. 720) stresses *humilitas* as a quality of King David, and Lupus of Ferrières advised Charles the Bald that humility and piety were the precondition of the exercise of royal power (see Wallace-Hadrill, *op. cit.* p 137.) The importance of *generosity* is discussed by D. Haskin, 'Food, Clothing and Kingship in *HD*' (*American Benedictine Review* (1973)).

41. See the Introduction by G. V. Smithers to his edition, Vol. II, (EETS, Original Series 257, 1953), pp. 28–40.

42. *Op. cit.* p. 149. The whole discussion (pp. 146–52) is valuable.

43. Trounce, Introduction to his edition (see (C) on *Ath.*, p. 187), p. 43.

44. *Op. cit.* p. 150.

45. He considers *Ath.* in the chapter with that heading (*op. cit.* pp. 120–58).

46. The three young men in the burning fiery furnace (Dan. 3). Interestingly, the tyrannical king in this book is Nebuchadnezzar (see note 50 below). Cf. also the OE *Daniel*, 345ff., for the 'pleasant fire'.

47. As with the sea in *King Horn* and *Emaré*, for example.

48. Athelston's crime is presumably to be seen as self-punishing, even if the medieval sense of justice is not our own.

49. III. iii. 35ff., esp. 97–8: 'My words fly up, my thoughts remain below,/Words without thoughts never to heaven go.' Claudius is also guilty of 'A brother's murder' (38).

50. *CT*, B, 2143–2182, especially line 2182: 'He knew [recognised, acknowledged] that God was ful off myght and grace'. The third stanza of this *tragedie* draws on Dan. 3 (see note 46 above) with its 'fourneys, ful of flambes rede'.

51. The authoritarian personality (of which the tyrant is an extreme example) is seen in Freudian psychology as often deeply neurotic and secretly tormented by feelings of anxiety and inadequacy. Freud, who acknowledged how much his insights owed to literature, would have found *Athelston* unusually interesting.

52. *Troilus and Criseyde*, I, 925–31, V, 1232–42, and discussion of latter in V, 1442ff.

53. E.g. *Cligès*, 625ff.; on Chrétien's mastery of 'le rôle du subconscient' see J. Frappier, *Chrétien de Troyes* (Paris, 1968), pp. 225–6. Chrétien's method reflects the rational psychology of his day. Cf. also *Ipom.* 905ff.

54. *Franklin's Tale*, esp. F 1474–9; *SGGK*, 619–64 (the 'Pentangle' passage), and see J. A. Burrow, *A Reading of SGGK* (London, 1966), esp. pp. 42–50.

55. *Op. cit.* p. 147.

56. See Mortimer J. Donovan's *The Breton Lays: a Guide to Varieties* (London, 1969) and the Introductions to A. J. Bliss's editions of *SO* (Oxford, 2nd edition 1966), *Sir Launfal* (London, 1960), and to Phyllis Hodgson's edition of *Franklin's Tale* (London, 1960). The main general articles are G. V. Smithers, 'Story Patterns in Some Breton Lays' (*MÆ* XXII (1953), 61–92), L. H. Loomis, 'Chaucer and the Breton Lays of the Auchinleck MS.' (*SP* XXXVIII (1941), 18–29) and Rachel Bromwich, 'A Note on the Breton Lays' (*MÆ* XXVI (1957), 36–8). See also Graham Johnston, 'The Breton Lays in Middle English' in *Iceland and the Medieval World: Studies in Honour of Ian Maxwell*, ed. G. Turville-Petre and J. S. Martin (Victoria, Australia, 1974) and John B. Beston, 'How Much was Known of the Breton Lai in Fourteenth Century England?' in *The Learned and the Lewed: Studies in Chaucer and Medieval Literature*, ed. L. D. Benson (Harvard, 1974), pp. 319–36.

57. Ed. Edith Rickert (EETS Extra Series 99, 1908).

58. Ed. K. Breul (Oppeln, 1886).

59. Ed. G. Lüdtke (Berlin, 1881).

60. The main subject of Breton lays, according to the Prologue to *SO* (18). The ref. to the events as having occurred (*SO* 21) probably follows Marie: *L'aventure k'aves oïe/Veraie fu . . .* (*Bisclavret*, 315–16).

61. See Loomis, *art. cit.*

62. *Ed. cit.* Bliss suspects Chestre may have been influenced by Chaucer.

63. The main studies of this most important single romance MS. collection are E. Kölbing, 'Vier Romanzenhandschriften' (*Englische Studien* VII (1884), 177–201) and A. J. Bliss, 'Notes on the Auchinleck MS.' (*Spec.* XXVI (1951), 652–8). An account of the likely milieu in which the MS. was produced is L. H. Loomis, 'The Auchinleck MS. and a possible London bookshop of 1330–1340' (*PMLA* LVII (1942), 595–627).

64. Ed. Margaret Wattie (Northampton, Mass., 1929), ll. 150–60.

65. *Ed. cit.* Intro. p. xli.

66. *Ibid.*

67. See Loomis, *art. cit.* (*SP* XXXVIII (1941), 18–29).

68. Cf. her description of Lanval's fairy mistress in *Lanval*, 100–6.

69. Cf. *YG* 1637–1708.

70. *SGGK* 700ff.

71. *Ed. cit.* p. xlii.

72. Bliss examines the use of suspense in this section (*ed. cit.* p. xliii) but finds no thematic significance in it. Indeed he shows no awareness that *SO* has a theme at all. A view of this incident similar to the one here proposed is offered by Peter J. Lucas in 'An Interpretation of *Sir Orfeo*' (*Leeds Studies in English* (1972)), p. 5ff.

73. He is already, like King David, a skilled harper, and like the Fairy King, a generous monarch ('Large and curteys he was also', 42); he now displays the Solomonian gift of wisdom.

74. Bliss prints all three texts in his edition. It may be that the apparent conflict between thematic purpose and dramatic propriety discernible here in these versions and totally lacking in Auchinleck is an implicit confirmation of the authenticity of that manuscript's text.

75. *SO*, 5–7.

Note on Selection of Texts and Editorial Procedure

The works in these volumes have been chosen both for their intrinsic merits and for their representativeness. One long and three short romances are printed entire, a 'romance' episode is extracted from a poem not itself a romance, and three medium-to-long romances have been presented in the form of linked extracts with extensive summaries. In the last instance, our aim has been to enable the reader to appreciate the *structure* of these works as well as can be done without printing them *in toto*: romances are narrative poems, and isolated extracts concentrate misleadingly on their weakest feature, which is style, and make it impossible to consider their narrative qualities adequately. The availability of *Ywain and Gawain* in a good modern edition might suggest that this text should have been omitted and more given of *Ipomadon* (which has long been out of print). However, we wished to include a typical tale of Arthurian adventure to complement the story of the fall of Arthur, and this was the obvious and only choice; further, given the extreme length of *Ipomadon*, a selection of even twice the size would scarcely have proved twice as satisfactory as the one we give. *Athelston* (rather than, say, *King Horn*) was chosen because of its brevity, excellence and value in illustrating the variety of mood, atmosphere and moral tone possible in the genre. In order to make the texts as readable as we could, we have printed glosses at the foot of the page and confined discussion of linguistic and textual points to the Commentary, printed at the back of the book and referred to by the abbreviation (C). All bibliographical references are given in full on their first appearance.

The texts are edited from the manuscripts or from photographic reproductions of them, collated with the existing editions. All editions may have errors, and no exception is claimed for the texts printed here. The text is generally conservative; not from a belief that if a scribe made a mistake he necessarily wrote nonsense, and that therefore any reading is acceptable from which any sense may be wrung,[1] but because the lack of a standard language and style in Middle English frequently makes it impossible to determine whether or not a reading is grammatically or stylistically possible: a piece of apparently bad writing may well be the fault of the poet rather than of the scribe. But where a manuscript is late and plainly corrupt (e.g. *Ipomadon*), we have felt more confidence in charging the scribes with responsibility for uncharacteristically muddled or technically incompetent passages, even though in many cases restorations can be only tentative. Romance scribes seem to have been particularly inclined to rewrite their material, consciously or unconsciously, often in an apparently arbitrary way and without detectable motivation. [2]

Divergences from the base manuscript used for the text of each poem are signalled in the margin or by italicisation. *Added* or *substituted* letters are italicised, but where letters have been *omitted,* the adjacent letters have *not* been italicised. Where letters have been substituted or omitted, the manuscript reading is recorded in the margin, but not where they have been added. In addition, certain idiosyncratic spellings which might cause confusion in particular texts have been corrected with italics but without marginal notes: these cases are specified in the introductions to individual texts. Unless otherwise stated, marginalia represent the readings of the base manuscript.

[1] See A. E. Housman, *D. Iunii Iuuenalis Saturae* (Cambridge, 1931), p. xi for a trenchant characterisation of this among other editorial ineptitudes.

[2] See, by contrast, G. Kane, *Piers Plowman: the A Version* (London, 1960), p. 115ff., where the expectation of wayward variation is shown to be unfulfilled. It would appear that purely secular material may have been treated with less respect.

I

HAVELOK

Herknet*h* to me, gode men,
Wives, maydnes, and alle men,
Of a tale þat Ich you wile telle,
*H*wo-so it wile here, and þer-to duelle.
Þe tale is of Havelok i-maked—   5
*H*wil he was litel, he yede ful naked.
Havelok was a ful god gome;
He was ful god in everi trome.
He was þe wicteste man at nede
Þat þurte riden on ani stede;   10
Þat ye mowen nou y-here,
And þe tale ye mowen y-lere.
At þe biginni*n*g of ure tale,
Fil me a cuppe of ful god ale,

Sk. adds y; her   And *Y* wile drinken, er Y spelle,   15
Þat Crist us shilde alle fro helle.
heuere   Krist late us evere so for to do
Þat we moten comen him to;
And, wit*h* that it mote ben so,
Benedicamus domino!   20
Here Y schal biginnen a rym—
Krist us yeve wel god fyn!
The rym is maked of Havelok,
A stalworþi man in a flok;

stalworþeste]   He was þe *wihtest* man at nede   25
wihtest *Sk*   Þat may riden on ani stede.
(cf. 9)

---

[4] *þer-to duelle*, wait for it.
[6] *yede*, went.
[7] *ful*, very, thoroughly.   *gome*, man.
[8] *trome*, company.
[9] *wicteste*, most vigorous (cf. *wihtest* 25, etc.).   *at nede*, when needed (rhyming tag).
[10] *þurte*, might.   *stede*, horse.
[11] *mowen*, may (cf. *mowe* 175, etc.).
[12] *y-lere*, learn.
[13] *ure*, our.
[15] *spelle*, recite.
[16] *shilde*, protect.
[17] *late*, let.
[18] *moten*, may (cf. *mote* 19, etc.).
[19] *with that*, so that.
[20] 'Let us bless God!'
[22] *yeve*, give (also *yive* 198, 300, etc.).   *fyn*, ending, death.
[24] *stalworþi*, valiant, strong.   *flok*, troop.

New para MS.	It was a king bi are-dawes,
	Þat in his time were gode lawes
holden	He dede maken, an ful wel holde;
holde	Hym lovede yung, him lovede olde, 30
kayn	Erl and barun, dreng and þayn,
	Knict, bondeman and swain,
	Wydues, maydnes, prestes and clerkes,
	And al for hise gode werkes.
	He lovede God with al his mic*ht*, 35
	And holi kirke and soth ant ric*ht*;
Rirth-	Ri*ht*wise men he lovede alle
	And over-al made hem for-to calle;
	Wreieres and wrobberes made he falle
	And hated hem so man doth galle. 40
	Utlawes and theves made he bynde,
	Alle that he mic*ht*e fynde,
	And heye hengen on galwe-tre—
	For hem ne yede gold ne fe.
	In þat time a man þat bore 45
No gap in MS.	* * * * * * *
	Of red gold upon hiis bac
with	In a male *hwit* or blac,
	Ne funde he non þat him misseyde,
N with iuele	N*e* hond on *him* with ivele leyde. 50
on hond leyde]	Þanne mic*ht*e chapmen fare
corr. Sk. (C)	Þuruth Englond wi*th* here ware
	And baldelike beye and sellen
	Over-al, þer he wilen dwellen,

---

27 *It was*, there was.   *are-dawes*, olden days (and cf. 2349).
28 'In whose time . . .'
29 'Which he caused to be made and well kept.'
31 *dreng*, free tenant (C) (ON).   *þayn*, thane (C).
32 *bondeman*, small farmer (C) (cf. 1018, etc.) (ON).   *swain*, peasant (C) (ON).
33 *clerkes*, minor clergy (C).
36 *soth ant richt*, truth and justice.
37 *rihtwise*, just.
38 'And had them summoned from everywhere.'
39 *wreieres*, traitors.   *wrobberes*, informers.
41 'he caused to be bound.'
42 *michte*, could.
44 *yede*, availed (cf. *gon* 1434).   *fe*, wealth, property (cf. 386, etc.).
48 *male*, pack, bundle.
49 *misseyde*, insulted.
50 *ivele*, wrong.
51 *þanne*, then.   *chapmen*, pedlars (cf. 1644).
52 *þuruth*, through.
53 *baldelike*, confidently ('boldly').
54 *over-al*, everywhere.   *þer*, where, wherever.   *he*, they (frequently).
dwellen, stop.

In gode burwes, and þer-fram   55
Ne funden he non þat dede hem sham,
Þat he ne weren sone to sorwe brouht,
An povere maked, and browt to nouht.
hayse   Þanne was Engelond at ayse;
Michel was suich a king to preyse   60
Þat held so Englond in grith—
Krist of hevene was him with!
He was Engelondes blome—
lond] loverd   Was non so bold loverd to Rome
Craigie   Þat durste upon his *londe* bringe   65
We add londe;   Hunger ne here, wicke þinge.
menie Sk.
bringhe 65   Hwan he felede hise foos,
þinghe 66   He made hem lurken and crepen in wros;
Þei hidden hem alle and helden hem stille
And diden al his herte wille.   70
Richt he lovede of alle þinge—
To wronge micht him no man bringe
Ne for silver ne for gold,
So was he his soule hold.
To þe faderles was he rath,   75
Hwo-so dede hem wrong or lath,
Were it clerc or were it knicht,
He dede hem sone to haven richt;
And hwo dide widuen wrong,
Were he nevere knicht so strong   80
Þat he ne made him sone kesten
So Z: and   In feteres, *and* ful faste festen;
before In *MS.*   And hwo-so dide maydne shame

---

⁵⁵ *burwes*, towns (sing. *borw, boru*).   *þer-fram*, from there.
⁵⁶ *funden*, found.   *dede hem sham*, injured, abused them.
⁵⁷ *sorwe*, sorrow.
⁵⁸ *povere*, poor.
⁶⁰ *michel*, much.   *to preyse*, worthy of praise.
⁶¹ *grith*, peace (cf. 512) (ON).
⁶³ *blome*, flower.
⁶⁴ *loverd*, lord.
⁶⁶ *here*, war, invasion.   *wicke*, evil, harmful.
⁶⁷ *felede*, put to flight, terrified (ON).
⁶⁸ *lurken*, hide (ON).   *wros*, corners (ON).
⁶⁹ 'kept themselves quiet.'
⁷⁰ 'all the desire of his heart.'
⁷⁴ *hold*, loyal (i.e. to his soul's good) (cf. 2786, etc.).
⁷⁵ *rath*, counsel, help (ON).
⁷⁶ *lath*, harm, injury (cf. 2723, etc.).
⁷⁹ *widuen*, widows.
⁸¹ *kesten*, cast (passive sense, cf. 82, etc.).
⁸² *faste*, firmly.   *festen*, bind, chain.

Of hire bodi, or brou*ht* in blame,
Bute it were bi hire wille, 85
Ke *H*e made him sone of limes spille.
Ke *H*e was te beste kni*ht* at nede
heuere Þat evere mic*ht*e riden on stede,
Or wepne wagge, or folc ut lede—
Of kni*ht* ne havede he nevere drede 90
Þat he ne sprong forth so sparke of glede,
Sk adds knawe And lete him *knawe*, of hise hand-dede,
Hw he cou*þ*e with wepne spede;
And o*þ*er he refte him hors or wede,
Or made him sone handes sprede 95
And 'Loverd, merci!' loude grede.
He was large, and no wic*ht* gnede;
Havede he non so god brede,
Ne on his bord non so god shrede,
Þat he ne wolde *þ*or-wit*h* fede 100
Povre þat on fote yede,
For-to haven of him þe mede
Þat for us wolde on rode blede,
Crist, that al kan wisse and rede
Þat evere woneth in ani þede. 105

Þe king was hoten A*þ*elwold;
Of word, of wepne he was bold.
In Engeland was nevre knic*ht*
Þat betere hel*d* þe lond to ric*ht*.
Of his bodi ne havede he eyr 110

[84] *blame*, disrepute.
[85] *Bute*, unless.
[86] *limes*, limbs, members.   *spille*, deprive (i.e. castrate).
[87] *was te*=*was þe.*
[89] *wagge*, brandish.   *folc*, army.
[91] *spronge*, leapt.   *so*, as.   *glede*, coal, ember.
[92] *knawe*, know.
[93] *hw*, how (cf. 120, etc.).   *spede*, succeed (past *spedde* 758, etc.).
[94] *oþer*, either.   *wede*, clothing, armour.
[96] *grede*, cry (past *gredde* 2322).
[97] *large*, generous.   *gnede*, stingy.
[98] *brede*, roast meat.
[99] *bord*, table.   *shrede*, morsel.
[100] *þor-with*, therewith (cf. *þore* 743, etc.).
[102] *mede*, reward.
[103] *rode*, Cross.
[104] *wisse*, guide, direct.   *rede*, counsel.
[105] *woneth*, dwell.   *þede*, nation, country (cf. 2895).
[106] *hoten*, called (cf. 284, etc.).
[110] *eyr*, heir.

Bute a mayden swiþe fayr
Þat was so yung þat sho ne couþe
Gon on fote, ne speke with mouþe.
Þan him tok an ivel strong,
Þat he wel wiste and under-fong   115
Þat his deth was comen him on,
And seyde, 'Crist, hwat shal Y don?
Loverd, hwat shal me to rede?
woth   I wot ful wel Ich have mi mede.
Hw shal nou mi douhter fare?   120
Of hire have Ich michel kare;
Sho is mikel in mi þouht—
Of me self is me riht nowt.
No selcouth is, þou me be wo;
Sho ne kan speke, ne sho kan go.   125
Yif scho couþe on horse ride,
And a thousande men bi hire syde,
helde   And sho were comen in-til elde,
And Engelond sho couþe welde
hem of þar] And don *of hem þat* hire were queme,   130
corr. Sk An hire bodi couþe yeme,
Ne wolde me nevere ivele like,
Me, -riche Ne þou ich were in hevene-rike.'

Quanne he havede þis pleinte maked,
Þer-after stronglike quaked,   135
He sende writes sone on-on
After his erles, evere-ich on,
And after hise baruns, riche and povre,
douere   Fro Rokesburw al in-to Dovre,

111 *swiþe*, very.
112 *couþe*, 'could', knew how to.
113 *gon*, walk.
114 *ivel*, sickness (cf. *yvel* 144, etc.).
115 *wiste*, knew (past of *wot*, as in 119, etc.).   *under-fong*, realized.
123 'For myself I care nothing' (cf. 313, 839, etc.).
124 *selcouth*, wonder (cf. 2124, etc.).   *þou me be wo*, if I am unhappy.
128 *in-til elde*, of age.
129 *welde*, govern.
130 'And do with them whatever was pleasing to her.'
131 *yeme*, take care of (cf. 172, etc.).
132 *ivele like*, displease (*like*='please') (cf. 1167) (C).
133 *hevene-rike*, kingdom of heaven.
134 *quanne*, when.   *pleinte*, complaint, lament.
135 *strongly*, terribly.
136 *writes*, messages, summons.   *on-on*, at once (also *anan*, *anon*).
137 *evere-ich*, every (and *evere-il* 219, etc.).
139 *Rokesburw*, Roxburgh (cf. 265).

That he shulden comen swiþe 140
Til him, that was ful unbliþe,
To þat stede þer he lay
In harde bondes, nicht and day.
He was so faste with yvel fest
Þat he ne mouhte haven no rest. 145
hete He ne mouhte no mete ete
Ne he ne mouchte no lyþe gete,
Ne non of his ivel þat couþe red—
Of him ne was nouht buten ded.

Alle þat þe writes herden 150
Sorful an sori til him ferden;
He wrungen hondes and wepen sore,
hore And yerne preyden Cristes ore
Sk adds wolde Þat he *wolde* turnen him
Ut of þat yvel þat was so grim. 155
Þanne he weren comen alle
Bi-for þe king into the halle
At Winchestre þer he lay,
'Welcome,' he seyde, 'be ye ay!
Sk adds Y Ful michel þank kan *Y* yow 160
That ye aren comen to me now!'

Quanne he weren alle set,
And þe king haveden i-gret,
He greten and gouleden and goven hem ille,
And he bad hem alle ben stille 165
And seyde, 'Þat greting helpeth nouht,
For al to dede am Ich brouht.
Bute nou ye sen þat I shal deye,
Nou Ich wille you alle preye
Of mi douhter þat shal be 170

140 *swiþe*, quickly (cf. 586, 684, etc.).
141 *unbliþe*, wretched.
142 *stede*, place.
145 *mouhte*, could (past of *mowe*).
147 *lyþe*, relief.
148 *couþe red*, could (offer) advice (cf. 180, etc.).
149 'There was nothing for him but death' (cf. 167, etc.).
153 *yerne*, earnestly, eagerly.   *ore*, mercy, grace (cf. 211).
160 *kan*, acknowledge, express (C).
162 *set*, sat down.
163 *i-gret*, greeted.
164 *greten*, wept (and *greting* 167, *i-groten*, p.p., 285).   *goulden*, cried (ON). *goven hem ille*, grieved.
165 *stille*, quiet.

Yure levedi after me,
*H*wo may yemen hire so longe,
Boþen hire and Engelonde,
Ʒ adds be   Til þat she *be* wman of elde
H adds hire   And þat she mowe *hire* yemen and welde?'   175
He ansuereden and seyden an-an,
ion] Iohan *H*   Bi Crist and bi seint Jo*h*an,
Þat þerl Godrigh of Cornwayle
Was trewe man, wit*h*-uten faile,
Wis man of red, wis man of dede—   180
And men haveden of him mikel drede.
'He may hire alþer-best yeme
Til þat she mowe wel ben quene.'

Þe king was payed of that rede;
A wol fair cloth bringen he dede   185
And þer-on leyde þe messe-bok,
Þe caliz and þe pateyn ok,
Þe corporaus, þe messe-gere:
Þer-on he garte þe erl suere
Þat he sholde yemen hire wel   190
With-uten lac, wit*h*-uten tel,
hold   Til þat she were tuelf winter old
And of speche were bold,
And þat she couþe of curteysye
Gon] Don *Sk*   *D*on, and speken of luve-drurye,   195
mithe   And til þat she loven m*ouh*te
*H*wom so hire to gode þoucte;
yeve   And þat he shulde hire yive
beste] hexte *Sk*   Þe *hexte* man þat mi*c*hte live,

---

[171] *levedi*, lady.
[172] *yemen*, look after.
[178] *þerl=þe erl*.
[180] *red*, counsel.
[182] *alþer-best*, best of all.
[184] *payed*, pleased.
[185] *wol*, 'well', very.
[186] *messe-bok*, missal.
[187] *caliz*, chalice.   *pateyn*, paten.   *ok*, also.
[188] *corporaus*, cloth on which Host was placed.   *messe-gere*, things used in celebration of the Mass (C).
[189] *garte*, made, compelled (cf. 1003, etc.) (ON).
[191] *lac*, fault.   *tel*, reproach (cf. 2224).
[194] *curteysye*, social attitudes/behaviour appropriate to the nobility.
[195] *luve-drurye*, courtship.
[196] 'whomsoever seemed proper to her'.
[199] *hexte*, highest.

Þe beste, fayreste, the strangest ok— 200
Þat dede he him sweren on þe bok—
And þanne shulde he Engelond
Al bi-techen into hire hond.

Ouanne; his]
þis *Sk*

Quanne þat was sworn on *þis* wise
Þe king dede þe mayden arise, 205
And þe erl hire bi-taucte
And al the lond he evere awcte,
Engelonde, everi del,
And preide, he shulde yeme hire wel.

Þe king ne mowcte don no more 210
But yerne preyede Godes ore,
And dede him hoslen wel and shrive,
woth I wot, fif hundred siþes and five,
An ofte dede him sore swinge
And wit*h* hondes smerte dinge, 215
So þat þe blod ran of his fleys
Þat tendre was, and swiþe neys.
218f. *couplet
transposed in
MS.; corr.* Z He made his quiste swiþe wel
And sone gaf it evere-il del.
*H*wan it was goven, ne micte men finde 220
So mikel, men micte him in winde,
Of his, in arke ne in chiste,
In Engelond, þat no man wiste;
For al was yoven, faire and wel,
Þat him was leved no catel. 225

Þanne he havede ben ofte swngen,
Ofte shriven and ofte dungen,
'In manus tuas,' loude he seyde,

200 *strangest*, strongest.
203 *bi-techen*, entrust, hand over (past *bi-tauhte*, cf. 206, etc.).
207 *awcte*, possessed (also *auhte* 745, etc.).
212 'had the last sacraments of Communion and Absolution administered to him'.
213 *siþes*, times.
214 *swinge*, whip (and p.p. *swngen* 226).
215 *smerte*, severely. *dinge*, beat (and p.p. *dungen* 227; past *dong* 1149).
216 *fleys*, flesh.
217 *neys*, soft.
218 *quiste*, will.
220 *goven*, given (and *yoven* 224, etc.).
221 'Enough for him to be wrapped in.'
222 *arke*, coffer. *chiste*, chest.
223 'as far as anyone knew'.
225 *leved*, left. *catel*, property (cf. 2028).
228 'Into thy hands' (C).

Her	Er þat he þe speche leyde;	
	To Ihesu Crist bigan to calle	230
	And deyede bi-forn his heymen alle.	
	Þan he was ded, þere micte men se	
	Þe meste sorwe that micte be;	
	Þer was sobbing, siking and sor,	
	Handes wringing, and drawing bi hor.	235
	Alle greten swiþe sore,	
	Riche and povre þat þere wore,	
	An mikel sorwe haveden alle,	
	Levedyes in boure, knictes in halle.	
	Quan þat sorwe was som-del laten	240
	And he haveden longe graten,	
	Belles deden he sone ringen,	
	Monkes and prestes messe singen,	
	And sauteres deden he manie reden	
	Þat God self shulde his soule leden	245
	Into hevene, bi-forn his sone —	
	And þer with-uten ende wone.	
	Þan he was to þe erþe brouht	
	Þe riche erl ne foryat nouht	
	Þat he ne dede al Engelond	250
	Sone sayse in-til his hond,	
leth	And in þe castels let he do	
	Þe knictes he micte tristen to,	
	And alle þe Englis dede he sweren	
ghod	Þat he shulden him god fey beren;	255
	He yaf alle men þat god þoucte,	
him] corr. Sk	Liven and deyen til þat he moucte,	
	Til þat þe kinges dowter wore	
hold	Tuenti winter old, and more.	

229 'Before he became speechless.'
231 *heymen*, nobles.
233 *meste*, greatest.
234 *siking*, sighing.   *sor*, grief.
235 'and tearing at hair'.
239 *boure*, private room.
240 *som-del*, somewhat, a little.   *laten*, abated.
241 *graten*, wept (cf. 164).
244 *sauteres*, psalters.
247 *wone*, dwell.
249 *foryat*, forgot.
251 *sayse*, take possession of (C).
252 *let*, caused.   *do*, 'to be placed' (*do*=place).
253 'whom he could trust'.
255 *fey*, faith, loyalty (cf. 1671).
256 '. . . what seemed good to him'.

New para MS   Þanne he havede taken þis oth   260
Of erles, baruns, lef and loth,
Of knictes, cherles, fre and þewe,
Justises dede he maken newe
Al Engelond to faren þorw
Fro Dovere into Rokesborw.   265
Schireves he sette, bedels and greyves,
Grith-sergeans wit*h* longe gleyves
To yemen wilde wodes and paþes
Fro wicke men þat wolde don scaþes;
And for-to haven alle at his cri,   270
At his wille, at hise merci,
Þat non durste ben him ageyn,
Erl ne barun, knict ne sweyn.
Wislike, for sothe, was him wel
Of folk, of wepne, of catel.   275
Soþlike, in a lite þrawe,
Al Engelond of him stod awe;

adred   Al Engelond was of him adr*a*d
MS., but Sk   So *is* þe beste fro þe gad.
claims that the
e *is altered to* a
279 his   Þe kinges douh*ter* bi-gan þrive   280
And wex þe fayrest wman on live.
Of alle þewes w*as* she wis
Þat gode weren, and of pris.
Þe mayden Goldeboru was hoten—
For hire was mani a ter i-groten.   285

Quanne þe erl Godrich him herde
Of þat mayden, hw we*l s*he ferde,
H*w* wis sho was, *h*w chaste, hw fayr,

²⁶¹ *lef and loth*, friend and foe.
²⁶² *cherles*, servants.   *þewe*, slaves.
²⁶⁴ *faren*, travel.
²⁶⁶ *schireves*, sheriffs (C).   *bedels*, beadles (C).   *greyves*, town officers (C) (ON).
²⁶⁷ *grith-sergeans*, officers of the watch.   *gleyves*, swords.
²⁶⁹ *scapes*, harm, injuries (cf. 1356) (ON).
²⁷⁰ *at his cri*, at his command.
²⁷² *ageyn*, against.
²⁷⁴ *wislike*, truly.   *wan him wel*, he was well provided.
²⁷⁶ *lite*, little.   *þrawe*, space of time.
²⁷⁷ 'All England was afraid of him' (C).
²⁷⁸ *adrad*, afraid.
²⁷⁹ *beste*, beast (and *best* 946).   *gad*, goad (cf. 1018).
²⁸¹ *wex*, grew (and p.p. *waxen* 302).
²⁸² *þewes*, manners.   *wis*, wise, discreet.
²⁸³ *of pris*, estimable.
²⁸⁵ *ter*, tear.

And þat sho was þe rihte eyr
Of Engelond, of al þe rike,   290
Þo bi-gan Godrich to sike,
And seyde, 'Hweþer she sholde be
Quen and levedi over me?
Hweþer sho sholde al Engelond,
And me, and mine, haven in hire hond?   295
Daþeit hwo it hire þave—
Shal sho it nevere more have!
Sholde Ic yeve a fol, a þerne,
Engelond, þou sho it yerne?

yeve   Daþeit hwo it hire yive   300
Evere-more hwil I live!
Sho is waxen al to prud
For gode metes and noble shrud

hic   Þat Ic have yoven hire to offte;
Hic   Ic have yemed hire to softe.   305
Shal it nouht ben als sho þenkes—
Hope maketh fol man ofte blenkes.
Ich have a sone, a ful fayr knave:
He shal Engelond al have.

Sk adds ben   He shal ben king, he shal ben sire,   310
So brouke I evere mi blake swire!'

Hwan þis trayson was al þouht,
Of his oth ne was him nouht.
He let his oth al over-ga—
Þerof ne yaf he nouht a stra,   315
Bute sone dede hire fete,

heten   Er he wolde eten ani mete,
Fro Winchestre, þer sho was,
Al-so a wicke traytur Judas,
And dede leden hire to Dovre   320

---

291 *sike*, sigh.
292 *hweþer*, interrogative particle.
296 *daþeit*, cursed be (he who . . .)   *þave*, allow, endure (cf. 2701).
298 *fol*, fool.   *þerne*, serving-wench, slut.
299 *yerne*, desire.
303 *for*, because of.   *metes*, food.   *shrud*, clothes.
305 'I have brought her up too delicately.'
307 'Hope often plays a fool tricks.'
308 *knave*, boy.
311 'As I wish to enjoy my white neck' (C).
314 *over-ga*, come to nothing.
315 *yaf* (past of *yive*), care (cf. 419, etc.).   *stra*, straw.
316 *fete*, fetch.
319 *al-so*, just like.

Þat standeth on þe seis ovre,

þerhinne   And þer-inne dede hire fede

Povrelike, in feble wede.

Þe castel dede he yemen so

Þat non ne micte comen hire to   325

Of hire frend, with to speken,

heuere   Þat evere micte hire bale wreken.

Of Goldeboru shul we nou laten,

Þat nouht ne blinneth for-to graten

Þer sho liggeth in prisoun: 330

Ihesu Crist, that Lazarun

To live broucte fro dede-bondes,

He lese hire with hise hondes,

mo] *corr.* Z   And leve sho mote him y-se

Heye hangen on galwe-tre   335

Þat hire haved in sorwe brouht,

So as sho ne misdede nouht!

hure   Say we nou forth in ure spelle!

In þat time, so it bi-felle,

Was in þe lond of Denemark   340

A riche king and swyþe stark.

Þe name of him was Birkabeyn;

He havede mani knict and sueyn.

He was fayr man and wicht;

Of bodi he was þe beste knicht   345

uth   Þat evere micte leden ut here,

Or stede onne ride, or handlen spere.

Þre children he havede bi his wif;

He hem lovede so his lif.

Sk adds and   He havede a sone *and* douhtres two,   350

---

321 *seis ovre*, sea's shore.
323 *feble*, wretched.
326 *frend*, relations, friends (cf. 2073).
327 'who could ever avenge her wrong'.
328 *laten*, leave (off).
329 *blinneth*, ceases (and past *blunne* 2675).   *graten*, weep.
330 *liggeth*, lies (cf. 804, etc.).
332 *live*, life.   *dede-bondes*, bonds of death.
333 *he lese*, may he set free.
334 *leve*, grant (cf. 406, 2812).
337 *so as*, whereas, when.
338 'Let us now go on with our story.'
341 *stark*, strong.
349 *so*, as.

Swiþe fayre, as fel it so.
He þat wile non forbere,
Riche ne povre, king ne kaysere,

wolde] wilde Hupe

Deth, him tok þan he best wilde

355 fulde] filde Hupe

Liven, but hyse dayes were filde,   355
Þat he ne moucte no more live
For gold ne silver, ne for no gyve.

Hwan he þat wiste, raþe he sende
After prestes fer an hende,
Chanounes gode and monkes boþe   360

rede] roþe Si

Him for-to wisse, and to roþe;

hoslon

Him for-to hoslen, an for-to shrive
Hwil his bodi were on live.

Hwan he was hosled and shriven,
His quiste maked, and for him gyven,   365
His knictes dede he alle site,
For þorw hem he wolde wite
Hwo micte yeme hise children yunge
Til þat he kouþen speken with tunge,
Speken and gangen, on horse riden,   370
Knictes an sweynes bi here siden.
He spoken þer-offe, and chosen sone

was] þat Z

A riche man, þat under mone
Was þe trewest, as he wende,
Godard, þe kinges oune frende;   375
And seyden, he mouchte hem best loke,
Yif þat he hem under-toke,
Til hise sone mouhte bere

---

351 'as it happened'.
352 *forbere*, spare, neglect (past *forbar* 766).
353 *kaysere*, emperor (cf. Germ. *Kaiser*).
354 'when he most desired . . .'.
355 *filde*, completed.
357 *gyve*, gift.
358 *raþe*, quickly.
359 *fer*, far (cf. 1868, etc).   *hende*, at hand, near (cf. 2280).
360 *chanounes*, canons.
361 *roþe*, advise (and *rathe* 1339) (ON).
368 *wite*, know (contrast 405).
370 *gangen*, walk, go (and *gonge* 692, etc.).
371 'With knights and retainers beside them.'
372 'They discussed the matter.'
374 *wende*, supposed.
375 *oune frende*, personal friend.
376 *loke*, take care of.
377 *under-toke*, took in charge.

Helm on heved, and leden ut here,
In his hand a spere stark,   380
And king ben maked of Denemark.
He wel trowede þat he seyde,
And on Godard handes leyde
And seyde, 'Here bi-teche I þe
Mine children alle þre,   385
Al Denemark, and al mi fe,
helde   Til þat mi sone of elde be;
But þat Ich wille, þat þou suere
On auter, and on messe-gere,
On þe belles þat men ringes,   390
On messe-bok þe prest on singes,
Þat þou mine children shalt wel yeme,
Þat hire kin be ful wel queme,
Til mi sone mowe ben knicht;
Þanne bi-teche him þo his richt,   395
Denemark, and þat þer-til longes,
Casteles and tunes, wodes and wonges.'

Godard stirt up, an swor al þat
Þe king him bad, and siþen sat
Bi þe knictes þat þer ware,   400
Þat wepen alle swiþe sare
For þe king þat deide sone.
Ihesu Crist, þat makede mone
On þe mirke niht to shine,
Wite his soule fro helle-pine,   405
And leve þat it mote wone
In hevene-riche with Godes sone!

Hwan Birkabeyn was leyd in grave,
Þe erl dede sone take þe knave,
eir] broþer *Si*   Havelok, þat was þe *broþer*,   410
helfled   Swanborow his sister, Elfled þe toþer,

---

[379] *helm*, helmet.   *heved*, head.   *here*, army.
[382] 'He faithfully accepted what they said.'   *trowede*, believed.
[389] *auter*, altar.
[393] 'So that it may be pleasing to their kinsmen.'
[396] *þer-til longes*, belongs to it, goes with it (cf. 1447).
[397] *wodes*, woods.   *wonges*, plains (formulaic; cf. 1448).
[398] *stirt*, leapt.
[404] *mirke*, dark.
[405] *wite*, protect.   *helle-pine*, torment of hell.
[411] *þe toþer*, the other.

And in þe castel dede he hem do,
Þer non ne micte hem comen to
were   Of here kyn, þer þei sperd w*o*re;
Þer he greten ofte sore,   415
Boþe for hunger and for kold,
hold   Or he weren þre winter old.
Feblelike he gaf hem cloþes—
He ne yaf a note of hise oþes.
Sk adds ne   He hem *ne* cloþede ri*ht*, ne fedde,   420
Ne hem ne dede richelike be-bedde.
Þanne Godard was sikerlike
Under God þe moste swike
Þat evre in erþe shaped was,
With-uten on, þe wike Judas.   425
Have he þe malisun to-day
Of alle þat evre speken may!
Of patriark and of pope
And of prest with loken kope,
Of monekes and hermites boþe   430
431 *No gap in*   *   *   *   *   *   *   *
MS.   And of þe leve holi rode
Þat God him-selve ran on blode!
Crist warie him with his mouth!
Waried wrthe he of norþ and suth!   435
man   Offe alle m*e*n þat speken kunne,
maude   Of Crist þat made mone and sunne!
Þanne he havede of al þe lond
Al þe folk tilled in-til his hond,
And alle haveden sworen him oth,   440
Riche and povre, lef and loth,

---

412 *do*, place, imprison.
414 *sperd*, locked up.
419 *note*, nut (and *noute* 1336).
421 *be-bedde*, provide with bed.
422 *sikerlike*, surely.
423 *swike*, traitor.
424 *shaped*, created.
425 *with-uten on*, except one.   *wike*, wicked.
426 *malisun*, curse.
429 *loken*, closed (cf. 1962).
432 *leve*, dear.
433 'On which God himself shed his blood.'
434 *warie*, curse.
435 *wrthe*, let him be.
436 *kunne*, can.
439 *tilled*, brought over.

Þat he sholden hise wille freme,
And þat he shulde him nou*h*t greme,
He þou*h*te a ful strong trechery,
A trayson and a felony   445
Of þe children for-to make—
Þe devel of helle him sone take!

Hwan þat was þou*h*t, on-on he ferde
To þe tour þer he woren sperde,
Þer he greten for hunger and cold.   450
Þe knave, þat was sum-del bold,
Kam him ageyn, on knes him sette,
And Godard ful feyre he þer grette;
And Godard seyde, '*H*wat is yw?
Hwi grete ye and goulen nou?'   455
'For us hungreth swiþe sore,'

Sk adds We
hete

Seyden he, '*We* wolden more:
We ne have to ete, ne we ne have
Her-inne neyther kni*h*t ne knave
Þat yeveth us drinken, ne no mete,   460
Halven-del þat we moun ete.
Wo is us þat we weren born!
Weilawei! nis it no korn
Þat men micte maken of bred?

þs] Us (Ws *Sk*):
Sk adds so

*W*s hungreth *so*, we aren ney ded.'   465

Godard herde here wa;
Ther-offe yaf he nou*h*t a stra,
But tok þe maydnes bothe samen
Al-so it were upon hiis gamen,
Al-so he wolde with hem leyke   470
Þat weren for hunger grene and bleike.
Of boþen he karf on-two here þrotes,

---

442 *freme*, do, accomplish.
443 *greme*, annoy.
449 *tour*, tower.
452 *ageyn*, towards.
454 'What is the matter with you?'
461 *halven-del*, (by) half.
463 *weilawei*, alas.   *nis it no korn*, is there no corn?
464 'of which men might make bread'.
465 *ney*, nearly.
466 *wa*, misery, woe.
469 'as it were in play'.
470 *leyke*, play (cf. 952) (ON).
471 *bleike*, pale (ON).
472 *karf*, cut.

And siþen hem, al to grotes.
Þer was sorwe, *h*wo so it sawe,
Hwan þe children bi þe wawe   475
Leyen and sprauleden in þe blod!
Havelok it saw, and þer-bi stod.
Ful sori was þat seli knave;
Mikel dred he mou*hte* have,
For at hise herte he saw a knif,   480
For-to reven him hise lyf.
But þe k*n*ave, þat litel was,
He knelede bifor þat Judas,
And seyde, 'Loverd, merci nou!
Manrede, loverd, biddi you!   485
yeue   Al Denemark I wile you y*i*ve,
To þat forward þu late me live.
hi   Here I wile on boke swere
Þat nevre more ne shal I bere
Ayen þe, loverd, shel*d* ne spere,   490
MS. has wepne Ne oþer wepne þat may you dere.
bere; *corr. Sk* Loverd, have merci of me!
To-day I wile fro Denemark fle,
Ne nevere more comen ageyn;
Sweren Y wole, þat Bircabein   495
Nevere yete me ne gat.'
Hwan þe devel he*r*de þat,
Sum-del bigan him for-to rewe;
With-drow þe knif, þat was lewe
Of þe seli children blod —   500
Þer was miracle fair and god,
Þat he þe knave nou*ht* ne slou
But fo*r* rewnesse him wi*th*-drow.
Of *H*avelok rewede him ful sore —

---

473 *grotes*, little pieces.
474 'for whoever saw it'.
475 *wawe*, wall.
476 *sprauleden*, sprawled.
478 *seli*, innocent (C).
481 *reven*, deprive.
485 *manrede*, homage.   *biddi*, I offer (= *bidde I*).
487 *forward*, condition, agreement (cf. 556).
491 *dere*, harm, injure (cf. 650, etc.).
496 'never begot me'.
498 *rewe*, pity (impersonal verb).
499 *lewe*, warm (cf. 2926).
502 *slou*, slew (also *slow*; inf. *slo* 513, p.p. *slawe* 1808).
503 *rewnesse*, pity.

þoucte] þouh	And _þouh_ he wolde þat he ded wore,	505
Napier	But on þat he _nolde_ wi_th_ his hend	
506 nouth]	Ne drepe him nou_h_t, þat fule fend.	
nolde _Sk_	Þoucte he, als he him bi-stod,	
	Starinde als he were wod,	
	'Yif Y late him lives go,	510
	He micte me wirchen michel wo.	
	Grith ne get Y nevere mo:	
Sk adds me	He may _me_ waiten for-to slo;	
	And yf he were brouct of live,	
	And mine children wolden thrive,	515
	Loverdinges after me	
	Of al Denemark micten he be.	
	God it wite, he shal ben ded—	
	Wile I taken non oþer red!	
she	I shal do casten him in þe se:	520
	Þer I wile þat he drench_ed_ be;	
	Abouten his hals an anker god,	
þad	Þa_t_ he ne flete in the flod.'	
	Þer an-on he dede sende	
	After a fishere, þat he wende	525
	Þat wolde al his wille do,	
	And sone an-on seyde him to:	
	'Grim, þou wost þu art mi þral;	
	Wilte don mi wille al	
	Þat I wile bidden þe,	530
Sk adds I	To-morwen _I_ shal maken þe fre,	
	And aucte þe yeven, and riche make,	
	With þan þu wilt þis child take	

[505] _þouh_, yet, even so.
[506] _but on_, save only (cf. 964).   _hend_, hands (cf. 2074, etc.).
[507] _drepe_, kill (past _drop_ 2234, p.p. _dropen_ 1788).   _fule_, foul (cf. 557, etc.).   _fend_, fiend, devil.
[509] _wod_, mad (cf. 1782, etc.).
[510] _lives_, alive (adverbial use of genitive) (cf. 1309).
[511] _wirchen_, do.
[513] _waiten_, lie in wait.
[514] _brouct of live_, killed.
[516] _loverdinges_, lords.
[518] 'Let God know it.'
[521] _drenched_, drowned.
[522] _hals_, neck (cf. 2515, etc.).
[523] _flete_, float.   _flod_, water.
[525–6] 'who he thought would do his will'.
[528] _þral_, servant, slave (contrast 1412) (ON).
[529] _wilte_, (if) you will.
[530] _bidden_, ask (cf. 912, etc.; past _bad_ 936, etc.).
[532] _aucte_, wealth.
[533] _with þan_, provided that.

	And leden him with þe to-nicht	
þan *all edd.; but* *MS. has* þai; se	Þan þou sest þe mone-li*ht*,	535
	In-to þe se, and don him þer-inne—	
Sk adds I	Al wile *I* taken on me þe sinne.'	
	Grim tok þe child, and bond him faste,	
	Hwil þe bondes micte laste,	
	Þat weren of ful strong line;	540
	Þo was Havelok in ful strong pine.	
her	Wiste he nevere er *h*wat was wo;	
	Ihesu Crist, þat makede to go	
speken	Þe halte, and þe doumbe speke,	
	Havelok, þe of Godard wreke!	545

	Hwan Grim him havede faste bounden,	
	And siþen in an eld cloth wnden,	
548 *Not in MS.;* *restored from* *Cambridge* *Fragments* (*reading* muþ) (C)	He þriste in his mo*u*þ wel faste	
	A kevel of clutes, ful unwraste,	
	Þat he *ne* mou*h*te speke ne fnaste,	550
	Hwere he wolde him bere or lede.	
	Hwan he havede don þat dede,	
550 *Sk adds* ne	*Als* þe swike him *bad*, he yede,	
553 Hwan, havede =] as, bad *Ho*	Þat he shulde him forth *lede*	
	And him dreinchen in þe se—	555
554 *Sk adds* lede	Þat forwarde makeden he.	
	In a poke, ful and blac,	
	Sone he caste him on his bac,	
	And bar him hom to hise cleve,	
	And bi-taucte him dame Leve,	560
	And seyde, 'Wite þou þis knave	
with] wilt *Garnett Ho* *adds* save	Al-so þou *wilt* mi lif have *save*.	
	I shal dreinchen him in þe se;	
	For him shole we ben maked fre,	

---

[537] 'I will take the responsibility on myself entirely.'
[540] *line*, cord.
[541] *pine*, pain.
[542] 'never before had he known what pain was'.
[544] *halte*, lame.
[545] 'May (Christ) take vengeance, Havelok, for your sake, upon Godard.'
[547] *wnden*, wrapped.
[548] *þriste*, thrust.
[549] *kevel*, gag (cf. *unkevelen* 603) (ON).   *clutes*, rags.   *unwraste*, filthy (cf. 2826).
[550] *fnaste*, breathe.
[551] *hwere*, wherever.
[557] *poke*, bag.
[559] *cleve*, cottage.
[560] *wite*, look after.
[562] *save*, safe (cf. 2231).

Gold haven ynou, and oþer fe—   565
Þat haveth mi loverd bi-hoten me.'

Sk adds Leue   Hwan dame *Leve* herde þat,
Up she stirte, and nouht ne sat,
569f. adoun so   And caste þe knave so harde adoune
harde/þat hise   Þat he crakede þer hise croune   570
croune he þer   Ageyn a gret ston, þer it lay;
crakede]   Þo Havelok micte sei, 'Weilawei!
corr. Morris   Þat evere was I kinges bern—
Þat him ne havede grip or ern,
Leoun or wlf, wlvine or bere,   575
Or oþer best þat wolde him dere!'
So lay þat child to middel nicht,
Þat Grim bad Leve bringen lict
For to don on his cloþes:
'Ne thenkeste nowt of mine oþes   580
Þat Ich have mi loverd sworen?
Ne wile I nouht be forloren.
I shal beren him to þe se;
Sk adds so bi-   Þou wost þat *so bi*-hoves me;
And I shal drenchen him þer-inne.   585
Ris up swiþe, an go þu binne,
And blou þe fir, and liht a kandel.'
Als she shulde hise cloþes handel
þer   On for-to don, and blawe þe fir,
She saw þer-inne a liht ful shir,   590
Al-so briht so it were day,
Aboute þe knave þer he lay.
Of hise mouth it stod a stem
Als it were a sunne-bem;
Al-so liht was it þer-inne   595
So þer brenden cerges inne.
wat] quath *Sk*   'Ihesu Crist!' *quath* dame Leve,

---

565 *ynou*, enough.
566 *bi-hoten*, promised (past ind. *bi-hetet* 679).
573 *bern*, child ('bairn').
574 *grip*, vulture.   *ern*, eagle.   On syntax, see (C).
575 *wlvine*, wolverine.
579 *don on*, put on ('don').
582 *forloren*, lost.
584 *bi-hoves*, is necessary.
586 *binne*, inside (C).
590 *shir*, bright.
591 *al-so*, just as (cf. 595, etc.).
593 *stem*, ray.
596 *brenden*, burned.   *cerges*, candles (also *serges* 2130).   *inne*, in there.

'Hwat is þat li*ht* in ure cleve?

Sir] *corr.* Ƶ   *Ris* up, Grim, and loke *h*wat it menes,

Hwat is þe li*ht*, as þou wenes?'   600

He stirten boþe up to the knave

(For man shal god wille have)

Unkeveleden him and swiþe unbounden,

Sk adds upon   And sone an-on *upon* him funden,

Als he tirveden of his serk,   605

On hise ri*ht* shuldre a kyne-merk,

A swiþe bri*ht*, a swiþe fair.

H adds is   'Goddot!' quath Grim, 'þis *is* ure eir

Sk adds ben   Þat shal *ben* loverd of Denemark;

He shal ben king, strong and stark.   610

He shal haven in his hand

A*l* Denemark and Engeland;

He shal do Godard ful wo—

He shal him hangen, or quik flo,

Or he shal him al quic grave: 615

Of him shal he no merci have.'

Þus seide Grim, and sore gret,

And sone fel him to þe fet

And seide, 'Loverd, have merci

Of me, and Leve, þat is me bi!   620

Loverd, we aren boþe þine,

Þine cherles, þine hine.

Lowerd, we sholen þe wel fede

Til þat þu cone riden on stede,

Til þat þu cone ful wel bere   625

Helm on heved, sheld and spere.

He ne shal nevere, sikerlike,

wite *trans-*   Godard, *wite*, þat fule swike.

posed from

after nevere in   Þoru oþer man, loverd, than þoru þe

627 *by Sk*   Sal I nevere freman be.   630

Þou shalt me, loverd, fre maken,

For I shal yemen þe, and waken;

Þoru þe wile I fredom have.'

Þo was Haveloc a bliþe knave;

---

605 *tirveden*, stripped (cf. *to-turven* 920).   *serk*, shirt (ON).

606 *kyne-merk*, royal mark (and *kunmerk* 2148) (C).

608 *Goddot*=God wot.

614 *quik*, alive.   *flo*, flay (past *flowe* 2438, p.p. *flawen* 2481).

615 *grave*, bury.

618 'fell at his feet'.

621 *hine*, servants.

624 *cone*, subjunctive of *can.*

629f. i.e. I will accept freedom only from you.

632 *waken*, watch over.

He sat him up, and cravede bred,   635
And seide, 'Ich am ney ded,
Hwat for hunger, *h*wat for bondes
Þat þu leidest on min hondes,

Sk adds þe   And for *þe* kevel at þe laste
Þat in mi mouth was þrist faste.   640
Y was þer-with so harde prangled
Þat I was þer-with ney strangled.'

hete   'Wel is me þat þu may*ht* ete;
Goddoth   Goddot!' quath Leve, 'Y shal þe fete
Bred an chese, butere and milk,   645
Pastees and flaunes; al with suilk
Shole we sone þe wel fede,
Loverd, in þis mikel nede;
Soth it is, þat men sey*th* and suereth:
Þer God wile helpen, nou*ht* ne dereth.'   650

Þanne sho havede brou*ht* þe mete,
Haveloc an-on bigan to ete
Grundlike, and was ful bliþe—
Couþe he nouht his hunger miþe.

het, woth   A lof he et, Y wot, and more,   655
For him hungrede swiþe sore.
Þre dayes þer-biforn, I wene,
Et he no mete—þat was wel sene!
Hwan he havede eten, and was fed,
Grim dede maken a ful fayr bed,   660
Uncloþede him, and dede him þer-inne,
And seyde, 'Slep, sone, with michel winne!
Slep wel faste, and dred þe nou*ht*:
Fro sorwe to joie art þu brou*ht*.'
Sone so it was li*ht* of day,   665
Grim it under-tok, þe wey
To þe wicke traitour Godard,

H adds of;   Þat was *of* Denemar*k* stiward,
Denemak a   And seyde, 'Loverd, don Ich have

[635] *cravede*, begged for.
[637] *hwat for*, cf. 'what with'.
[641] *prangled*, tied, pinched.
[642] *strangled*, choked.
[646] *flaunes*, custard- or cheese-cakes ('flans').   *suilk*, such.
[653] *grundlike*, heartily (cf. 2664).
[654] *miþe*, conceal (cf. 950, etc.).
[658] 'that was clearly visible!'
[662] *winne*, joy.
[666] *under-tok*, took (went).
[668] *stiward*, cf. *SO* 205 (C).

Þat þou me bede of þe knave;   670
He is drenched in þe flod,
Abouten his hals an anker god;
He is witerlike ded—
Eteth he nevre more bred;
He liþ drenched in þe se;   675

Sk adds and   Yif me gold *and* oþer fe
Þat Y mowe riche be,
And with þi chartre make fre,
For þu ful wel bi-hetet me
Þanne I last spak with þe.'   680
Godard stod and lokede on him
Þoruth-like, with eyne grim,
And seyde, 'Wiltu ben erl?
Go hom swiþe, fule drit-cherl;
Go heþen, and be evere-more   685
Þral and cherl, als þou er wore.

Shal] Shaltu *Sk*   Shal*tu* have non oþer mede;
Sk adds shal   For litel *shal* I do þe lede
To þe galues, so God me rede,
For þou haves don a wicke dede.   690
Þou mai*h*t stonden her to longe,
Bute þou swiþe *h*eþen gonge.'

Grim thouc*h*te to late þat he ran
Fro þat traytour, *þ*at wicke man,
rede] roþe *H*   And þoucte, '*H*wat shal me to *roþe*?   695
beþe] boþe *H*,   Wite he him on live, he wile *us boþe*
and adds us   Heye hangen on galwe-tre;
(*after*   Betere us is of londe to fle
Wittenbrinck)   And berwen boþen ure lives,
And mine children and mine wives.'   700
Grim solde sone al his corn,

[670] *bede*, commanded.
[673] *witerlike*, certainly.
[679] *bihetet=bihete it* (cf. *havedet* 716).
[684] *drit-cherl*, filthy slave.
[685] *heþen*, hence.
[686] 'As you were before.'
[691] i.e. for your own good.
[692] *heþen*, from here.
[693] 'It seemed to G. that he couldn't get away quickly enough . . .
[695] *to roþe*, as advice (C) (i.e. 'what shall I do?').
[696] 'if he discovers him to be alive'.
[699] *berwen*, save (and *burwe* 2875; past *barw* 2027).
[700] 'and those of my children and my wife'.

neth	Shep wit*h* wolle, net wit*h* horn,
Sk adds and geet	Hors and swin *and geet* wit*h* berd,
	Þe gees, þe hennes of þe yerd:
	Al he solde, þat ou*ht* dou*hte*, 705
	Þat he evre selle moucte,
	And al he to peni drou.
	Hise ship he greyþede wel inow;
	He dede it tere an ful wel pike,
	Þat it ne doutede sond ne krike; 710
	Þer-inne dide a ful god mast,
	Stronge kables and ful fast,
	Ores gode, an ful god seyl;
	Þer-inne wantede nou*ht* a nayl
	Þat evere he sholde þer-inne do. 715
	Hwan he havedet greyþed so,
	Havelok þe yunge he dede þer-inne,
	Him and his wif, hise sones þrinne,
	And hise two dou*h*tres, þat faire wore;
	And sone dede he leyn in an ore, 720
	And drou him to þe heye se
	Þere he mi*ht* alþer-best fle.
	Fro londe woren he bote a mile,
Sk adds it	Ne were *it* nevere but ane hwile
	Þat it ne bigan a wind to rise 725
	Out of þe north, men calleth bise,
	And drof hem in-til Engelond
	Þat al was siþen in his hond,
	His, þat Havelok was þe name;
	But or, he havede michel shame, 730

702 *net*, cattle (also sing. 'ox', 810, 1028, etc.).
703 *geet*, goats.
705 *ouht*, anything.   *douhte*, was worth, was good (cf. 835, etc.).
707 'turned into cash'.
708 *greyþede*, made ready (ON).
709 *tere*, tar (v).   *pike*, pitch (v).
710 *doutede*, feared (subjunctive).   *sond*, sandbank? strait? ('sound').   *krike*, creek.
714 *wantede*, lacked.
715 'that he needed to put into it'.
718 *þrinne*, three (ON).
720 *leyn in*, put in (*sc*. the water).
721 *drou him to*, made for, betook himself to.
723 *bote*, only, 'but'.
724 *hwile*, little time.
726 *bise*, the French name of the wind.
728 'That was afterwards all in his possession.
730 *or*, before (that).

Michel sorwe and michel tene—
þrie] yete *Sk*   And *yete* he gat it al bidene,
here] lere *Sk*   Als ye shulen nou forthward *l*ere,
Yf that ye wilen þer-to here.

In Humber Grim bigan to lende,   735
In Lindeseye, ri*ht* at þe north ende.
Þer sat *his* ship up-on þe sond,
But Grim it drou up to þe lond,
And þere he made a litel cote
To him and to hise flote.   740
erþe (*see* (*C*))   Bigan he þere for-to er*d*e,
A litel hus to maken of erþe,
So þat he wel þore were
Of here herboru herborwed þere;
And for þat Grim þat place au*h*te,   745
Þe stede of Grim þe name lau*h*te,
calleth alle]   So þat Grimesbi *it calle*
corr. Ƶ   Þat þer-offe speken alle,
And so shulen men it callen ay
Bituene þis and domesday.   750

Grim was fishere swiþe god,
And mikel couþe on the flod.
Mani god fish þer-inne he tok,
neth   Boþe with net, and with hok.
He tok þe sturgiun, and þe qual,   755
And þe turbut, and lax with-al.
hwel] el *Sk*   He tok þe sele, and þe *el*;
He spedde ofte swiþe wel:
Keling he tok, and tumberel,
Hering, and þe makerel,   760
Þe butte, þe schulle, þe þornebake;

731 *tene*, grief.
732 *bidene*, presently.
733 *forthward*, in due course.   *lere*, learn.
735 *lende*, dwell.
740 *flote*, company.
741 *erde*, inhabit.
744 *herboru*, shelter, lodging.
746 *lauhte*, received.
752 *mikel couþe*, was skilled, experienced.
755 *qual*, whale, dolphin? starfish? (C).
756 *lax*, salmon.
757 *sele*, seal.   *el*, eel.
759 *keling*, cod.   *tumberel*, porpoise?
761 *butte*, halibut.   *schulle*, plaice.   *þornebake*, skate.

Gode paniers dede he make,
On til him, and oþer þrinne
Til hise sones, to beren fish inne,

fonge] chonge
H
Up o londe to selle and *ch*onge;   765
For-bar he neyþer tun ne gronge
Þat he ne to yede with his ware;
Kam he nevere hom hand-bare
Þat he ne broucte bred and sowel
In his shirte, or in his couel,   770
In his poke benes and korn—
Hise swink ne havede he nowt for-lorn.
And hwan he tok þe grete laumprei,
Ful we*l* he couþe þe ri*ht*e wei
To Lincolne, þe gode boru;   775
Ofte he yede it þoru and þoru,
Til he havede wol wel sold
And þer-fore þe penies told.
Þanne he com þenne, he were bliþe,
For hom he brou*ht*e fele siþe   780
Wastels, simenels wiþ þe horn,
Hise pokes fulle of mele an korn,
Netes flesh, shepes and swines,
And hemp to maken of gode lines,
And stronge ropes to hise netes—   785

se weren]
seweres *Sm*
In þe sewere*s* he ofte setes.

Þus-gate Grim him fayre ledde;
Him and his genge wel he fedde
Wel twelf winter oþer more.
Havelok was war þat Grim swank sore   790
For his mete, and he lay at hom;

762 *paniers*, baskets.
763 'One for himself, and three others.'
765 *chonge*, exchange.
766 *gronge*, farmhouse ('grange').
768 *hand-bare*, empty-handed.
769 *sowel*, something eaten with bread.
770 *couel*, cloak.
772 *swink*, labour (cf. *swank* 790 (worked)).   *for-lorn*, wasted.
773 *laumprei*, lamprey.
776 *þoru and þoru*, throughout.
777 *wol*, thoroughly, very.
778 *told*, counted.
781 *wastels*, fine loaves (cf. Fr. *gâteau*).   *simenels*, loaves, cakes?   *wiþ þe horn*, three-cornered?
786 *seweres*, water-channels (C).   *setes*, set them?
787 *him ledde*, lived ('led his life').
788 *genge*, household, company (cf. 798).

þhouthe (*sic*)	Þhou*h*t he, 'Ich am nou no grom;
	Ich am wel waxen, and wel may eten
	More þan evere Grim may geten.
	Ich ete more, bi God on live,
	Þan Grim an hise children five!
longe	It ne may nou*ht* ben þus lenge;
gange (*see* (*C*))	Goddot! Y wile with þe genge
	For-to leren sum god to gete—
	Swinken Ich wolde for mi mete.
	It is no shame for-to swinken;
	Þe man þat may wel eten and drinken
þat] þar *H*	Þar nou*ht* ne have but on swink long;
	To liggen at hom it is ful strong.
	God yelde him, þer I ne may
	Þat haveth me fed to þis day!
	Gladlike I wile þe paniers bere;
woth	Ich wot, ne shal it me nou*ht* dere,
	Þey þer be inne a birþene gret
neth	Al-so hevi als a net.
	Shal Ich nevere lengere dwelle;
	To-morwen shal Ich forth pelle.'

Line numbers: 795, 800, 805, 810

On þe morwen, hwan it was day,
He stirt up sone, and nou*ht* ne lay,
And cast a panier on his bac
With fish giveled als a stac;
Al-so michel he bar him one
So he foure, bi mine mone!
Wel he it bar, and solde it wel;
Þe silver he brou*te* hom il-del,
Al þat he þer-fore tok—
With-held he nou*ht* a ferþinges nok.
So yede he forth ilke day,
Þat he nevere at home lay;

Line numbers: 815, 820

792 *grom*, boy.
797 *lenge*, longer.
803 *þar*, ought. *on . . . long*, through ('along of').
804 *strong*, shameful.
805 *yelde*, repay. *þer*, insofar as.
809 *birþene*, burden, weight.
812 *pelle*, hurry.
813 *morwen*, next day.
816 *giveled*, piled up.
817 *him one*, by himself (cf. 938).
818 'as the four of them, in my opinion'.
820 *il-del*, every bit (=*ilk-del*).
822 'a fraction of a farthing'.

So wolde he his mester lere. 825
Bifel it so, a strong dere
Bigan to rise of korn of bred,
Þat Grim ne couþe no god red,
Hw he sholde his meiné fede;
Of Havelok havede he michel drede, 830
For he was strong, and wel mouhte ete
heuere More þanne evere mouhte he gete,
Ne he ne mouhte on þe se take
Neyþer lenge ne þornbake;
Ne non oþer fish þat douhte 835
His meyne feden with he mouhte.
Of Havelok he havede kare,
Hwil-gat þat he michte fare;
Of his children was him nouht—
On Havelok was al hise þouht; 840
And seyde, 'Havelok, dere sone,
I wene that we deye mone
For hunger, þis dere is so strong,
hure And ure mete is uten long.
Betere is þat þu henne gonge 845
Þan þu here dwelle longe;
Heþen þow mayht gangen to late.
Thou canst ful wel þe richte gate
To Lincolne, þe gode borw—
Þou havest it gon ful ofte þoru. 850
Of me ne is me nouht a slo;
Betere is þat þu þider go,
For þer is mani god man inne
Þer þou mayht þi mete winne.
But wo is me! þou art so naked; 855
Of mi seyl Y wolde þe were maked

---

825 *mester*, trade.
826 *dere*, dearth.
827 'corn to make bread'.
829 *meiné*, household.
830 *of Havelok*, on Havelok's account.
834 *lenge*, ling.
835f. 'nor with any other ... could he ...'
838 *hwil-gat*, how (=*hwilk-gat*, cf. 848).
839 'it mattered little to him' (cf. 851).
842 *mone*, must.
843 *strong*, severe.
844 *uten*, exhausted.
845 *henne*, from here.
848 *canst*, know.   *gate*, way, road (cf. 891, etc.).
851 *slo*, sloe.

gongen	A cloth, þou mi*ht*est inne gonge,	
	Sone, no cold þat þu ne fonge.'	
	He tok þe sh*e*res of þe nayl	
	And made him a couel of þe sayl,	860
	And Havelok dide it sone on;	
	Havede neyþer hosen ne shon,	
	Ne none kines oþ*er* wede;	
	To Lincolne bar-fot he yede.	
	Hwan he kam þ*er*, he was ful wil;	865
	Ne havede he no frend to gangen til.	
	Two dayes þer fastinde he yede,	
	Þat non for his werk wolde him fede;	
	Þe þridde day herde he calle,	
	'Bermen, bermen, hider forth alle!'	870
871 *No gap in MS.* (C)	* * * * * * *	
	Sprongen forth so sparke on glede.	
	Havelok shof dun nyne or ten	
	Ri*ht* amidewarde þe fen,	
	And stirte forth to þe kok	875
876 *No gap in MS.* (C)	* * * * * *	
	Þat he bou*ht*e at þe brigge;	
	Þe bermen let he alle ligge,	
	And bar þe mete to þe castel,	
	And gat him þere a ferþing wastel.	880
	Þet oþer day kepte he ok	
	Swiþe yerne þe erles kok,	
	Til þat he say him on þe brigge,	
	And bi him mani fishes ligge.	
herles	Þe erles mete havede he bou*ht*	885
	Of Cornwalie, and kalde oft:	
	'Bermen, bermen, hider swiþe!'	

858 *fonge*, take, catch.
859 *of*, from, off.
861 *dide . . . on*, put on ('don'=do on).
862 *hosen*, stockings.   *shon*, shoes.
863 *none kines*, of no kind.
865 *wil*, lost, bewildered (ON).
866 *til*, to.
870 *bermen*, porters.
873 *shof dun*, pushed down.
874 *amidewarde*, in the midst of.   *fen*, mud.
875 *kok*, cook.
877 *brigge*, bridge.
881 *oþer*, next.   *kepte*, looked out for.   *ok*, also (ON).
883 *say*, saw.

Havelok it herde, and was ful bliþe
Þat he herde 'bermen' calle;
Alle made he hem dun falle   890
Þat in his gate yeden and stode,
Wel sixtene laddes gode.
Als he lep þe kok til,
He shof hem alle upon an hyl,
Astirte til him with his rippe   895
And bigan þe fish to kippe.
He bar up wel a carte-lode
Of segges, laxes, of playces brode,
Of grete laumprees and of eles;
Sparede he neyþer tos ne heles   900
Til þat he to þe castel cam,
Þat men fro him his birþene nam.
Þan men haveden holpen him doun
With þe birþene of his croun,
Þe kok stod, and on him low,   905
And þouhte him stalworþe man ynow,
And seyde, 'Wiltu ben with me?
Gladlike wile Ich feden þe;
Wel is set þe mete þu etes,
And þe hire þat þu getes.'   910

Soddot   'Goddot!' quoth he, 'leve sire,
Bidde Ich you non oþer hire;
But yeveþ me inow to ete,
Fir and water Y wile yow fete,
Þe fir blowe, an ful wele maken;   915
Stickes kan Ich breken and kraken,
And kindlen ful wel a fyr
And maken it to brennen shir.
Ful wel kan Ich cleven shides,

---

891 *gate*, 'way' (ON; cf. street-names such as *Micklegate* in N. England).
892 *laddes*, serving-men.
893 *lep*, leapt.
894 *hyl*, heap.
895 *astirte*, sprang.   *rippe*, basket (ON).
896 *kippe*, snatch up (ON).
898 *segges*, cuttlefish.
902 *nam*, took.
903 *holpen*, helped.
905 *low*, smiled ('laughed').
909 'The food you eat is well invested.'
910 *hire*, wages.
919 *cleven*, split.   *shides*, kindling-wood.

Eles to-turven of here hides;   920
Ful wel kan Ich dishes swilen
And don al þat ye evere wilen.'
Quoth þe kok, 'Wile I no more;
Go þu yunder, and sit þore,
And Y shal yeve þe ful fair bred   925
And make þe broys in þe led.
Sit now doun and et ful yerne:
Daþeit hwo þe mete werne!'

Havelok sette him dun anon,
Al-so stille als a ston,   930
Til he havede ful wel eten;
Þo havede Havelok fayre geten.
Hwan he havede eten inow,
He kam to þe welle, water up-drow
And filde þer a michel so;   935
Bad he non ageyn him go,
But bi-twen his hondes he bar it in
Al him one, to þe kichin.
Bad he non him water to fete
Ne fro brigge to bere þe mete;   940
He bar þe turves, he bar þe star,
Þe wode fro the brigge he bar;
Al that evere shulden he nytte,

So Sk; MS.   Al he drow, and al he *k*itte;
has citte *or*   Wolde he nevere haven rest,   945
titte *(C)*   More þan he were a best.
Of alle men was he mest meke,
Lauhwinde ay, and bliþe of speke;
Evere he was glad and bliþe;
His sorwe he couþe ful wel miþe.   950
It ne was non so litel knave

---

920 *to-turven*, flay.   *hides*, skins.
921 *swilen*, wash ('swill').
926 *broys*, soup, broth.   *led*, cauldron.
927 *ful yerne*, to your heart's content.
928 *werne*, refuse (cf. 1349).
935 *so*, tub.
936 *ageyn him*, to meet him.
941 *star*, sedge (C) (ON).
943 *nytte*, use.
944 *kitte*, cut.
948 *lauhwinde*, laughing, smiling.   *speke*, speech.
951 'There was no boy so small . . .'

For-to leyken, ne for-to plawe,
Þat he ne wolde with him pleye;
Þe children þat yeden in þe weie
Of him he deden al her wille, 955
And with him leykeden here fille.
Him loveden alle, stille and bolde,

holde   Knictes, children, yunge and olde.
sowen   Alle him loveden þat him sowe,
Boþen heye men and lowe. 960
Of him ful wide þe word sprong
Hw he was mikel, hw he was strong,
Hw fayr man God him havede maked,
But on þat he was almest naked—
For he ne havede nouht to shride 965
But a kouel ful unride

Sk adds was   Þat was ful, and swiþe wicke—
Was it nouht worth a fir-sticke.
Þe cok bigan of him to rewe,
And bouhte him cloþes, al span-newe; 970
He bouhte him boþe hosen and shon,
And sone dide him dones on.
Hwan he was cloþed, hosed and shod,
Was non so fayr under God
Þat evere yete in erþe were, 975
Non þat evere moder bere;
It was nevere man þat yemede
In kinneriche, þat so wel semede
King or cayser for-to be,
Þan he was shrid, so semede he; 980
For þanne he weren alle samen
At Lincolne, at þe gamen,
And þe erles men woren al þore,

þan was]   Was Havelok bi þe shuldren more
orr. H   Þan þe meste þat þer kam; 985
In armes him no man nam

[952] *leyken*, play (cf. 956; also *layke* 1013) (ON).   *plawe*, play.
[959] *sowe*, saw.
[964] *but on*, except only (cf. 506).
[965] *shride*, clothe himself (p.p. *shrid* 980).
[966] *unride*, coarse.
[970] *span-newe*, brand new (ON).
[972] *dones=don es*, put them.
[977] *yemede*, ruled.
[978] *kinneriche*, kingdom.   *so wel semed*, seemed so fit.
[981] *samen*, together.
[984] *more*, bigger.
[986] *nam*, took on.

Þat he doune sone ne caste—
Havelok stod over hem als a mast.
al] als *Sk*   Als he was heie, al*s* he was long
He was boþe stark and strong.   990
Sk adds was   In Engelond *was* non hise per
Of strengþe þat evere kam him ner.
Als he was strong, so was he softe;
Þey a man him misdede ofte,
misdede]   Nevere more he him mis*seyde*,   995
misseyde   Ne hond on him with yvele leyde.
Ellis
Of bodi was he mayden clene:
Nevere yete in game ne in grene
hire] hore   Wit*h* hore ne wolde leyke ne lye,
Kölbing
No more þan it were a strie.   1000
hengelond   In þat time al Engelond
Þerl Godrich havede in his hond,
And he gart komen into þe tun
Mani erl and mani barun,
And alle þat lives were   1005
In Englond, þanne wer*e* þere,
Þat þey haveden after sent
To ben þer at þe parlement.
With hem com mani chambioun,
Mani wi*ht* ladde, blac and brown;   1010
An fel it so, þat yunge men,
Wel abouten nine or ten,
Bigunnen þer for-to layke;
Þider komen boþe stronge and wayke.
Þider komen lesse and more,   1015
Þat in þe borw þanne weren þore,
Chaunpiouns and starke laddes,
Bondemen with here gaddes
Als he comen fro þe plow—
Þere was sembling inow!   1020

[991] *per*, equal, rival ('peer').
[993] *softe*, gentle.
[997] *mayden*, virgin.
[998] *game*, play.   *grene*, lust (ON).
[999] *hore*, whore.
[1000] *strie*, witch.
[1002] *þerl*=*þe erl*.
[1007] 'after whom they had sent'.
[1009] *chambioun*, champion.
[1010] *wiht*, strong.   *blac and brown*, *sc*. -haired.
[1014] *wayke*, weak.
[1015] *lesse and more*, small and great.
[1020] *sembling*, gathering, 'assembling'.

For it ne was non horse-knave,
Þo þei sholden on honde have,
Þat he ne kam þider, þe leyk to se.
Biforn here fet þanne lay a tre,
pulten] putten And pu*t*ten with a mikel ston   1025
Sk Þe starke laddes, ful god won.
greth Þe ston was mikel and ek gret,
neth And al-so hevi as a net;
Grund-stalwrþe man he sholde be
Þat mou*h*te liften it to his kne;   1030
Was þer neyþer clerc ne prest
Þat mi*h*te liften it to his brest.
Þerwi*t*h putten the chaunpiouns
Þat þider comen with þe barouns.
Hwo-so mi*h*te putten þore   1035
Biforn anoþer, an inch or more,
hold Wore he yung, wore he old,
He was for a kempe told.
stareden] Al-so þei stoden, an ofte sta*d*den,
stadden *Si* Þe chaunpiouns and ek þe ladden,   1040
And he maden mikel strout
Abouten þe alþer-beste but,
Havelok stod and lokede þer-til,
And of puttingge he was ful wil,
For nevere yete ne saw he or   1045
Putten the stone, or þanne þor.
Hise mayster bad him gon þer-to,
Als he couþe þer-with do.
Þo hise mayster it him bad,
He was of him sore adrad;   1050
Þer-to he stirte sone anon
And kipte up þat hevi ston
Þat he sholde puten wiþe;

1021 *horse-knave*, groom.
1022 'when they were bound on their business'.
1024 *tre*, beam, bar (cf. 1811, etc.).
1025 *putten*, cf. 'putting the shot'.
1026 *ful god won*, in great numbers.
1027 *ek*, also.
1029 *grund-stalwrþe*, very strong.   *sholde*, would have to.
1038 *kempe*, champion.   *told*, accounted.
1039 *stadden*, looked on.
1041 *strout*, contention, debate (and as verb, 1784).
1042 *but*, throw.
1044 *wil*, inexperienced (ON).
1046 *or þanne þor*, before then and there.
1047f. 'join in as best he could'.
1049 *þo*, when.

He putte at þe firste siþe
Over alle þat þer wore   1055
Twel-fote, and sum-del more.
Þe chaunpiouns þat put sowen;
Shuldreden he ilc oþer and lowen;
Wolden he no more to putting gonge
gange
But seyde, 'We dwellen her to longe!'   1060
Þis selkouth mihte nouht ben hyd;
Ful sone it was ful loude kid
Of Havelok, hw he warp þe ston
Over þe laddes everilkon,
Hw he was fayr, hw he was long,   1065
Hw he was wiht, hw he was strong.
speche] corr.   Þoruth England yede þe speke
Sk   Hw he was strong and ek meke;
In þe castel, up in þe halle,
Þe knihtes speken þer-of alle,   1070
So that Godrich it herde wel,
speken] corr.   Þe speke of Havelok, everi del,
Sk   Hw he was strong man and hey,
sri (fri edd.)]   Hw he was strong and ek slei,
slei Ellis   And þouhte Godrich, 'Þoru þis knave   1075
þouthte   Shal Ich Engelond al have,
And mi sone after me,
For so I wile þat it be.
Þe king Aþelwald me dide swere
Upon al þe messe-gere   1080
yeve   Þat Y shulde his douhter yive
Þe hexte þat mihte live,
Þe beste, þe fairest, þe strangest ok—
Þat gart he me sweren on þe bok.
Hwere mihte I finden ani so hey   1085
So Havelok is, or so sley?
Þou Y souhte heþen into Ynde,
So fayr, so strong, ne mihte Y finde;
Havelok is þat ilke knave
Þat shal Goldeborw have!'   1090
Þis þouhte with trechery,

1055 over, beyond.
1058 shuldreden, nudged.   ilc oþer, one another.
1062 kid, made known.
1063 warp, threw.
1067 speke, rumour, word.
1073 hey, tall.
1074 slei, skilful (cf. 1086, 2121).
1087 'from here to India.'

With traysoun and wit*h* felony,
For he wende þat Havelok wore
Sum cherles sone, and no more:
Ne shulde he haven of Engellond   1095
Onlepi forw in his hond
With hire, þat was þer-of eyr,
Þat boþe was god and swiþe fair.
He wende þat Havelok wer a þral;
Þer-þoru he wende haven al   1100
In Engelond, þat hire ri*ht* was;
He was werse þan Sathanas
Þat Ihesu Crist in erþe swoc:
Hanged worþe he on an hok!

After Goldebo*r*w sone he sende,   1105
Þat was boþe fayr and hende,
And dide hire to Lincolne bringe*n*;
Belles dede he ageyn hire ringen,
And joie he made hire swiþe mikel,
But neþeles he was ful swikel.   1110
yeve   He seyde þat he sholde hire y*i*ve
                Þe fayrest man that mi*ht*e live.
anon   She answerede and seyde an*a*n,
                Bi Crist, and bi seint Iohan,
                Þat hire sholde no man wedde,   1115
to hire]   Ne no man bringen *hire to* bedde,
transp. H   But he were king or kinges eyr,
                Were he nevere man so fayr.

Godrich þe erl was swiþe wroth
Þat she swor swilk an oth,   1120
And seyde, 'Hwor þou wilt be
Quen and levedi over me?
Þou shalt haven a gadeling—
Ne shalt þou haven non oþer king.
Þe shal spusen mi cokes knave;   1125

1096 *onlepi*, a single (and *anlepi* 2112).   *forw*, furrow.
1097 *with hire*, i.e. as her dowry.
1100 *þer-þoru*, by means of this.
1103 *swoc*, betrayed (C).
1104 *worþe*, may he be.
1106 *hende*, gracious (C).
1108 *ageyn*, to greet ('against her coming').
1110 *neþeles*, nonetheless.   *swikel*, treacherous.
1121 *hwor*, interrogative particle.
1123 *gadeling*, ruffian.

Ne shalt þou non oþer loverd have!
yeve Daþeit þat þe oþer yive
Evere-more, hwil I live!
weddeth To-morwe ye sholen ben weddet
beddeth And, maugré þin, to-gidere beddet.'   1130
Goldeborw gret, and was hire ille;
She wolde ben ded bi hire wille.
On the morwen, hwan day was sprungen,
And day-belle at kirke rungen,
After Havelok sente þat Judas,   1135
Þat werse was þanne Sathanas,
And seyde, 'Mayster, wilte wif?'
'Nay,' quoth Havelok, 'bi my lif!
Hwat sholde Ich with wif*e* do?
I ne may hire fede, ne cloþe, ne sho.   1140
*H*wider sholde Ich wimman bringe?
I ne have none kines þinge.
I ne have hws, Y ne have cote,
Ne I ne I ne have stikke, Y ne have sprote,
I ne have neyþer bred ne sowel,   1145
hold with Ne cloth, but of an old *whit* couel.
Þis cloþes, þat Ich onne have
Aren þe kokes, and Ich his knave.'
Godrich stirt up, and on him dong

No gap in MS.   *   *   *   *   *   *   *   1150
And seyde, 'But þou hire take
Þat Y wole yeven þe to make,
I shal hangen þe ful heye,
uth, heie Or Y shal þristen ut þin eie.'
one or oue; Havelok was one, and was odra*d*,   1155
odrat And grauntede him al þat he bad.
Þo sende he after hire sone,
Þe fayrest wymman under mone,
Sk adds fals And seyde til hire, *fals* and slike,
Þat wicke þral, þat foule swike,   1160

[1130] *maugré þin*, like it or not (C).
[1131] 'it went ill with her'.
[1133] *sprungen*, cf. 'dayspring' = 'dawn'.
[1134] *day-belle*, morning bell.
[1137] *wilte*, do you want?
[1140] *sho*, shoe (verb).
[1144] *sprote*, twig.
[1155] *one*, alone: but see C.
[1158] *mone*, moon.
[1159] *slike*, plausible? ('slick').

'But þu þis man under-stonde,
I shal flemen þe of londe,
Or þou shalt to þe galwes renne,
And þer þou shalt in a fir brenne.'
Sho was adrad, for he so þrette,   1165
And durste nouht þe spusing lette;
But þey hire likede swiþe ille,

Sk adds sho   *Sho* þouhte, it was Godes wille;
God, þat makes to growen þe korn,
Formede hire wimman to be born.   1170
Hwan he havede don him, for drede,
Þat he sholde hire spusen and fede,
And þat she sholde til him holde,
Þer weren penies þicke tolde,
Mikel plenté upon þe bok—   1175

as   He ys hire yaf, and she *is* tok.
He weren spused fayre and wel;

he deden]   Þe messe *dede* everi-del
corr. H   Þat fel to spusing, a god clerk,
uth   Þe erchebishop ut of Yerk,   1180
Þat kam to þe parlement,
Als God him havede þider sent.

Hwan he weren togydere in Godes lawe,
Þat þe folc ful wel it sawe,
mouthen   He ne wisten hwat he mouhte,   1185
Ne he ne wisten hwat hem douhte,
Þer to dwellen, or þenne to gonge.
Þer ne wolden he dwellen longe,
For he wisten and ful wel sawe
hawe   Þat Godrich hem hatede, þe devel him awe!   1190
And yf he dwelleden þer ouht
(Þat fel Havelok ful wel on þouht)
Men sholde don his leman shame,

1161 *under-stonde*, receive (cf. 2819, etc.).
1162 *flemen*, banish.
1163 *renne*, go (run).
1166 *spusing*, marriage.   *lette*, prevent, hinder (and 2258; cf. 'let' in tennis).
1171 *don*, compelled.
1179 *fel*, was proper.   *clerk*, cleric.
1180 *Yerk*, York.
1185 'what they could do'.
1186 'what was best for them'.
1190 *awe*, possess (and *owe*, 1294, etc.).
1192 'That came into Havelok's mind.'
1193 *leman*, mistress, 'love' (C).

Or elles bringen in wicke blame;
Þat were him levere to ben ded;　　　　　　1195
For-þi he token anoþer red,
Þat þei sholden þenne fle
Til Grim, and til hise sones þre;
Þer wenden he alþer-best to spede,
Hem for-to cloþe and for-to fede.　　　　　1200
Þe lond he token under fote—
Ne wisten he non oþer bote—

Sk adds sti;
MS. erased And helden ay the ri*hte* sti
Til he comen to Grimesby.
Þanne he komen þere, þanne was Grim ded;　1205
Of him ne haveden he no red,
But hise children alle fyve
Alle weren yet on live,
Þat ful fayre ayen hem neme
Hwan he wisten þat he keme,　　　　　　1210
And maden joie swiþe mikel—
Ne weren he nevere ayen hem fikel.
On knes ful fayre he hem setten,
And Havelok swiþe fayre gretten
And seyden, 'Welcome, loverd dere!　　　　1215
And welkome be þi fayre fere!
Blessed be þat ilke þrawe
Þat þou hire toke in Godes lawe!

hus　　Wel is us we sen þe on lyve;
Þou mihte us boþe selle and yive.　　　　1220
Þou may*h*t us boþe yeve and selle
With þat þou wilt here dwelle.
We haven, loverd, alle gode,

neth　Hors and net and ship on flode,
Gold and silver and michel auchte,　　　　1225
Þat Grim ure fader us bi-tawchte:
Gold and silver and oþer fe
Bad he us bi-taken þe.

1195 'so that he would rather be dead'.
1197 *þenne*, from there.
1201 i.e. set out.
1202 *bote*, remedy, course.
1203 *helden*, kept to.　　*sti*, road.
1206 i.e. there was no help for him.
1209 *neme*, went (past of *nime*, 1936, etc., and past subj. *neme* 2206).
1210 *keme*, came (C).
1215 *fere*, companion.
1217 *þrawe*, time, occasion.
1219 'we are glad that . . .'
1220 *with þat*, provided that.
1228 *bi-taken*, give.

We haven shep, we haven swin;
Bi-leve her, loverd, and al be þin!   1230
Þou shalt ben loverd, þou shalt ben syre,
And we sholen serven þe and hire,
hure   And ure sistres sholen do
Al that evere biddes sho;
cloþen] clopes   He sholen hire cloþes washen and wringen   1235
Sk
And to hondes water bringen;
He sholen bedden hire and þe
For levedi wile we þat she be.'
Hwan he þis joie haveden maked,
Sithen stikes broken and kraked,   1240
And þe fir brouht on brenne,
Ne was þer spared gos ne henne,
Ne þe ende, ne þe drake:
Mete he deden plenté make—
Ne wantede þere no god mete.   1245
Wyn and ale deden he fete,
And made hem glade and bliþe;
Wesseyl ledden he fele siþe.

On þe niht, als Goldeborw lay,
Sory and sorwful was she ay,   1250
For she wende she were bi-swike,
shere] corr. Sk   Þat she were yeven unkyndelike.
O niht saw she þer-inne a liht,
A swiþe fayr, a swiþe bryht—
Al-so briht, al-so shir   1255
So it were a blase of fir.
She lokede norþ, and ek south,
And saw it comen ut of his mouth
Þat lay bi hire in þe bed—
No ferlike þou she were adred!   1260
Þouhte she, '*H*wat may this bi-mene?
He beth heyman yet, als Y wene;
He beth heyman er he be ded.'
On hise shuldre, of gold red

1230 *bi-leve*, stay (past *bi-lefte* 2967).
1241 *brouht on brenne*, lit. 'brought on fire'.
1242 *gos*, goose.
1243 *ende*, duck.
1248 *wesseyl*, toast.
1251 *bi-swike*, betrayed.
1252 *unkyndelike*, against nature (C).
1260 *ferlike*, wonder (cf. *ferli* in *SO* 4).
1261 *bi-mene*, mean.

She saw a swiþe noble croiz;   1265
Of an angel she herde a voyz:

'Goldeborw, lat þi sorwe be,
For Havelok, þat haveþ spuset þe,
He] Is *Sk*   *Is* kinges sone and kinges eyr—
Þat bi-kenneth þat croiz so fayr.   1270
Iit bi-kenneth more, þat he shal
Denemark haven, and Englond al;
He shal ben king, strong and stark,
Of Engelond and Denemark;
Þat shal*t* þu wi*th* eyne sen,   1275
And þou shalt quen and levedi ben.'

Þanne she havede herd the stevene
uth   Of þe angel ut of hevene,
She was so fele siþes blithe
Þat she ne mi*ht*e hire joie mythe,   1280
But Havelok sone anon she kiste—
And he slep, and nou*ht* ne wiste
Hwan] *corr.* Ƶ   Hwa*t* þat aungel havede seyd.
Of his slep anon he brayd,
And seide, 'Lemman, slepes þou?   1285
A selkuth drem dremede me nou.

Herkne nou hwat me haveth met:
Me þou*ht*e Y was in Denemark set,
But on on þe moste hil
Þat evere yete kam I til.   1290
It was so hey þat Y wel mou*ht*e
Al þe werd se, als me þou*ht*e.
Als I sat upon þat lowe,
awe] *or read*   I bi-gan Denemark for-to *o*we,
lawe *in* 1293   Þe borwes and þe castles stronge;   1295
And mine armes weren so longe

1270 *bi-kenneth*, signifies.
1275 *eyne*, eyes.   *sen*, see.
1277 *stevene*, voice.
1280 *mythe*, conceal.
1282 *slep*, slept (strong past).
1284 *brayd*, started, awoke.
1287 *met*, dreamt (impersonal, cf. 1286, 1306).
1289 *on þe moste*, 'one of the greatest'.
1292 *werd*, world.
1293 *lowe*, hill (cf. 1704).

That I fadmede, al at ones,
Denemark with mine longe bones;
And þanne Y wolde mine armes drawe
Til me, and hom for-to have,   1300
Al that evere in Denemark liveden
On mine armes faste clyveden,
And þe stronge castles alle
On knes bigunnen for-to falle;
Þe keyes fellen at mine fet.   1305
Anoþer drem dremede me ek,
Þat Ich fley over þe salte se
Til Engeland, and al with me
Þat evere was in Denemark lyves,
But bondemen and here wives;   1310
And þat Ich kom til Engelond,
Al closede it in-til min hond,—

Sk adds it   And, Goldeborw, Y gaf *it* þe—
Deus! Lemman, hwat may þis be?'
Sho answerede and seyde sone,   1315
'Ihesu Crist, þat made mone,
Þine dremes turne to joye

No gap in MS.   *   *   *   *   *   *   *
               *   *   *   *   *   *   *

Þat wite þw that sittes in trone!   1320
Ne non strong king, ne caysere
So þou shalt be, for þou shalt bere
In Engelond corune yet;
Denemark shal knele to þi fet;
Alle þe castles þat aren þer-inne   1325
Shaltow, lemman, ful wel winne.

woth   I wot, so wel so Ich it sowe,
To þe shole comen heye and lowe,
And alle þat in Denemark wone,
Em and broþer, fader and sone,   1330

kayn   Erl and baroun, dreng an þayn,
Knihtes and burgeys and sweyn,

mad] *corr. Sk*   And *make þe* king heyelike and wel—
Denemark shal be þin evere-ilc del.

1297 *fadmede*, embraced (fathom=arm-span).
1300 see C.
1302 *clyveden*, clung.
1307 *fley*, flew.
1320 *trone*, throne.
1323 *corune*, crown.
1330 *em*, uncle.

douthe	Have þou nouht þer-offe doute, 1335
nouthe (*end of line*)	Nouht þe worth of one noute:
	Þer-offe with-inne þe firste yer
of evere-il del (*cf.* 1334)] *em. Sk*	Shalt þou ben king *with-outen were*.
Nim in witl	But do nou als I wile rathe:
þe] Nimen wit *Z*	*Nimen wit* to Denemark baþe, 1340
	And do þou nouht on frest þis fare;
Lith] Hiht *H*	*Hiht* and selthe felawes are.
	For shal Ich nevere bliþe be
	Til I with eyen Denemark se,
woth	For Ich wot þat al þe lond 1345
	Shalt þou haven in þin hond.
	Prey Grimes sones, alle þre,
	That he wenden forþ with þe;
	(I wot, he wilen þe nouht werne;
	With þe wende shulen he yerne, 1350
	For he loven þe hertelike)
	Þou maght, til he aren quike,
	Hwore-so he o worde aren;
þere	*H*ere ship þou do hem swithe yaren,
	And loke þat þou dwelle nouht— 1355
	Dwelling haveth ofte scaþe wrouht.'
	Hwan Havelok herde þat she radde,
	Sone it was day, sone he him cladde,
	And sone to þe kirke yede
	Or he dide ani oþer dede, 1360
	And bifor þe rode bigan falle,
bi] bi-gan *Sk*	Croiz and Crist bi*gan* to kalle,
	And seyde, 'Loverd, þat al weldes,
	Wind and water, wodes and feldes,
	For the holi milce of you 1365
	Have merci of me, loverd, nou,

1338 *were*, doubt.
1340 *nimen wit*, let us two go (see C).   *baþe*, both.
1341 *do on frest*, postpone, delay (ON).   *fare*, journey.
1342 *hiht*, speed.   *selthe*, success.
1348 *wenden*, go.
1349 *werne*, refuse.
1352f. 'You could ask them that favour as long as they are alive, wherever in the world they are' (*worde=worlde*).
1354 *yaren*, make ready.
1355 *dwelle*, delay.
1356 *wrouht*, brought about.
1357 *radde*, advised (cf. *red* 148, etc.).
1358 *cladde*, dressed.   *sone*, at once (cf. 1712).
1365 *milce*, mercy, compassion.

And wreke me yet on mi fo
Þat Ich saw biforn min eyne slo
Mine sistres with a knif,
And siþen wolde me mi lyf   1370
Have reft, for in the se
Bad he Grim have drenched me.

Sk adds haldes   He *haldes* mi lond with mikel unri*ht*,
(*cf.* 1386)   With michel wrong, with mikel pli*ht*—
                    For I ne misdede him nevere nou*ht*—   1375
haued   And have*th* me to sorwe brou*ht*.
                    He haveth me do mi mete to þigge,
                    And ofte in sorwe and pine ligge.
                    Loverd, have merci of me,
                    And late wel passe þe se,   1380
ihc, douthe   Þat I*ch* have ther-offe dou*te* and kare,
                    Withuten stormes over-fare,
Sk adds be   Þat Y ne drenched *be* þer-ine,
                    Ne forfaren for no sinne,
                    And bringge me wel to þe lond   1385
                    Þat Godard haldes in his hond,
                    Þat is mi ri*ht*, everi del:
                    Ihesu Crist, þou wost it wel!'

                    Þanne he havede his bede seyd,
                    His offrende on þe auter leyd,   1390
                    His leve at Ihesu Crist he tok
                    And at his suete moder ok,
                    And at þe croiz, þat he biforn lay;
                    Siþen yede sore grotinde awey.

                    Hwan he com hom, he wore yare,   1395
                    Grimes sones, for-to fare
                    Into þe se, fishes to gete
                    Þat Havelok mi*hte* wel of ete;
                    But *H*avelok þou*hte* al anoþer:
heldeste   First he ka*l*de þe eldeste broþer,   1400

1374 *pliht*, injury, harm (cf. 2007).
1377 *þigge*, beg.
1380 *passe*, cross.
1381 *þat . . . ther-offe*, 'of which'.   *doute*, fear, anxiety.
1382 *over-fare*, pass over.
1384 *forfaren*, lost.
1389 *bede*, prayer.
1390 *offrende*, offering.
1394 *grotinde*, weeping.
1399 'had other plans'.

name] naven *Si*

Roberd þe Rede, bi his na*ven*,

wenduth,
hauen (*sic*)

Wiliam Wendut, and H*uwe R*aven,

Grimes sones alle þre,

And seyde, 'Liþes nou alle to me:

sheue] *em. Si*

Loverdinges, Ich wil you sh*awe*   1405

A þing of me þat ye wel kn*awe*.

knewe] knawe
Si

Mi fader was king of Denshe lond;

Denemark was al in his hond

Þe day þat he was quik and ded,

But þanne havede he wicke red,   1410

Þat he me and Denemark al

And mine sistres bi-tawte a þral:

hus

A develes lime h*e* us bi-tawte,

And al his lond, and al hise au*h*te;

Fro Y saw that fule fend   1415

Mine sistres slo with hise hend;

First he shar a-two here þrotes,

And siþen hem, al to grotes,

And siþen bad in þe se

Grim, youre fader, drenchen me;   1420

Deplike dede he him swere

On bok, þat he sholde me bere

Unto þe se, an drenchen ine,

Sk adds he

And *he* wolde taken on him þe sinne.

But Grim was wis and swiþe hende;   1425

Wolde he nou*ht* his soule shende.

Levere was him to be for-sworen

Þan drenchen me and ben for-lor*en*;

But sone bigan he for-to fle

Fro Denemark, for-to berwen me—   1430

yis

For yi*f* Ich havede þer ben funden,

Havede ben slayn, or harde bunden,

And heye ben henged on a tre—

Havede go*n* for him gold ne fe.

1401 *naven*, name (cf. 2534) (ON).
1404 *liþes*, listen (pl. imperative; cf. 2209, etc.).
1405 *shawe*, show.
1407 *Denshe*, Danish.
1410 *wicke*, here 'bad' in the sense 'ill-conceived', 'unfortunate'.
1412 *þral*, here as term of insult (cf. 528, etc.).
1413 'to a limb of Satan'.
1417 *shar*, cut.   *a-two*, in two.
1421 *deplike*, deeply.
1426 *shende*, injure (past *shente*, 2754).
1427 *levere*, preferable (dial. 'liefer').
1432 *havede=havede he* but not in 1434.

For-þi fro Denemark hider he fledde, 1435
And me ful fayre and ful wel fedde,

Sk adds ilke, So þat unto þis day
perhaps rightly Have Ich ben fed and fostred ay.

helde But nou Ich am up to þat elde
Cumen, that Ich may wepne welde, 1440

yeve And Y may grete dintes yive,
Sshal I nevere, hwil Ich lyve,
Ben glad, til that Ich Denemark se.
I preie you þat ye wende with me,
And Ich may mak you riche men: 1445
Ilk of you shal have castles ten,
And þe lond þat þor-til longes,
Borwes, tunes, wodes and wonges.

A leaf has been torn from the MS. here. It would have contained 180 lines, the substance of which must have been that Havelok, his wife and the sons of Grim sail to Denmark, come to the castle of Ubbe, a great Danish lord, and ask his permission to make a living by trade in that region.

another line * * * * * * *
lost somewhere 'With swilk als Ich byen shal: 1630

Z adds Y Þer-of biseche *Y* you nou leve;
Wile Ich speke with non oþer reve

þe] you *H* But with *you*, þat justise are,
seken] sellen Þat Y mi*h*te se*ll*en mi ware
Sk In gode borwes up and doun, 1635
And faren Ich wile fro tun to tun.'
A gold ring drow he forth anon —
An hundred pund was worth þe ston,
And yaf it Ubbe for-to spede —
He was ful wis þat first yaf mede — 1640
And so was Havelok ful wis here:
He sold his gold ring ful dere —
Was nevere non so dere sold

For] Fro *H* F*ro* chapmen, neyþer yung ne old.
shoren; Þat sho*l*en ye forthward ful wel *leren* 1645
heren] leren *H* Yif þat ye wile þe storie heren.

Hwan Ubbe havede þe gold ring,

1435 *for-þi*, therefore.
1441 *dintes*, blows.
1630 'with what I shall buy'.
1632 *reve*, official.
1639 *for-to spede*, so that he might succeed?

Havede he yovenet for no þing,
Nou*ht* for þe borw evere-il del.
Havelok bi-hel*d* he swiþe wel,   1650
Hw he was wel of bones maked,
Brod in þe scholdres, ful wel schaped,
Þicke in þe brest, of bodi long;
He semede wel to ben wel strong.

hwat] quath
'Deus!' *quath* Ubbe, 'qui ne were he kni*ht*?   1655
Sk
woth
I wot þat he is swiþe wi*ht*.
Betere semede him to bere
Helm on heved, sheld and spere
Þanne to beye and selle ware;
Allas! þat he shal þer-with fare!   1660
Goddot! wile he trowe me,
Chaffare shal he late be.'
Neþeles he seyde sone,
'Havelok, have þi bone,
And Y ful wel rede þe   1665
Þat þou come and ete with me
To-day, þou and þi fayre wif
Þat þou lovest al-so þi lif;
And have þou of hire no drede:
Shal hire no man shame bede.   1670
Bi þe fey þat Y owe to þe,
me serf
Þer-of shal I m*i*-se*lf* borw be.'

Havelok herde þat he bad;
And thow was he ful sore drad
With him to ete, for hise wif;   1675
For him wore levere þat his lif
Him wore reft, þan she in blame
Felle, or lau*hte* ani shame.
þat] yat
Hwanne he havede his wille *y*at,
Stratmann
Þe stede þat he onne sat   1680
Smot Ubbe with spures faste,
And forth awey, but at þe laste,

[1648] 'He would not have given it away for anything.'
[1652] *brod*, broad.
[1655] *qui*, why.
[1657] 'it would befit him better . . .'
[1660] *fare*, live.
[1661] 'if he will trust me'.
[1662] *chaffare*, trade.
[1664] *bone*, request ('boon').
[1670] *bede*, offer.
[1672] *borw*, surety.
[1679] *yat*, granted (ON).

Sk adds ferre	Or he *ferre* from him ferde,
	Seyde he, þat his folk herde,
beye](*sic*); *corr. Si*	'Loke þat ye comen boþe,
rede] *corr. Si*	For Ich it wile, and Ich it roþe.'

Or he *ferre* from him ferde,
Seyde he, þat his folk herde,
'Loke þat ye comen boþe,   1685
For Ich it wile, and Ich it roþe.'

Havelok ne durste, þey he were adrad,
Nouht with-sitten þat Ubbe bad.
His wif he dide with him lede;
Unto þe heye curt he yede.   1690
Roberd hire ledde, þat was red,

þarned] þoled   Þat havede *þoled* for hire þe ded
Sk   Or ani havede hire misseyd
Or hand with ivele onne leyd.
William Wendut was þat oþer   1695
Þat hire ledde, Roberdes broþer,
Þat was wiht at alle nedes—
Wel is him þat god man fedes!
Þan he weren comen to þe halle
Biforen Ubbe and hise men alle,   1700
Ubbe stirte hem ageyn,
And mani a kniht and mani a sweyn,

shewe   Hem for-to se and for-to showe;
Þo stod Havelok as a lowe
Aboven þat þer-inne wore   1705
Riht al bi þe heved more
Þanne ani þat þer-inne stod;
Þo was Ubbe bliþe of mod
Þat he saw him so fayr and hende.
Fro him ne mihte his herte wende   1710
Ne fro him, ne fro his wif;
He lovede hem sone so his lif.
Weren non in Denemark þat him þouhte
Þat he so mikel love mouhte;
More he lovede Havelok one   1715

1683 *ferre*, further.   *ferde*, went.
1685 *loke*, be sure.
1686 *roþe=rede*.
1687 *þey*, though.
1688 *with-sitten*, resist.
1690 *curt*, court.
1691 *red*, red-headed.
1692 *havede þoled*, would have endured.
1693 *or*, rather than.
1703 *showe*, look at.
1705 'above those who . . .'
1710 *wende*, turn (and p.p. *went* 2143, 2455).

Þan al Denemark, bi mine wone!
Loke nou hw God helpen kan
O mani wise wif and man.

Hwan it was comen time to ete,
Hise wif dede Ubbe sone in fete   1720
And til hire seyde, al on gamen,
'Dame, þou and Havelok shulen ete samen,
And Goldeboru shal ete with me,
Þat is so fayr so flour on tre;
is] nis *Sk* In al Denemark *n*is wimman   1725
So fayr so sche, bi seint Johan!'
Þanne he were set, and bord leyd,
And þe beneysun was seyd,
Biforn hem com þe beste mete
Þat king or cayser wolde ete: 1730
Kranes, swannes, veneysun,
Lax, lampreys and god sturgun,
Pyment to drinke and god claré,
Win hwit and red ful god plenté;
Was þer-inne no page so lite   1735
Þat evere wolde ale bite.
Of þe mete for-to telle,
metes] win *Sk* Ne of þe *win*, bidde I nou*h*t dwelle.
Þat is þe storie for-to lenge—
It wolde anuye þis fayre genge.   1740
But hwan he haveden þe kil-þing deyled,
And fele siþes haveden wosseyled
And with gode drinkes seten longe,
And it was time for-to gonge,
Il-man to þer he cam fro,   1745
Þou*h*te Ubbe, 'Yf I late hem go
Þus one foure, withuten mo,

[1716] *wone*, opinion.
[1718] *wise*, ways.
[1721] *on gamen*, joking (cf. 2140 and contrast 2255).
[1728] *beneysun*, grace.
[1730] *wolde*, 'could wish to'.
[1731] *kranen*, cranes? herons?
[1733] *pyment*, mulled wine; also *claré*.
[1736] *bite*, taste (C).
[1738] 'I do not wish to delay.'
[1739] *lenge*, prolong.
[1740] *anuye*, annoy.
[1741] *kil-þing*, drink? (C).   *deyled*, distributed.
[1745] *il-man*=*ilk man*.
[1747] *one foure*, four by themselves.   *mo*, more.

So mote Ich brouke finger or to,
For þis wimman bes mikel wo;
For hire shal men hire loverd slo.'   1750
He tok sone kni*ht*es ten,
And wel sixti oþer men
Wit*h* gode bowes and with gleives,
And sende him unto þe greyves,
Þe beste man of al þe toun,   1755
Þat was named Bernard Brun,
And bad him, als he lovede his lif,
Havelok wel ye*m*en, and his wif,
And wel do wayten al þe ni*ht*
Til þe oþer day, þat it were li*ht*.   1760
Bernard was trewe, and swiþe wi*ht*;
In al þe borw ne was no kni*ht*
riden   Þat betere couþe on stede ride,
Helm on heved, ne swerd bi side.
Havelok he gladlike under-stod   1765
With mike*l* love and herte god,
And dide greyþe a super riche,
chinche   Al-so he was no wi*ht* chiche,
To his bihove ever-il del,
Þat he mi*ht*e supe swiþe wel.   1770

Al-so he seten, and sholde soupe,
So comes a ladde in a joupe,
And with him sixti oþer stronge
With swerdes drawen and knives longe,
Ilkan in hande a ful god gleive,   1775
And seyde, 'Undo, Bernard þe greyve!
Undo swiþe and lat us in,
Or þu art ded, bi seint Austin!'
Bernard stirt up, þat was ful big,
And caste a brinie up-on his rig,   1780
ar] ax *Sk*   And grop an a*x*, þat was ful god;
Lep to þe dore, so he wore wod,
And seyde, 'Hwat are ye, þat are þer-oute,
Þat þus biginnen for-to stroute?

1748 *brouke*, use, enjoy.
1754 'to the official's house'.
1767 *greyþe*, prepare.
1768 *al-so*, as, seeing that.   *chiche*, niggardly.
1769 *bihove*, need.
1772 *joupe*, loose jacket.
1778 *Austin*, Augustine.
1780 *brinie*, coat of mail.   *rig*, back (ON).
1781 *grop*, seized (and pres. imp. *gripeth* 1887, past plur. *gripen* 1795).

Goth henne swiþe, fule þeves,   1785
For, bi þe Loverd þat man on leves,
Shol Ich casten þe dore open,
drepen: Summe of you shal Ich *have* dropen;
Huþe adds   And þe oþre shal Ich kesten
have, reads   In feteres, and ful faste festen!'   1790
dropen   'Hwat have ye seid?' quoth a ladde,
'Wenestu þat we ben adradde?
We shole at þis dore gonge
Maugre þin, carl, or ouht longe.'
He gripen sone a bulder-ston,   1795
And let it fleye, ful god won,
Agen þe dore, þat it to-rof:
*H*avelok it saw, and þider drof,
And þe barre sone ut-drow,
Þat was unride and gret ynow,   1800
And caste þe dore open wide,
And seide, 'Her shal Y now abide;
MS. has   Comes swiþe unto me!
daþeit at end   Datheyt hwo you henne fle!'
of line, as well 'No,' quoþth on, 'þat shaltou coupe,'   1805
as Daþeyt *in*   And bigan til him to loupe,
the next   In his hond *h*is swerd ut-drawe—
1805 quodh   Havelok he wende þore have slawe;
Sk adds him   And with *him* comen oþer two
Þat him wolde of live have do.   1810
Havelok lifte up þe dore-tre,
And at a dint he slow hem þre—
Was non of hem þat hise hernes
Ne lay þer-ute ageyn þe sternes.
Þe ferþe þat he siþen mette   1815

1786 'in whom men believe'.
1788 *dropen,* slain (C).
1794 *carl,* slave (ON).   *or ouht longe,* before long.
1795 *bulder-stone,* cobble-stone.
1796 *ful god won,* with great force (?).
1797 *to-rof,* split.
1798 *drof,* rushed ('drove').
1800 *unride,* huge.
1804 'Curse on anyone who runs away from you (from here)!'
1805 *coupe,* pay for (ON).
1806 *loupe,* rush (ON).
1810 *of live . . . do,* kill.
1811 *dore-tre,* bar of door.
1812 'with one blow'.
1813 *hernes,* brains.
1814 *ageyn þe sternes,* beneath the stars (?).

With þe barre so he him grette,
Bi-for þe heved, þat þe riht eye
Ut of þe hole made he fleye,
And siþe clapte him on þe crune
So þat he stan-ded fel þor dune.   1820
Þe fifte þat he over-tok
Gaf he a ful sor dint ok,
Bitwen þe sholdres, þer he stod,

spen] speu
Sm (C)
Þat he speu his herte-blod.
Þe sixte wende for-to fle,   1825
And he clapte him with þe tre
Riht in þe fule necke so
Þat he smot hise necke on to.

ut his swerd]
up . . . scheld
Dobson
Þanne þe sixe weren doun feld,
Þe sevenþe brayd up his *scheld*,   1830
And wolde Havelok riht in þe eye;

haue le] *Sk*
restores
And Havelok let þe barre fleye,
And smot him sone ageyn þe brest,
Þat havede he nevere schrifte of prest;
For he was ded on lesse hwile   1835
Þan men mouhte renne a mile.
Alle þe oþere weren ful kene;
A red þei taken hem bitwene
Þat he sholde him bi-halve,
And brisen so, þat with no salve   1840
Ne sholde him helen leche non:
Þey drowen ut swerdes ful god won,
And shoten on him, so don on bere
Dogges þat wolden him to-tere,
Þanne men doth þe bere beyte;   1845

[1816] *grette*, assailed.
[1817] *bi-for*, in front.
[1820] *stan-ded*, stone-dead.
[1821] *over-tok*, caught (and pres. inf. *over-take* 1861).
[1824] *speu*, spewed, vomited.
[1829] *feld*, felled.
[1830] *brayd*, moved quickly.
[1831] *riht*, slash, cut.
[1834] *schrifte*, confession, absolution.
[1837] *kene*, bold (ironic?).
[1838] 'They made a plan among themselves.'
[1839] *bi-halve*, surround.
[1840] *brisen*, beat.   *salve*, ointment.
[1841] *leche*, doctor.
[1843] *shoten*, assailed? rushed on?
[1844] *to-tere*, tear apart.
[1845] *beyte*, bait.

Þe laddes were kaske and teyte
un-   And umbiyeden him ilkon:
Sum smot with tre and sum with ston;
Sum putten with gleyve in bac and side,
And yeven wundes longe and wide   1850
In twenti stedes and wel mo,
Fro þe croune til þe to.
Hwan he saw þat, he was wod;
And was it ferlik, hw he stod,
For the blod ran of his sides   1855
So water þat fro þe welle glides;
But þanne bigan he for-to mowe
shewe] showe   With the barre, and let hem showe
Si (-n H)   Hw he cowþe sore smite;
For was þer non, long ne lite,   1860
Þat he mouhte over-take,
Þat he ne garte his croune krake,
So þat, on a litel stund,
Felde he twenti to þe grund.

Þo bigan gret dine to rise,   1865
For þe laddes on ilke wise
Him asayleden with grete dintes:
stoden]   Fro fer he stonden him with flintes,
stonden Sm   And gleyves schoten him fro ferne,
For drepen him he wolden yerne,   1870
But dursten he newhen him no more
Þanne he bor or leun wore.

Huwe Raven þat dine herde,
And þowhte wel þat men misferde
With his loverd, for his wif;   1875
And grop an ore and a long knif,

1846 *kaske*, vigorous (ON).   *teyte*, eager (cf. 2336) (ON).
1847 *umbiyeden*, surrounded.
1849 *putten*, thrust.
1854 'it was marvellous'.
1856 *welle*, spring.   *glides*, flows.
1858 *showe*, see.
1863 *stund*, time.
1864 *dine*, din.
1868 *stonden*, stoned.
1869 *ferne*, afar.
1871 *newhen*, approach.
1872 *bor*, boar.   *leun*, lion.
1876 *ore*, oar.

cham

And þider drof al-so an hert,
And cam þer on a litel stert,
And saw how þe laddes wode
Havelok his loverd umbistode,   1880
And beten on him so doth þe smith
With þe hamer on þe stith.

hwat] quath
Sk

'Allas!' *quath* Hwe, 'þat Y was boren,
Þat evere et Ich bred of koren,
Þat Ich here þis sorwe se!   1885
Roberd! Willam! hware ar ye?
Gripeth eyþer unker a god tre,
And late we nouht þise doges fle

Ƶ adds be

Til ure loverd wreke *be*;
Cometh swiþe and folwes me!   1890
Ich have in honde a ful god ore:
Datheit hwo ne smite sore!'
'Ya, leve, ya!' quod Roberd sone,
'We haven ful god liht of þe mone.'
Roberd grop a staf, strong and gret   1895
Þat mouhte ful wel bere a net,
And Willam Wendut grop a tre

þre

Mikel grettere þan his þe,
And Bernard held his ax ful faste—
I seye, was he nouht þe laste—   1900
And lopen forth so he weren wode
To þe laddes, þer he stode,
And yaf hem wundes swiþe grete.
Þer mihte men wel se boyes bete,
And ribbes in here sides breke,   1905
And Havelok on hem wel wreke.
He broken armes, he broken knes,
He broken shankes, he broken þes;
He dide þe blode þere renne dune

[1877] *hert*, hart.
[1878] *stert*, moment, time.
[1880] *umbistode*, surrounded.
[1882] *stith*, anvil.
[1884] *koren*, corn.
[1887] *unker*, of you (two) (C).
[1889] *wreke*, avenged.
[1893] *ya*, yes.
[1897] *tre*, beam.
[1898] *þe*, thigh.
[1901] *lopen*, leapt.
[1904] *boyes*, men (fellows, rascals).   *bete*, beaten.
[1908] *shankes*, calves.

To þe fet riht fro the crune,   1910
For was þer spared heved non;
He leyden on hevedes ful god won,
And made croune breke and crake
Of þe broune and of þe blake;
He maden here backes al-so bloute   1915
Als here wombes, and made hem rowte
Als he weren kradel-barnes;
So dos þe child þat moder þarnes.

Daþeit þe recke, for he it servede!
Hwat dide he þore? Weren he werewede!   1920
So longe haveden he but and bet
With neves under hernes set,
Þat of þo sixti men and on
Ne went þer awey lives non.

On þe morwen, hwan it was day,   1925
Ilc on other wirwed lay
Als it were dogges þat weren henged,
And summe leye in dikes slenged,
And summe in gripes bi þe her
Drawen ware, and laten ther.   1930
Sket cam tiding in-til Ubbe
Þat Havelok havede with a clubbe
Of hise slawen sixti and on
Sergaunz, þe beste þat mihten gon.
'Deus!' quoth Ubbe, 'hwat may þis be?   1935
Betere is I nime mi-self and se
Hwat þis baret oweth on wold,
Þanne I sende yung or old.
For yif I sende him unto,
I wene men sholde him shame do,   1940
And þat ne wolde Ich for no þing;

Left margin glosses:
hhan (1925)
slenget (1928)
his (1936)
þat] Hwat *H*;
on hwat is]
haveth on *H*,
oweth on *Si* (1937)

1915 *bloute*, soft (ON).
1916 *wombes*, bellies.   *rowte*, roar.
1918 *þarnes*, is without (cf. 2497 'lose') (ON).
1919 *þe recke*, who cares.   *servede*, deserved.
1920 *werewede*, mauled, mangled (cf. 1926).
1921 *but*, thrust.   *bet*, beaten.
1922 *neves*, fists (ON).   *hernes*, ears? brains? (C).
1928 *dikes*, ditches.   *slenged*, slung.
1929 *gripes*, gutters.
1931 *sket*, quickly (cf. 1965, etc.) (ON).
1933 *of hise*, of his men.
1934 *sergaunz*, retainers, (foot-) soldiers.
1937 *baret*, fighting.   *oweth on wold*, means ('has in meaning').

I love him wel, bi hevene king!
Me wore levere I wore lame
Þanne men dide him ani shame,
Or tok, or onne handes leyde
Vnornelske Unornelike, or shame seyde.'   1945
He lep upon a stede liht,
And with him mani a noble kniht,
And ferde forth unto þe tun
And dide calle Bernard Brun   1950
Ut of his hus, hwan he þer cam;
Sk adds him And Bernard sone ageyn *him* nam,
Al to-tused and al to-torn,
Ner al-so naked so he was born,
And al to-brised, bac and þe.   1955
Quoth Ubbe, 'Bernard, hwat is þe?
Hwo haves þe þus ille maked,
Þus to-riven and al mad naked?'

Iouerd 'Loverd, merci,' quoth he sone,
'To-nicht, al-so ros þe mone,   1960
Comen her mo þan sixti þeves
With lokene copes and wide sleves,
Me for-to robben and to pine,
And for-to drepe me and mine.
Mi dore he broken up ful sket   1965
And wolde me binden, hond and fet.
Hwan þe godemen þat sawe,
wowe Havelok, and he þat bi þe wawe
Leye, he stirten up sone onon,
And summe grop tre, and sum grop ston,   1970
And drive hem ut, þei he weren crus,
So dogges ut of milne-hous.
Havelok grop þe dore-tre
Sk adds at And *at* a dint he slow hem thre.
He is þe beste man at nede   1975
Þat evere-mar shal ride stede.
Als helpe God, bi mine wone,
þhousend, his A þousend of men is he worth one.

1946 *unornelike*, roughly.
1947 *liht*, swift? nimbly?
1953 *to-tused*, mauled.
1955 *to-brised*, bruised.
1959 *to-riven*, torn.
1969 *leye*, lay (pl.).
1971 *crus*, fierce (ON).
1972 *milne-hous*, mill.

Yif he ne were, Ich were nou ded,
So have Ich don mi soule red!   1980

hof   But it is of him mikel sinne:
He maden him swilke woundes þrinne
Þat of þe alþer-leste wounde
Were a stede brouht to grunde.
He haves a wunde in the side,   1985
With a gleyve, ful unride;
And he haves on þoru his arum—
Þer-of is ful mikel harum;

þhe   And he haves on þoru his þe,
Þe unrideste þat men may se;   1990
And oþere wundes haves he stronge
Mo than twenti, swiþe longe;
But siþen he havede lauht þe sor
Of þe wundes, was nevere bor
Þat so fauht, so he fauht þanne.   1995
Was non þat havede þe hern-panne

-cruhsse   So hard þat he ne dede al to-crusshe,
And al to-shivere, and al to-frusshe.
He folwede hem so hund dos hare—
Daþeyt on he wolde spare,   2000

Sk adds he   Þat *he* ne made hem everilk on
Ligge stille so doth þe ston;
And þer nis he nouht to frie,
For oþer sholde he make hem lye
Ded, or þei him havede slawen,   2005
Or al to-hewen, or al to-drawen.

Loverd, havi no more pliht
Of þat Ich was greyþed þus to-niht.
Þus wolde þe theves me have reft,
But, God þank, he havenet sure keft.   2010

1980 *red*, help.
1981 *sinne*, pity (cf. 2380).
1988 *harum*, harm, pity (cf. 2414).
1996 *hern-panne*, skull.
1998 *to-shivere*, shatter.   *to-frusshe*, break in pieces.
1999 *hund*, hound (cf. 2440).
2000 *daþeyt*, cf. 'the devil a one'.
2003 *frie*, blame (ON).
2004 'either he had to . . .'
2006 *to-hewen*, cut to pieces.   *to-drawen*, torn apart.
2007 *pliht*, harm.
2008 *greyþed*, ill-treated (ON).
2009 *reft*, robbed.
2010 *sure*, bitterly ('sourly').   *keft*, paid for (ON).

93

But it is of him mikel scaþe;
woth   I wot þat he bes ded ful raþe!'

Quoth Ubbe, 'Bernard, seyst þou soth?'
lepe] leye   'Ya, sire, that I ne leƴe oth.
Sm (C)   Yif Y, loverd, a word leye,   2015
To-morwen do me hengen heye.'
Þe burgeys þat þer-bi stode þore
Grundlike and grete oþes swore,
holde   Litle and mikle, yunge and olde,
Þat was soth þat Bernard tolde: 2020
Soth was þat he wolden him bynde,
And trusse al þat he mi*ht*en fynde
Of hise, in arke or in kiste,
Þat he mou*ht*e in seckes þriste:
'Loverd, he haveden al awey born   2025
His þing, and him-self al to-torn,
But al-so God self barw him wel,
Þat he ne tinte no catel.
Hwo mi*ht*e so mani stonde ageyn
Bi ni*ht*er-tale, kni*ht* or swein?   2030
He weren bi tale sixti and ten
Starke laddes, stalworthi men,
And on, þe mayster of hem alle,
Þat was þe name Giffin Galle.
Hwo mou*ht*e ageyn so mani stonde   2035
But als þis man of ferne londe,
Haveth hem slawen with a tre?
Mikel joie have he!
God yeve him mikel god to welde
Boþe in tun and ek in felde!'   2040
he etes met]   'We*l* is set *þe mete he etes,*'
em. H   Quoth Ubbe, '*gos,* him swiþe fete*s,*
doth, fete]   Þat Y mou*ht*e his woundes se,
gos, fetes Si   Yf that he mou*ht*en holed be;
(C)

2014 *leye,* violate (C), lie.
2022 *trusse,* pack up.
2023 *kiste,* chest.
2024 *secken,* sacks.
2025 *haveden,* would have.
2027 *but al-so,* except that.
2028 *tinte,* lost.
2030 *bi nihter-tale,* at dead of night.
2031 *bi tale,* in number.
2043 *holed,* healed.

For yf he mou*ht*e covere yet   2045
And gangen wel upon hise fet,
Mi-self shal dubben him to kni*ht*
For-þi þat he is so wi*ht*;
And yif he livede, þo foule theves,
Þat weren of Kaym kin and Eves,   2050
He sholden hange bi þe necke;
Of here ded daþeit *h*wo recke,
Hwan he yeden þus on ni*ht*es
To binde boþe burgmen and kni*ht*es,
For bynderes love Ich nevere mo—   2055
Of hem ne yeve Ich nouht a slo.'

Havelok was bifore Ubbe browht,
Þat havede for him ful mikel þou*ht*,
And mikel sorwe in his herte
For hise wundes, þat we*re* so smerte.   2060

shewed   But hwan hise wundes weren sh*a*wed,
And a leche havede knawed
Þat he hem mou*ht*e ful wel hele,
Wel make him gange, and ful wel mele,
And wel a palefrey bi-stride,   2065
And wel upon a stede ride,
Þo let Ubbe al his care
And al his sorwe over-fare,
And seyde, 'Cum now forth with me,
And Goldeboru, þi wif, with þe,   2070
And þine serjaunz alle þre,
For nou wile Y youre warant be;
Wile Y non of here frend
Þat þu slowe with þin hend
Sk adds to   Moucte wayte þe *to* slo   2075
Al-so þou gange to and fro.
I shal lene þe a bowr
Þat is up in þe heye tour
Til þou mowe ful wel go,

2045 *covere*, recover.
2050 *Kaym*, Cain.
2061 *shawed*, examined.
2062 *knawed*, pronounced, made known.
2064 *mele*, speak.
2065 *palefrey*, riding-horse (C).
2068 *over-fare*, pass.
2072 *warant*, surety.
2077 *bowr*, room.
2079 'Until you are able to walk.'

And wel ben hol of al þi wo.   2080
It ne shal no þing ben bi-twene
Ði bour and min, al-so Y wene,
But a fayr firrene wowe—
Speke Y loude or spek Y lowe
sahalt, the
second a
cancelled with
a dot instead of
the first
Ðou s*h*alt ful wel heren me,   2085
And þan þu wilt, þou shalt me se.
A rof shal hile us boþe o ni*h*t,
Þat none of mine, clerk ne kni*h*t,
Ne sholen þi wif no shame bede,
No more þan min, so God me rede!'   2090

He dide unto þe borw bringe
The i *of*
ioyinge *erased*
Sone anon, al with joy*i*nge,
His wif and his serganz þre,
Þe beste men þat mou*h*te be.
Þe firste ni*h*t he lay þer-inne,   2095
Hise wif, and his serganz þrinne,
Aboute þe middel of þe ni*h*t
Wok Ubbe, and saw a mikel li*h*t
þat] þer edd.
In þe bour þer Havelok lay,
Al-so bri*h*t so it were day.   2100

'Deus!' quoth Ubbe, 'hwat may þis be?
Betere is I go mi-self, and se,
Hweþer he sitten nou and wesseylen,
shot-
Or of ani sotshipe to-deyle*n*
Ðis tid nihtes, al-so foles;   2105
birþe
Ðan birþ men casten hem in poles,
Or in a grip, or in þe fen;
Nou ne sitten none but wicke men,
Glotouns, revres or wicke þeves,
Bi Crist, þat alle folk on leves!'   2110

He stod and totede in at a bord
Her, anilepi
Er he spak anlepi word,
And saw hem slepen faste ilk-on
And lye stille so þe ston,

2080 *hol*, healed.
2083 *firrene*, of fir-wood.   *wowe*, wall.
2087 *A*, a single.   *hile*, cover.
2104 *sotshipe*, foolishness.   *to-deylen*, take part in.
2105 *foles*, fools.
2106 *birþ*, ought (impersonal) (past *birde* 2766).   *poles*, pools.
2108 *sitten*, sc. awake.
2111 *totede*, peeped.   *bord*, plank (i.e. through a chink).

Wittenbrinck
adds þat

And saw *þat* al þat mikel li*ht*   2115
Fro Havelok cam, þat was so bri*ht*.
Of his mouth it com il-del—
Þat was he war ful swiþe wel.
'Deus!' quoth he, 'hwat may þis mene?'
He calde boþe arwe men and kene,   2120
Kni*ht*es and serganz swiþe sleie,
Mo þan an hundred, with-uten leye,
And bad hem alle comen and se
Hwat þat selcuth mi*ht*e be.

Als þe kni*ht*es were comen alle   2125
Þer Havelok lay, ut of þe halle,
So stod ut of his mouth a glem,
Riht al swilk so þe sunne-bem,
Þat al so li*ht* wa*s* þare, bi hevene,
So þer brenden serges sevene   2130

serges] *H*
sugg. torches

And an hundred serges ok—
Þat durste hi sweren on a bok.
He slepen faste alle five,
So he weren brou*ht* of live,
And Havelok lay on his lift side,   2135
In his armes his bri*ht*e bride.
Bi þe pappes he leyen naked—
So faire two weren nevere maked
In a bed to lyen samen;
Þe kni*ht*es þouht of hem god gamen,   2140
Hem for-to shewe and loken to.
Ri*ht* al-so he stoden alle so,

wend

And his bac was toward hem went,
So weren he war of a croiz ful gent

swe] *corr. Sk*
Brithter

On his riht shuldre, swiþe bri*ht*,   2145
Bri*ht*er þan gold ageyn þe li*ht*,
So þat he wiste, heye and lowe,

kunrik]
kunmerk *Si;*
sawe

Þat it was kun*merk* þat he sowe.
It sparkede, and ful bri*ht* shon
So doth þe gode charbucle-ston,   2150

2120 *arwe*, sluggish, timid.
2127 *glem*, ray.
2130 *serges*, wax tapers.
2135 *lift*, left.
2137 *bi þe pappes*, down to the breasts.
2140 *gamen*, sport (C).
2141 *shewe*, look (and *shawe* 2789).
2144 *gent*, fair.
2149 *sparkede*, sparkled.
2150 *charbucle*, carbuncle (C).

Þat men mou*h*te se, by þe li*h*t,
A peni chesen, so was it bri*h*t.
Þanne bi-helden he him faste
So þat he knewen at þe laste
Þat he was Birkabeynes sone   2155
Þat was here king, þat was hem wone
Wel to yeme, and wel were
Ageynes uten-laddes here;
'For it was nevere yet a broþer
In all Denemark so lich anoþer   2160
So þis man, þat is so fayr
Als Birkabeyn: he is hise eyr.'

He fellen sone at hise fet—
Was non of hem þat he ne gret,
Of joie he weren alle so fawen   2165
So he him haveden of erþe drawen.
Hise fet he kisten an hundred syþes,
Þe tos, þe nayles and þe lithes,
So þat he bigan to wakne,
And wit*h* hem ful sore to blakne,   2170
For hc wende he wolden him slo,
Or elles binde him, and do wo.

Quoth Ubbe, 'Loverd, ne dred þe now*h*t:
Me þinkes that I se þi þou*h*t.
Dere sone, wel is me   2175
Þat Y þe with ey*e*n se.
Manred, loverd, bede Y þe;
Þi man auht I ful wel to be,
For þu art comen of Birkabeyn,
Þat havede mani kni*h*t and sweyn;   2180
And so shalt þou, loverd, have,
Þou þu be yet a ful yung knave.
Þou shalt be king of al Denemark,
Was þer-inne nevere non so stark.
To-morwen shaltu manrede take   2185
Of þe brune and of þe blake,

2151f. 'could see to choose a penny'.
2157 *were*, defend (cf. 2303).
2158 'against the armies of foreigners'.
2164 *gret*, wept.
2165 *fawen*, glad.
2166 'as if they had brought him back from the grave.'
2168 *lithes*, tips of toes.
2170 *with hem*, i.e. at the sight of them.   *blakne*, turn pale.
2179 *comen*, descended.

Of alle þat aren in þis tun,
Boþe of erl and of barun,
And of dreng, and of thayn,
And of kni*h*t, and of sweyn,   2190
And so shaltu ben mad kni*h*t
Wit*h* blisse, for þou art so wi*h*t.'

Þo was Havelok swiþe bliþe
And þankede God ful fele siþe.
On þe morwen, *h*wan it was li*h*t   2195
And gon was þisternesse of þe niht,
Ubbe dide upon a stede
A ladde lepe, and þider bede
Erles, barouns, drenges, theynes,
Klerkes, kni*h*tes, bur*g*eys, sweynes,   2200
Þat he sholden comen anon
Bi-foren him sone everilk-on
loven] loveden   Al-so he lov*ed*en here lives,
ʒ   And here children, and here wives.

Hise bode ne durste he non at-sitte   2205
meme   Þat he ne *n*eme, for-to wite
Sone, hwat wolde þe justise;
Sk adds he   And *he* bigan anon to rise
And seyde sone, 'Liþes me
Alle samen, þeu and fre.   2210
A þing Ich wile you here shauwe
he   Þat *y*e alle ful wel knawe.
Ye witen wel þat al þis lond
Was in Birkabeynes hond
Þe day þat he was quic and ded,   2215
And how þat he, bi youre red,
Bi-tauhte hise children þre
Godard to yeme, and al his fe.
Havelok his sone he him tauhte,
And hise two douhtres, and al his auhte.   2220
Alle herden ye him swere
On bok, and on messe-gere,
Þat he shulde yeme hem wel,
Withuten lac, withuten tel.

2196 *þisternesse*, darkness.
2205 'none of them dared disobey his command'.
2206 *neme*, went.
2210 *þeu*, serf.
2224 *tel*, reproach.

New para MS   He let his oth al over-go—   2225
Evere wurþe him yvel and wo!
For þe maydnes here lif
Refte he boþen with a knif,
And him shulde ok have slawen—
Þe knif was at his herte drawen.   2230
But God him wolde wel have save;
He havede reunesse of þe knave,
So þat he with his hend
Ne drop him nou*ht*, þat sori fend!
But sone dide he a fishere   2235
Swiþe grete oþes swere
Þat he sholde drenchen him
In þe se, þat was ful brim.

Hwan Grim saw þat he was so fayr,
And wiste he was þe ri*ht* eir,   2240
Fro Denemark ful sone he fledde
In-til Englond, and þer him fedde
Mani winter, þat til þis day
Haves he ben fed and fostred ay.
Lokes hware he stondes her!   2245
In al þis werd ne haves he per,
Non so fayr ne non so long,
Ne non so mikel, ne non so strong;
In þis middel-erd nis so kni*ht*
Half so strong, ne half so wi*ht*.   2250
Bes of him ful glad and bliþe,
And cometh alle hider swiþe
Manrede youre loverd for-to make,
Boþe þe brune and þe blake.
I shal mi-self do first þe gamen,   2255
And ye siþen, alle samen.'

O knes ful fayre he him sette—
Mou*ht*e no þing him þer-fro lette—
And bi-cam *his* man ri*ht* þare;
Þat alle sawen þat þere ware.   2260

After him stirt up laddes ten
And bi-comen hise men,
And siþen everilk a baroun

[2229] 'and would also have killed Havelok'.
[2238] *brim*, raging.
[2249] *middel-erd*, world (C).
[2255] *gamen*, joyful ceremony.

Þat evere weren in al that toun,
And siþen drenges, and siþen thaynes,　　　　2265
And siþen knihtes, and siþen sweynes,
So þat, or þat day was gon,
In al þe tun ne was nouht on
Þat it ne was his man bi-comen—
Manrede of alle havede he nomen.　　　　2270

Hwan he havede of hem alle
Manrede taken in the halle,
Grundlike dide he hem swere
Þat he sholden him god feyth bere
Ageynes alle þat woren on live;　　　　2275
Þer-yen ne wolde never on strive
Þat he ne maden sone þat oth,
Riche and poure, lef and loth.
Hwan þat was maked, sone he sende,
Ubbe, writes fer and hende,　　　　2280
After alle þat castel yemede,
Burwes, tunes, sibbe an fremde,
Þat þider sholden comen swiþe
Til him, and heren tiþandes bliþe
Þat he hem alle shulde telle.　　　　2285
Of hem ne wolde nevere on dwelle
Þat he ne come sone plattinde—
gangande　　Hwo hors ne havede, com ganginde.
So þat with-inne a fourteniht
In al Denmark ne was no kniht,　　　　2290
Ne conestable, ne shireve,
Þat com of Adam and of Eve,
Þat he ne com bi-forn sire Ubbe—
þhes　　He dredden him so þef doth clubbe.

Hwan he haveden alle þe king gret,　　　　2295
And he weren alle dun set,
Þo seyd Ubbe, 'Lokes here

2269 *it ne was = he ne was.*
2273 *grundlike*, solemnly (cf. 2312).
2276 *þer-yen*, against that (= *þer-ageyn*).
2280 *writes*, writs, summons.
2282 *sibbe*, kinsmen.　　*fremde*, strangers.
2284 *tiþandes*, news (ON).
2287 *plattinde*, spurring.
2288 *ganginde*, walking, on foot.
2291 *conestable*, keeper of castle.
2294 *þef*, thief.

Ure loverd swiþe dere,
Þat shal ben king of al þe lond
And have us alle under hond!   2300
For he is Birkabeynes sone,
Þe king þat was umbe stonde wone
H adds Us *Us* for-to yeme*n* and wel were
Wit*h* sharp swerd and longe spere.
Lokes nou, hw he is fayr—   2305
Sikerlike he is hise eyr.
Falles alle to hise fet;
Bicomes hise men ful sket!'
He weren for Ubbe swiþe adrad
And dide sone al þat he bad,   2310
And yet deden he sum-del more;
O bok ful grundlike he swore
Þat he sholde with him halde,
bolde Boþe ageynes stille and ba*l*de,
Þat evere wo*l*de his bodi dere: 2315
Þat dide hem o boke swere.

Hwan he havede manrede and oth
Taken of lef and of loth,
Ubbe dubbede him to kni*ht*
With a swerd ful swiþe bri*ht*,   2320
And þe folk of al þe lond
Bi-tauhte him al in his hond,
Þe cunnriche everil-del,
And made him king heylike and wel.
Hwan he was king, þer mou*ht*e men se   2325
Þe moste joie þat mouhte be:
Buttinge with sharpe speres,
Skirming with talevaces þat men beres,
Wrastling with laddes, putting of ston,
Harping and piping ful god won,   2330
Leyk of mine, of hasard ok,
Romanz-reding on þe bok.
Þer mou*ht*e men here þe gestes singe,

[2302] *umbe stonde*, formerly.
[2314] *balde*, bolde.
[2324] *heylike*, nobly.
[2326] *moste*, greatest.
[2327] *buttinge*, thrusting.
[2328] *skirming*, fencing. *talevaces*, shields.
[2331] *leyk*, playing (ON). *mine*, a game like backgammon. *hasard*, dice.
[2333] *gestes*, epics ('chansons de geste').

Þe gleumen on þe tabour dinge;
Þer mouhte men se þe boles beyte,   2335
And þe bores, with hundes teyte;
Þer mouhte men se everil gleu,
Þer mouhte men se hw grim greu—
Was nevere yete joie more
In al þis werd, þan þo was þore.   2340
Þer was so mikel yeft of cloþes
Þat, þou I swore you grete othes,
troud] trod   I ne wore nouht þer-offe trod—
H   Þe may I ful wel swere, bi God!
Þere was swiþe gode metes,   2345
And of wyn, þat men fer fetes,
Riht al-so mikel and gret plenté
So it were water of þe se.
Þe feste fourti dawes sat;
So riche was nevere non so þat.   2350
Þat king made Roberd þere kniht,
Þat was ful strong and ful wiht;
hec   And Willam Wendut ec, his broþer,
And Huwe Raven, þat was þat oþer,
And made hem barouns alle þre,   2355
And yaf hem lond and oþer fe,
So mikel, þat ilker twenti knightes
Havede of genge, dayes and nihtes.

Hwan þat feste was al don,
A thusand knihtes ful wel o bon   2360
With-held þe king, with him to lede,
Þat ilk-an havede ful god stede,
Helm and sheld and brinie briht,
And al þe wepne þat fel to kniht;
With hem five thusand gode   2365
Sergaunz, þat weren to fyht wode,
With-held he, al of his genge;

2334 *gleumen*, minstrels.   *tabour*, small drum.
2335 *boles*, bulls.
2336 *teyte*, eager, keen.
2337 *gleu*, amusement.
2338 *grim*, excitement.   *greu*, increased.
2341 *yeft*, gift.
2343 *trod*, believed (cf. inf. *tro* 2867).
2346 *fer*, from afar.
2357 *ilker*, each of them (for *ilk her*).
2358 *of genge*, in his retinue.
2360 *wel o bon*, in good condition (cf. 2576, and contrast 2510) (*bon* is ON).
2361 *with-held*, retained (*king* is subject).

Wil I na-more þe storie lenge.
Yet hwan he havede of al þe lond
Þe casteles alle in his hond,   2370
And conestables don þer-inne,
He swor, he ne sholde never blinne
Til þat he were of Godard wreken,
Þat Ich have of ofte speken.
Half hundred knihtes dede he calle,   2375
And hise fif thusand sergaunz alle,
And dide sweren on þe bok
Sone, and on þe auter ok,
Þat he ne sholde nevere blinne,
Ne for love, ne for sinne,   2380
Til þat he haveden Godard funde,
And brouht bi-forn him faste bunde.

Þanne he haveden sworn þis oth,
Ne leten he nouht, for lef ne loth,
Þat he ne foren swiþe rathe   2385
Þer he was, unto þe paþe
Þer he yet on hunting for
With mikel genge, and swiþe stor.
Robert, þat was of al þe ferd
Mayster, was girt with a swerd,   2390
And sat upon a ful god stede
Þat under him riht wolde wede;
He was þe firste þat with Godard
Spak, and seyde, 'Hede, cavenard!
Hwat dos þu here at þis paþe?   2395
Cum to þe king, swiþe and raþe,
Þat sendes he þe word, and bedes
Þat þu þenke hwat þu hem dedes
Hwan þu reftes with a knif
Hise sistres here lif,   2400
An siþen bede þu in þe se
Drenchen him—þat herde he!
He is to þe swiþe grim;
Cum nu swiþe unto him
-riche   Þat king is of þis kunerike,   2405
Þu fule man, þu wicke swike!

2368 *lenge*, spin out, delay.
2387 *for*, went (past of *fare*).
2388 *stor*, proud.
2389 *ferd*, army (cf. 2540, etc.).
2392 *wede*, gallop (madly) (cf. 2646).
2394 *hede*, take heed.   *cavenard*, coward?

And he shal yelde þe þi mede,
Bi Crist þat wolde on rode blede!'

Sk adds he Hwan Godard herde þat *he* þer þrette,
With þe neve he Robert sette   2410
Bi-forn þe teth a dint ful strong;
And Robert kipt ut a knif long
And smot him þoru þe ri*ht* arum—
Þer-of was ful litel harum!

Hwan his folk þat sau and herde,   2415
Hwou Robert with here loverd ferde,
He haveden him wel ner brow*ht* of live,
Ne weren his two breþren and oþre five
Sk adds þat *Þat* slowen of here laddes ten,
Of Godardes alþer-beste men.   2420
fledden Hwan þe oþre sawen þat, he fledde,
And Godard swiþe loude gredde,
'Mine kni*ht*es, hwat do ye?
Sule ye þus-gate fro me fle?
Ich have you fed, and yet shal fede,   2425
Helpe me nu in þis nede,
And late ye nou*ht* mi bodi spille,
Ne Havelok don of me hise wille.
id Yif ye *it* do, ye do you shame
And bringeth you-self in mikel blame.'   2430
Hwan he þat herden, he wenten ageyn,
And slowen a kni*ht* and a sweyn
Of þe kinges oune men,
And woundeden abuten ten.

Þe kinges men, hwan he þat sawe,   2435
lowe Sc*h*uten on hem, heye and l*a*we,
And everilk fot of hem slowe
But Godard one, þat he flowe,
So þe þef, men dos henge,
Or hund men shole in dike slenge.   2440
He bunden him ful swiþe faste,
Hwil þe bondes wolden laste,

[2414] 'That was nothing to be sorry about!'
[2424] *sule*, shall, will. *þus-gate*, thus.
[2427] *spille*, destroy.
[2436] *schuten*, rushed.
[2437] *everilk fot*, every man.
[2438] 'whom they [afterwards] flayed'.

Þat he rorede als a bole

he wore — Þat wore parrede in an hole

With dogges for-to bite and beite— 2445

Were þe bondes nou*ht* to leite.

He bounden him *so* fele sore

Þat he gan crien Godes ore,

Sk adds ne — Þat he *ne* sholde of his hend plette.

Wolden he nouht þer-fore lette 2450

Þat he ne bounden hond and fet—

Daþeit þat on þat þer-fore let!

But dunten him so man doth bere,

And keste him on a scabbed mere,

crice — Hise nese went unto þe cri*c*e: 2455

So ledden he þat fule swike,

Til he was bi-forn Havelok brou*ht*,

Þat he have*de* ful wo wrowht,

hungred — Boþe with hungre and with cold,

Or he were twel winter old, 2460

And with mani hevi swink,

With poure mete and feble drink,

with not in — And *with* swiþe wikke cloþes,

MS.; see (C) — For al hise manie grete othes.

holde — Nu beyes he his olde blame— 2465

Old sinne makes newe shame!

*H*wan he was so shamelike

Brouht bi-forn þe king, þe fule swike,

Þe king dede Ubbe swiþe calle

Hise erles and hise barouns alle, 2470

Dreng and thein, burgeis and kni*ht*,

And bad he sholden demen him ri*ht*,

For he kneu þe swike-dam

Everil-del—God was him gram!

He setten hem dun bi þe wawe, 2475

lowe — Riche and povere, heye and l*a*we,

helde — Þe elde men and ek þe grom,

And made þer þe ri*ht*e dom,

And seyden unto þe king anon,

2444 *parrede*, penned.
2446 *leite*, seek (i.e. one did not have to look hard for them) (ON).
2449 *of . . . plette*, strike off.
2450 *lette,* desist (and *let* 2452).
2453 *dunten*, beat.
2455 *crike*, anus (anal cleft, cf. 710).
2465 *beyes*, pays dear for.
2474 *gram*, angry.
2477 *grom*, young man.

	Þat stille sat, so þe ston,	2480
slawen	'We deme þat he be al quic *f*lawen,	
	And siþen to þe galwes drawen	
	At þis foule mere tayl,	
	Þoru *h*is fet a ful strong nayl,	
	And þore ben henged wit*h* two feteres,	2485
	And þare be writen þise leteres:	
	"Þis is þe swike þat wende wel	
	Þe king have reft þe lond il-del,	
	And hise sistres with a knif	
	Boþe refte here lif."	2490
	Þis writ shal henge bi him þare;	
more	Þe dom is demd, seye we na m*a*re.'	
	Hwan þe dom was demd and give,	
	And he was wit*h* þe prestes shrive,	
	And it ne mou*ht*e ben non oþer,	2495
	Ne for fader ne for broþer,	
Sk adds But	*But* þat he sholde þarne lif,	
	Sket cam a ladde with a knif,	
	And bigan ri*ht* at þe to	
	For-to ritte and for-to flo;	2500
rore] rare *Sm*	And he bigan for-to r*a*re	
	So it were grim or g*a*re,	
gore] gare *Sm*	Þat men mi*ht*e þeþen a mile	
	Here him rore, þat fule file.	
	Þe ladde ne let no wi*ht* for-þi	2505
	Þey he criede, 'Merci, merci!'	
Sk adds he, him	Þat *he* ne flow *him* everil-del	
	With knif mad of grunden stel.	
	Þei garte bringe þe mere sone,	
Skabbeb	Skabbe*d* and ful ivele o bone,	2510
	And bunden him ri*ht* at hire tayl	
	With a rop of an old seyl,	
	And drowen him unto þe galwes,	
	Nou*ht* bi þe gate but over þe falwes,	
	And henge*d* þore bi þe hals.	2515
	Daþeit hwo recke—he was fals!	

2481 *quic flawen*, flayed alive.
2500 *ritte*, cut.
2501 *rare*, roar.
2502 *grim or gare*, rage or fury (C).
2504 *file*, scoundrel.
2508 *grunden*, ground, sharpened.
2514 *gate*, road (ON).   *falwes*, ploughed fields.

New para MS	Þanne he was ded, þat Sathanas,	
	Sket was seysed al þat his was	
	In þe kinges hand il-del,	
	Lond and lith and oþer catel,	2520
	And þe king ful sone it yaf	
	Ubbe in þe hond, wit*h* a fayr staf,	
	And seyde, 'Her Ich sayse þe	
	In al þe lond, in al þe fe.'	
	Þo swor Havelok he sholde make,	2525
	Al for Grim, of monekes blake	
	A priorie to serven inne ay	
	Ihesu Crist, til domes-day,	
haueden (*C*)	For þe god he havede him don	
we] ivel *Sk*	Hwil he was povere and *ivel* o bon.	2530
oth] hot *Si*	And þer-of held he wel his *hot*,	
woth	For he it made, God it wot,	
	In þe tun þer Grim was graven,	
name	Þat of Grim yet haves þe na*ven*.	
	Of Grim bidde Ich na more spelle,	2535
	But *h*wan Godrich herde telle,	
	Of Cornwayle þat was erl,	
	Þat fule traytour, that mixed cherl,	
	Þat Havelok was king of Denemark,	
ferde	And ferd with him, strong and stark,	2540
	Comen Engelond with-inne,	
	Engelond al for-to winne,	
	And þat she þat was so fayr,	
	Þat was of Engelond ri*ht* eir,	
	Was comen up at Grimesbi,	2545
	He was ful sorful and sori	
	And seyde, 'Hwat shal me to raþe?	
Goddoth	Goddot I shal do slon hem baþe;	
	I shal don hengen hem ful heye,	
	So mote Ich brouke mi ri*ht*e eie,	2550
	But yif he of mi lond fle —	
	Hwat wenden he to desherite me?'	

[2520] *lith*, people (ON).
[2522] *staf*, mace? (C).
[2526] *monekes*, monks.
[2531] *hot*, promise.
[2538] *mixed*, filthy (cf. 'mixen', dunghill).
[2541] *comen*, *sc.* was.
[2545] *comen up*, landed.
[2546] *sorful*, sad.
[2547] *raþe*, advice (cf. verb 1339) (ON)
[2550] cf. 311, etc.

bidde] bede *Stratmann*	He dide sone ferd ut *bede*,
	Þat al þat evere mouhte o stede
	Ride, or helm on heved bere, 2555
	Brini on bac, and sheld and spere,
	Or ani oþer wepne bere,
	Hand-ax, syþe, gisarm or spere,
	Or aunlaz and god long knif,
	Þat, als he lovede leme or lif, 2560
	Þat þey sholden comen him to
	With ful god wepne ye ber so,
	To Lincolne, þer he lay,
	Of Marz þe seventenþe day,
	So þat he couþe hem god þank; 2565
rang	And yif ani were so ran*k*
anon	Þat he ne þanne ne come an*a*n,
	He swor bi Crist and seint Johan
	Þat he sholde maken him þral,
	And al his of-spring forth with-al. 2570

Þe Englishe þat herde þat,
Was non þat evere his bode sat,
For he him dredde swiþe sore,
So runci spore, and mikle more.
At þe day he come sone 2575
Þat he hem sette, ful wel o bone,
To Lincolne, with gode stedes
And al þe wepne þat kni*ht* ledes.

þare] *Sk reads* yare *or* þare	Hwan he wore come, sket was þe erl *y*are
	Ageynes Denshe men to fare, 2580
	And seyde, 'Lyþes nu alle samen:
	Have Ich gadred you for no gamen,
	But Ich wile seyen you for-*h*wi;
	Lokes hware here at Grimesbi
comen	Hise uten-laddes here c*u*men, 2585
	And haves nu þe priorie numen.
	Al þat evere mi*ht*en he finde,

2553 *bede*, summon.
2558 *syþe*, scythe.   *gisarm*, halberd.
2559 *aunlaz*, dagger.
2560 *leme*, limb.
2562 *ye ber*, see (C).
2565 'would be grateful to them'.
2566 *rank*, stubborn.
2572 *sat*, withstood.
2574 'as a horse does the spur'.
2576 *sette*, appointed.

He brenne kirkes, and prestes binde;
He strangleth monkes and nunnes boþe:

Rede] roþe *Si*   *H*wat wile ye, frend, her-offe roþe?   2590
Yif he regne þus-gate longe,

-gange   He moun us alle over-gonge;
slo] flo *Si*   He moun us alle quic henge or *f*lo,
Or þral maken and do ful wo,
Or elles reve us ure lives,   2595
And ure children, and ure wives.
But dos nu als Ich wile you lere,
Als ye wile be with me dere:
Nimes nu swiþe forth and raþe,
And helpes me and yu-self baþe,   2600
And slos upo*n* þe dogges swiþe;

Sk adds I   For shal *I* nevere more be bliþe,
Ne hoseled ben, ne of prest shriven,
Til þat he ben of londe driven.
Nime we swiþe and do him fle,   2605
And folwes alle faste me;
For Ich am he, of al þe ferd,
Þat first shal slo with drawen swerd.
Daþeyt hwo ne stonde faste
Bi me, hwil hise armes laste!'   2610

couth] quoth   'Ye, lef, ye!' *quoth* þe erl Gunter;
Sk   'Ya!' quoth þe erl of Cestre, Reyner;
And so dide alle þat þer stode,
And stirte forth, so he were wode.
Þo mou*ht*e men se þe brinies brihte   2615
On backes keste, and late ri*ht*e,
Þe helmes heye on heved sette;
To armes al so swiþe plette
Þat þei wore on a litel stunde

Greþet   Grey*þe*d, als men mi*ht*e telle a pund,   2620
And lopen on stedes sone anon,
And toward Grimesbi, ful god won,
He foren softe bi þe sti,
Til he come ney at Grimesbi.

2590 *roþe*, advise.
2592 *he moun*, they may.   *over-gonge*, overrun.
2601 *slos*, strike.
2612 *Cestre*, Chester.
2616 *late rihte*, adjust, straighten.
2618 *plette*, hurried.
2620 *telle*, count out.
2623 *softe*, stealthily.

New para MS	Havelok, þat havede spired wel	2625
	Of here fare, everil-del,
	With al his ferd cam hem ageyn—
	For-bar he noþer kniht ne sweyn.
	Þe firste kniht þat he þer mette
	With þe swerd so he him grette	2630
For] Þat *edd.*	Þat his heved of he plette—
	Wolde he nouht for sinne lette.
	Roberd saw þat dint so hende;
	Wolde he nevere þeþen wende
	Til þat he havede anoþer slawen	2635
	With þe swerd he held ut-drawen.
	Willam Wendut his swerd ut-drow,
	And þe þredde so sore he slow
	Þat he made upon the feld
swerd] sheld	His lift arm fleye with the *shel*d.	2640
Madden	
	Huwe Raven ne forgat nouht
	Þe swerd he havede þider brouht;
	He kipte it up, and smot ful sore
	An erl þat he saw priken þore
	Ful noblelike upon a stede,	2645
	Þat with him wolde al quic wede.
	He smot him on þe heved so
	Þat he þe heved clef a-two,
	And þat bi þe shu*l*dre-blade
	Þe sharpe swerd let *he* wade	2650
	Þorw the brest unto þe herte;
	Þe dint bigan ful sore to smerte,
	Þat þe erl fel dun anon,
	Al-so ded so ani ston.
	Quoth Ubbe, 'Nu dwelle Ich to longe,'	2655
leth	And let his stede sone gonge
	To Godrich, with a god spere
	Þat he saw anoþer bere,
smoth	And smot Godrich, and G*odrich* him,
	Hetelike, with herte grim,	2660
	So þat he boþe felle dune

2625 *spired*, enquired, found out.
2626 *fare*, course.
2631 *plette*, struck.
2644 *priken*, spur, charge.
2646 *al quic*, vigorously.
2468 *clef*, split (cf. 2735).
2650 *wade*, pass, go.
2660 *hetelike*, furiously.

To þe erþe, first þe croune.

dun boþen]
lowe *Dobson* (C)
-drowen
Þanne he woren fallen *lowe*,
Grundlike here swerdes *he* ut-drowe
Þat weren swiþe sharp and gode,   2665
And fouhten so þei woren wode,
Þat þe swot ran fro þe crune

No gap in MS.   *   *   *   *   *   *   *

Þer mouhte men se to knihtes bete
Ayþer on oþer dintes grete,   2670
So þat with *þe* alþer-lest dint
Were al to-shivered a flint.
So was bi-twenen hem a fiht
Fro þe morwen ner to þe niht,

blinne] *corr.*
Stratmann
So þat þei nouht ne blunne   2675
Til þat to sette bigan þe sunne.
Þo yaf Godrich þorw þe side
Ubbe a wunde ful unride,
So þat þorw þat ilke wounde
Havede ben brouht to þe grunde,   2680
And his heved al of-slawen,
Yif God ne were, and Huwe Raven,
Þat drow him fro Godrich awey,
And barw him so þat ilke day.

her
But er he were fro Godrich drawen,   2685
Þer were a þousind knihtes slawen
Bi boþe halve, and mo ynowe,
Þer þe ferdes to-gidere slowe.
Þer was swilk dreping of þe folk
Þat on þe feld was nevere a polk   2690
Þat it ne stod of blod so ful
Þat þe strem ran intil þe hul.
Þo tarst bigan Godrich to go
Upon þe Danshe, and faste to slo,

2662 'head first'.
2667 *swot*, sweat? blood?
2672 'a flint would have been shattered'.
2678 *unride*, huge.
2680 *havede* = *havede he*.
2681 *of-slawen*, struck off.
2687 'on both sides'.
2688 'clashed together'.
2689 *dreping*, slaughter.
2690 *polk*, puddle.
2692 *hul*, hollow (i.e. down the slope?).
2693 *tarst*, first (= *at arst*).

	And forth-ri*ht,* al-so levin fares	2695
	Þat nevere kines best ne spares,	
his; *Sk adds* he	Þanne is *he* gon, for he garte alle	
	Þe Denshe men bi-forn him falle.	
	He felde browne, he felde blake,	
	Þat he mou*hte* over-take;	2700
	Was nevere non þat mou*hte* þave	
	His dintes, noyþer kni*ht* ne knave,	
Sk adds ne;	Þat he ne felden so dos þe gres	
feldem (C)	Bi-forn þe syþe þat ful sharp *es.*	
2704 is	Hwan Havelok saw his folk so brittene,	2705
	And his ferd so swiþe littene,	
	He cam drivende upon a stede	
	And bigan til him to grede,	
	And seyde, 'Godrich, *h*wat is þe	
	Þat þou fare þus with me	2710
	And mine gode knightes slos?	
	Sikerlike þou mis-gos.	
	Þou wost ful wel, yif þu wilt wite,	
	Þat Aþelwold þe dide site	
	On knes, and sweren on messe-bok,	2715
messe hok]	On caliz and on *pateyn ok,*	
corr. Sk (cf.	Þat þou hise douhter sholdest yelde,	
187)	Þan she were wimman of elde,	
	Engelond, everil-del—	
	Godrich þe erl, þou wost it wel!	2720
	Do nu wel, with-uten fiht,	
	Yeld hire þe lond, for þat is ri*ht*;	
	Wile Ich forgive þe þe lathe,	
mi] þi *Ƶ* (C)	Al *þ*i dede and al mi wrathe,	
	For Y se þu art so wi*ht*,	2725
	And of þi bodi so god kni*ht.*'	
	'Þat ne wile Ich nevere mo,'	
	Quoth erl Godrich, 'for Ich shal slo	
	Þe, and hire for-henge heye.	
	I shal þrist ut þi rihte eye	2730
	Þat þou lokes with on me,	
	But þu swiþe heþen fle.'	

2695 *levin,* lightning (C).
2703 *gres,* grass.
2704 *es,* is.
2705 *brittene,* cut to pieces.
2706 *littene,* diminish.
2712 *mis-gos,* do wrong.
2723 *lathe,* enmity (cf. 2981)

He grop þe swerd ut sone anon
And hew on Havelok, ful god won,
So þat he clef his sheld on-two.   2735
Hwan Havelok saw þat shame do
His bodi, þer bi-forn his ferd,
He drow ut sone hise gode swerd
And smot him so upon þe crune
Þat Godrich fel to þe erþe a-dune.   2740
But Godrich stirt up swiþe sket—
Lay he nowht longe at hise fet—
And smot him on þe sholdre so
Þat he dide þare undo
Of his brinie ringes mo   2745
Þan þat Ich kan tellen fro,
And woundede him riht in þe flesh,
þat tendre was and swiþe nesh,
So þat þe blod ran til his to;
Þo was Havelok swiþe wo,   2750
drawem   Þat he havede of him drawen
Blod, and so sore him slawen.
Hertelike til him he wente,
And Godrich þer fullike shente,
For his swerd he hof up heye   2755
And þe hand he dide of-fleye
Þat he smot him with so sore—
Hw mihte he don him shame more?

Hwan he havede him so shamed,
His hand of-plat, and yvele lamed,   2760
He tok him sone bi þe necke
Als a traytour, daþeyt hwo recke!
And dide him binde and fetere wel
With gode feteres al of stel,
And to þe quen he sende him,   2765
Þat birde wel to him ben grim,
And bad, she sholde don him gete,
And þat non ne sholde him bete
Ne shame do, for he was kniht,
Til knihtes haveden demd him riht.   2770

2746 *fro*, concerning
2754 *fullike*, shamefully.
2757 'with which he had struck him so hard'.
2760 *lamed*, mutilated, disabled.
2767 *gete*, guard (ON).
2770 *demd*, judged.

Þan þe Englishe men þat sawe,
Þat þei wisten, heye and lawe,
Þat Goldeboru, þat was so fayr,
Was of Engeland ri*ht* eyr,
And þat þe king hire havede wedded,   2775
And haveden ben samen bedded,
He comen alle to crie merci
Unto þe king, at one cri,
And beden him sone manrede and oth,
Þat he ne sholden, for lef ne loth,   2780
Nevere more ageyn him go
Ne ride, for wel ne for wo.

Þe king ne wolde nou*ht* for-sake
Þat he ne shulde of hem take
Manrede þat he beden, and ok   2785
Hold oþes sweren on þe bok;
But or bad he þat þider were brou*ht*
Þe quen, for hem (swilk was his þou*ht*)
For-to se and for-to shawe,
Yif þat he hire wolde knawe,   2790
Þoruth hem witen wolde he
Yif þat she aucte quen to be.

Sixe erles weren sone yare
After hire for-to fare.
He nomen onon, and comen sone,   2795
And brou*ht*en hire, þat under mone
In al þe werd ne havede per
Of hendeleik, fer ne ner.
Hwan she was come þider, alle
Þe Englishe men bi-gunne to falle   2800
O knes, and greten swiþe sore,
And seyden, 'Levedi, K*r*istes ore
And youres! We haven mis-do mikel,
Þat we ayen you have be fikel;
youres *at end* For Englond auhte for-to ben   2805
of 2805; and *Youres*, and we youre men.
youres *at end* Is non of us, yung ne old,
of 2806   Þat we ne wot þat Aþelwold
                 Was king of þis kunerike,

2778 'with one voice'.
2783 *for-sake*, refuse.
2786 *hold oþes*, oaths of loyalty (cf. 2821).
2798 *hendeleik*, courtesy.
2804 *fikel*, disloyal.

And ye his eyr, and þat þe swike   2810
Haves it halden with mikel wronge:
God leve him sone to honge!'

Quoth Havelok, 'Hwan þat ye it wite,
Nu wile Ich þat ye doun site,
And, after Godrich haves wrouht,   2815
Þat haves in sorwe him-self brouht,
Lokes þat ye demen him riht,
For dom ne spareth clerk ne kniht;   spared
And siþen shal Ich under-stonde
Of you, after lawe of londe,   2820
Manrede, and holde oþes boþe,
Yif ye it wilen and ek rothe.'
Anon þer dune he hem sette,
For non þe dom ne durste lette,
And demden him to binden faste   2825
Upon an asse swiþe un-wraste,
Ande-long, nouht over-þwert,
His nose went unto þe stert,
And so to Lincolne lede
Shamelike, in wicke wede;   2830
And hwan he came unto þe borw,
Shamelike ben led þer-þoru,
Bi-souþe þe borw, unto a grene—
Þat þare is yet, als Y wene—
And þere be bunden til a stake,   2835
Abouten him ful gret fir make,
And al to dust be brend riht þore;   þere
And yet demden he þer more,
Oþer swikes for-to warne,
Þat hise children sulde þarne   2840
Evere-more þat eritage
Þat his was, for hise utrage.

Hwan þe dom was demd and seyd,
Sket was þe swike on þe asse leyd

2815 'according to what G. has done'.
2819 *understonde*, receive.
2826 *un-wraste*, wretched.
2827 *ande-long*, lengthwise.   *over-þwert*, across (cf. 'athwart') (*þwert* is ON).
2828 *stert*, tail.
2833 *bi-souþe*, to the south of.
2841 *eritage*, inheritance.
2842 *utrage*, crime.

And him til]
em. Sk

And *led un*-til þat ilke grene   2845
And brend til asken al bidene.
Þo was Goldeboru ful bliþe;
She þanked God fele syþe
Þat þe fule swike was brend,
Þat wende wel hire bodi have shend;   2850
And seyde, 'Nu is time to take
Manrede of brune and of blake
Þat Ich se ride and go,
Nu Ich am wreke of mi fo.'

Havelok anon manrede tok   2855
Of alle Englishe, on þe bok,
And dide hem grete oþes swere
Þat he sholden him god feyth bere
Ageyn alle þat woren lives,
And þat sholde ben born of wives.   2860

Þanne he haveden sikernesse
Taken of more and of lesse,
Al at hise wille, so dide he calle
Þe erl of Cestre, and hise men alle,
Þat was yung kni*ht* wit*h*-uten wif,   2865
And seyde, 'Sire erl, bi mi lif,
And þou wile mi conseyl tro,
Ful wel shal Ich with þe do;
For Ich shal yeve þe to wive
Þe fairest þing that is o-live: 2870
Þat is Gunnild of Grimesby,
Grimes dou*h*ter, bi seint Davy,
Þat me forth brou*h*te and wel fedde,
And ut of Denemark with me fledde,
Me for-to burwe fro mi ded.   2875
Sikerlike, þoru his red
Have Ich lived in-to þis day—
Blissed worþe his soule ay!
I rede þat þu hire take,
And spuse, and curteysé make,   2880
For she is fayr, and she is fre,
And al-so hende so she may be.

2846 *asken*, ashes.   *bidene*, at once.
2861 *sikernesse*, assurance, security.
2875 *burwe*, save (? for *berwe*).
2880 *curteysé make*, treat graciously.

Þertekene she is wel with me;
Þat shal Ich ful wel shewe þe,
For Ich give þe a give,   2885
Þat evere-more, hwil Ich live,
For hire shaltu be with me dere—
Þat wile Ich þat þis folc al here.'
Þe erl ne wolde nouht ageyn
Þe king be, for kniht ne sweyn,   2890
Ne of þe spusing seyen nay,
But spusede þat ilke day.

H adds in   Þat spusinge was *in* god time maked,
For it ne were nevere clad ne naked
In a þede samened two   2895
Þat cam to-gidere, livede so,
So þey dide al here live;
He geten samen sones five,
Þat were þe beste men at nede
Þat mouhte riden on ani stede.   2900
Hwan Gunnild was to Cestre brouht,
Havelok þe gode ne forgat nouht
Bertram, þat was the erles kok,

H adds him   Þat he ne dide *him* callen ok,
And seyde, 'Frend, so God me rede,   2905
Nu shaltu have riche mede
For wissing, and þi gode dede
Þat tu me dides in ful gret nede;

cuuel   For þanne Y yede in mi couel,
haue] hauede   And Ich ne have*de* bred ne sowel,   2910
Sk   Ne Y ne havede no catel,
Þou feddes and claddes me ful wel.
Have nu for-þi of Cornwayle
Þe erldom il-del, with-uten fayle,
And al þe lond þat Godrich held,   2915
Boþe in towne and ek in feld;
And þer-to wile Ich þat þu spuse,
And fayre bring hire un-til huse,
Grimes douhter, Levive þe hende,
For þider shal she with þe wende.   2920
Hire semes curteys for-to be,

2883 *þertekene*, furthermore.   *wel with me*, in favour with me.
2885f. *Ich give þe a give/þat*, I give you assurance that.
2895 *samened*, united.
2907 *wissing*, guidance, advice.
2913 *for-þi*, in recompense for that.
2921 *semes*, befits.

For she is fayr so flour on tre;
Þe heu is swilk in hire ler
So þe rose in roser,
Hwan it is fayr sprad ut newe   2925
Ageyn þe sunne bri*ht* and lewe.'
And girde him sone with þe swerd
Of þe erldom, bi-forn his ferd,
And with his hond he made him kni*ht*
And yaf him armes, for þat was riht,   2930
And dide him þere sone wedde
Hire þat was ful swete in bedde.

After þat he spused wore,
Wolde þe erl nou*ht* dwelle þore,
But sone nam un-til his lond,   2935
And seysed it al in his hond,
And livede þer-inne, he and his wif,
An hundred winter in god lif,
And gaten mani children samen,
And liveden ay in blisse and gamen.   2940

boþe] baþe H   Hwan þe maydens were spused ba*þe*,
Havelok anon bigan ful rathe
His Denshe men to feste wel
Wit*h* riche landes and catel,
So þat he weren alle riche;   2945
chinche   For he was large and nou*ht* chiche.

Þer-after sone, with his here,
For he to Lundone, for-to bere
Corune, so þat it sawe
Henglishe,   Englishe ant Denshe, heye and *l*awe,   2950
lowe
Hwou he it bar with mikel pride,
For his barnage þat was unride.

Þe feste of his coruni*ng*
Laste with gret joying
Fourti dawes and sumdel mo;   2955
Þo bigunnen þe Denshe to go
Unto þe king, to aske leve;

2923 *heu*, colour.   *ler*, cheek, face.
2924 *roser*, rose-garden.
2926 *lewe*, warm.
2943 *feste*, establish, endow.
2946 *large*, generous.
2952 *barnage*, baronage.   *unride*, numerous.
2957 *leve, sc.* to go.

And he ne wolde hem nou*ht* greve,
For he saw þat he woren yare
Into Denemark for-to fare,   2960
anon But gaf hem leve sone an*a*n
And bi-tauhte hem seint Johan,
And bad Ubbe, his justise,
Þat he sholde on ilke wise
Denemark yeme and gete so   2965
Þat no pleynte come him to.

Hwan he wore parted alle samen,
Havelok bi-lefte wit*h* joie and gamen
In Engelond, and was þer-inne
Sixti winter king with winne,   2970
And Goldeboru quen, þat I wene
So mikel love was hem bi-twene
Þat al þe werd spak of hem two:
He lovede hire, and she him so,
Þat neyþer oþer mi*ht*e be   2975
Fro oþer, ne no joie se
togidede But yf he were to-gide*r*e boþe;
Nevere yete ne weren he wroþe,
For here love was ay newe —
Nevere yete wordes ne grewe   2980
ne Bi-twene hem, hwar-of n*o* lathe
Mi*ht*e rise, ne no wrathe.

He geten children hem bi-twene,
Sones and dou*ht*res ri*ht* fivetene,
Hwar-of þe sones were kinges alle —   2985
So wolde God it sholde bi-falle —
And þe dou*ht*res alle quenes;
Him stondes wel, þat god child strenes.
Nu have ye herd þe gest al þoru
Of Havelok and of Goldeborw;   2990
Hw he weren born, and hw fedde,
And hwou he woren with wronge ledde
In here youþe, with trecherie,
With tresoun and with felounye;
thit And hwou þe swikes haveden ti*h*t   2995
Reven hem þat was here ri*ht*;
And hwou he weren wreken wel
Have Ich sey*d* you everil-del.

2968 *bi-lefte*, remained.
2970 *with winne*, with joy.
2988 'It is well with him who begets a good child.'
2995 *tiht*, intended.

And for-þi Ich wolde biseken you
Þat haven herd þe rim nu,   3000
Þat ilke of you, with gode wille,
Seye a pater-noster stille
For him þat haveth þe rym maked,
And þer-fore fele nihtes waked,
Þat Iesu Crist his soule bringe   3005
Bi-forn his fader at his endinge! Amen.

[3004] *waked*, stayed awake.

II

ATHELSTON

1. Lord, þat is off myȝtys most,
   Fadyr and sone and holy gost,
       Bryng us out off synne,
   And lene us grace so for-to wyrke,
   To love boþe God and holy kyrke
       Þat *we* may hevene wynne.

Ƶ adds we

   Lystnes, lordyngys þat ben hende,
   Off ffalsnesse, hou it wil ende
       A man þat ledes hym þer-in.
   Off ffoure weddyd breþeryn I wole ȝow tel,
   Þat wolden yn Yngelond go dwel,

kynde] kyn *T*

       Þat sybbe were nouȝt off *kyn*.

2. And alle foure messangeres þey were
   Þat wolden yn Yngelond lettrys bere,
       As it wes here kynde.
   By a fforest gan þey mete
   Wiþ a cros, stood in a strete,
       Be leff undyr a lynde.
   And, as þe story telles me,
   Ylke man was of dyvers cuntre —
       In book i-wreten we ffynde —
   For love of here metyng þare

binding covers
all but eu ma

   Þey swoor hem weddyd breþeryn for e*ve*rma*re*,
       In trewþe trewely dede hem bynde.

1.1 *myȝtys*, power.
1.4 *lene*, grant (and past *lent* 42.6).
1.7 *hende*, pleasant, 'nice' (cf. 19.12).
1.9 'for a man who practises it'.
1.10 *weddyd*, sworn (C).
1.12 *sybbe*, related (cf. 'sibling').

2.3 *kynde*, proper occupation (cf. *SD* 101).
2.4 *gan þey mete*, they met (cf. 11.10).
2.5 *wiþ*, beside.   *stood*, which stood (cf. 5.8, 34.6, 71.11) (C).   *strete*, high road.
2.6 *leff*, leaf.   *lynde*, lime-tree ('linden') (C).
2.8 *ylke*, each.   *dyvers*, different.
2.10 *here*, their (cf. 6.11, etc.).
2.12 *trewþe*, true faith, honour.   *dede hem bynde*, bound themselves.

3. Þe eldeste off hem ylkon,
   He was hyȝt Athelston,
       Þe kyngys cosyn dere;
   He was off þe kyngys blood—
   Hys eemes sone, I undyrstood—
       Þerfore he neyȝyd hym nere.
   And at þe laste, weel and fayr,
   Þe kyng hym dyyd withouten ayr;
       Þenne was þer non hys pere
   But Athelston, hys eemes sone.

scho only
visible; schone Z
   To make hym kyng wolde þey nouȝt scho*ne*,
       To corowne hym with gold so clere.

4. Now was he kyng, semely to se;
   He sendes afftyr hys breþeryn þre
       And gaff hem here warysoun.
   Þe eldest broþir he made eerl of Dovere—
   And þus þe pore man gan covere—
       Lord off tour and toun.
   Þat oþer broþer he made eerl of Stane—
   Egelond was hys name,
       A man off gret renoun—

end of line
unclear
   And gaff hym tyl hys weddy*d* wy*ff*
   Hys owne sustyr, dame Edyff,
       Wiþ gret devocyoun.

5. Þe ferþe broþir was a clerk—
   Mekyl he cowde off Goddys werk—
       Hys name it was Alryke.

3.1 *hem ylkon*, them all.
3.2 *hyȝt*, called.
3.5 *eemes*, uncle's.
3.6 *neyȝyd hym nere*, was close to him.
3.8 *ayr*, heir.
3.9 *pere*, equal, match (cf. 6.9).
3.11 *schone*, hesitate ('shun').
3.12 *clere*, bright.

4.1 *semely*, fair ('seemly').
4.3 *warysoun*, reward (cf. 37.10).
4.5 *covere*, recover (favour, position) (cf. 30.11).
4.7 *Stane*, Stone (C).
4.8 *tyl*, as (cf. 'to wife').
4.12 *devocyoun*, solemnity, ceremony.

5.1 *ferþe*, fourth.   *clerk*, cleric.
5.2 *mekyl*, much.   *cowde*, knew, was skilled, experienced.

vacant	Cauntyrbury was vacan*d* And fel into þat kyngys hand; He gaff it hym, þat wyke,
e *of* cowde *obscure* lyche	And made hym bysschop of þat stede, Þat noble clerk, on book cowde rede — In þe world was non hym ly*k*e. Þus avaunsyd he hys broþer þorwʒ Goddys gras, And Athelston hymselven was
ryche	A good kyng and a ry*k*e.

6. And he þat was eerl off Stane —
   Sere Egeland was hys name —
      Was trewe, as ʒe schal here.
   Þorwʒ þe myʒt off Goddys gras
   He gat upon þe countas
      Twoo knave-chyldren dere.
   Þat on was ffyfftene wyntyr old,
   Þat oþer þryttene, as men me told —
      In þe world was non here pere —
   Al-so whyt so lylye-fflour,
   Red as rose off here colour,
      As bryʒt as blosme on brere.

7. Boþe þe eerl and hys wyff,
      Þe kyng hem lovede as hys lyff,
         And here sones twoo,
      And offten-syþe he gan hem calle
      Boþe to boure and to halle,
         To counsayl whenne þey scholde goo.
      Þer-at sere Wymound hadde gret envye,

Þ, *with space* *for two letters*	Þ*e* eerl off Dovere, wyttyrlye; In herte he was ful woo. He þouʒte al for here sake

5.6 *wyke*, city? office? (C).
5.10 *avaunsyd*, helped, advanced.   *brother*, prob. plural here.
5.12 *ryke*, powerful (cf. 32.5).

6.4 *gras*, grace.
6.5 *gat*, begot.   *countas*, countess (and *cuntas* 18.10).
6.6 *knave-chyldren*, boys (cf. 27.5, and Germ. *Knabe*).
6.10 *al-so*, just as.
6.12 *blosme*, blossom (cf. 27.5–7).   *brere*, briar.

7.4 *offten-syþe*, often.
7.5 *boure*, chamber.
7.8 *wyttyrlye*, truly (C).
7.9 *woo*, sad (cf. 11.7, 23.12).

False lesyngys on hem to make,
　　To doon hem brenne and sloo.

8. And þanne sere Wymound hym be-þouȝte,
　'Here love þus endure may nouȝte;
　　Þorwȝ wurd oure werk may sprynge.'
　He bad hys men maken hem ȝare;
　Unto Londone wolde he fare
　　To speke wiþ þe kynge.
　Whenne þat he to Londone come,
　He mette with þe kyng ful sone;
　　He sayde, 'Welcome, my derelyng.'
　Þe kyng hym fraynyd soone anon
　Be what way he hadde i-gon,
　　Wiþouten ony dwellyng.

9. 'Come þou ouȝt be Cauntyrbery,
　Þere þe clerkys syngen mery
　　Boþe erly and late?
in margin, same
hand
　Hou faryth þat noble clerk
　Þat mekyl can on Goddys werk?
　　Knowest þou ouȝt hys state?
　And come þou ouȝt be þe eerl off Stane,
　Þat wurþy lord in hys wane?
　　Wente þou ouȝt þat gate?
　Hou fares þat noble knyȝt
　And hys sones fayr and bryȝt,
　　My sustyr, ȝiff þat þou wate?'

10. 'Sere,' þanne he sayde, 'wiþouten les,
　Be Cauntyrbery my way I ches;

7.11 *lesyngys*, lies.
7.12 'To cause them to be burnt and slain.'

8.3 *wurd*, speech, slander.　*sprynge*, proceed, prosper.
8.4 *ȝare*, ready (cf. 22.1).
8.9 *derelyng*, dear friend ('darling').
8.10 *fraynyd*, asked.
8.12 *ony*, any.　*dwellyng*, delay (cf. 16.9).

9.1 'did you come at all by way of Canterbury?'
9.8 *wurþy*, noble, honourable.　*wane*, dwelling (and *wone* 22.4, 71.3).
9.9 *gate*, way (ON).
9.12 *ȝiff*, if.　*wate*, know.

10.1 *les*, deceit (cf. *lesyngys*).
10.2 *ches*, took ('chose').

Þere spak I wiþ þat dere.

Ry3t weel gretes þee þat noble clerk,
Þat mykyl can off Goddys werk—
    In þe world is non hys pere.
And al-so be Stane my way I drow3;
Wiþ Egeland I spak inow3
    And with þe countesse so clere.
þey fare weel, is nou3t to layne,
And boþe here sones.' Þe king was fayne
    And in his herte made glad chere.

11. 'Sere kyng,' he sayde, '3iff it be þi wille
To chaumbyr þat þou woldest wenden tylle,
    Counsayl for to here,
I schal þe tellen a swete tydande—
Þer comen nevere non swyche in þis lande
    Off al þis hundryd 3ere.'
Þe kyngys herte þan was ful woo
Wiþ þat traytour for to goo;
    Þey wente boþe forþ in ffere,
And whenne þat þey were þe chaumbyr
                withinne,
False lesyngys he gan begynne
    On hys weddyd broþer dere.

12. 'Sere kyng,' he sayde, 'woo were me
Ded þat I scholde see þe,
    So moot I have my lyff;
For, by hym þat al þis worl wan,
Þou hast makyd me a man
    And i-holpe me ffor to þryff.

10.3 *dere*, dear man.
10.7 *al-so*, likewise.   *drow3*, took ('drew') (cf. 10.2 and 61.7).
10.8 *inow3*, enough.
10.10 *layne*, conceal (cf. 14.3).
10.11 *fayne*, glad.

11.2 *wenden*, go
11.3 *counsayl*, (something in) secret, private (cf. 14.3) (C).
11.4 *tydande*, piece of news ('tidings'); *swete tydande* 'a fine bit of news' (ironic?).
11.5 *swyche*, such.
11.9 *in ffere*, together.
11.11 *gan begynne*, began (cf. 2.4, etc.).
11.12 *On*, against.

12.3 *moot*, may.
12.4 *worl*, world.   *wan*, redeemed.
12.6 *i-holpe*, helped.   *þryff*, prosper ('thrive').

For in þy land, sere, is a fals traytour;
He wole doo þe mykyl dyshonour
      And brynge þe off lyve.
He wole deposen þe slyly;
Sodaynly þan schalt þou dy,
      Be Crystys woundys ffyve.'

on

13. Þenne sayde þe kyng, 'So moot þou the,
     Knowe I þat man, and I hym see?
        His name þou me telle.'
     'Nay,' says þat traytour, 'þat wole I nouȝt
     For al þe gold þat evere was wrouȝt,
        Be masse-book and belle,
     But ȝiff þou me þy trowþe wil plyȝt
     Þat þou schalt nevere bewreye þe knyȝt
        Þat þe þe tale schal telle.'
     Þanne þe kyng his hand up rauȝte,
     Þat ffalse man his trowþe be-tauȝte—
        He was a devyl off helle!

me blurred

schalt,
bewreye very
unclear

kn only visible

14. 'Sere kyng,' he sayde, 'þou madyst me knyȝt,
     And now þou hast þy trowþe me plyȝt
        Oure counsayl for to layne.
     Sertaynly, it is non oþir
     But Egelane, þy weddyd broþir:
        He wolde þat þou were slayne.
     He dos þy sustyr to undyrstande
     He wole be kyng off þy lande,
        And þus he begynnes here trayne;
     He wole þe poysoun ryȝt slyly—
     Sodaynly þanne schalt þou dy,
        Be hym þat suffryd payne.'

12.9 *off lyve*, i.e. to death.
12.10 *slyly*, by stealth (cf. 14.10).
12.11 *Sodaynly*, suddenly.

13.1 'so may you prosper' (C).
13.2 *and*, if
13.8 *be-wreye*, make known.
13.9 *tale*, story, 'facts'.
13.10 *rauȝte*, stretched.
13.11 'He gave his word to that traitor.'

14.7 *dos*, causes.
14.9 *trayne*, treason, plot.

15. Þanne swoor þe kyng be cros and roode,
     'Meete ne drynk schal do me goode
          Tyl þat he be dede;
     Boþe he and hys wyff, hys soones twoo,
     Schole þey nevere be no moo
          In Yngelond on þat stede.'
     'Nay,' says þe traytour, 'so moot I the,
     Ded wole I nouȝt my broþer se;
          But do þy beste rede.'
     No lengere þere þen wolde he lende;
     He takes hys leve, to Dovere gan wende —
          God geve hym schame and dede!

or schames dede

16. Now is þat traytour hom i-went;
     A messanger was afftyr sent
          To speke with þe kyng.
     I wene he bar his owne name:
     He was hoten Athelstane;
          He was foundelyng.
     Þe lettrys were i-maad fullyche þare
     Unto Stane for to ffare
          Wiþouten ony dwellyng,
     To ffette þe eerl and his sones twoo,
     And þe countasse alsoo,
          Dame Edyve, þat swete þyng.

17. And in þe lettre ȝit was it tolde
     Þat þe kyng þe eerlys sones wolde
          Make hem boþe knyȝt;
     And þer-to his seel he sette;
     Þe messanger wolde nouȝt lette —
          Þe way he rydes ful ryȝt.

15.2 'Neither food nor drink . . .' (G).
15.5 *schole*, shall.   *no moo*, any more.
15.7 'as I hope to prosper' (cf. 13.1).
15.9 *þy beste rede*, 'what seems best to you.'
15.10 *lengere*, longer.   *lende*, remain.
15.12 *dede*, death (and *ded* 29.5).

16.2 *afftyr sent*, sent for.
16.4 *wene*, believe.   *bar*, bore.
16.5 *hoten*, called (cf. *hyȝt* 3.2).
16.10 *ffette*, fetch (cf. 54.1).

17.1 *ȝit was it tolde*, it was further stated.
17.4 'he put his seal to it'.
17.5 *lette*, delay (cf. 20.5, 21.2 and noun *lettyng* 19.5).
17.6 *ryȝt*, straight.

18. Þe messanger, þe noble man,
    Takes hys hors and forþ he wan,
        And hyes a ful good spede.
    Þe eerl in hys halle he fande;
    He took hym þe lettre in his hande,
        Anon he bad hym rede.
    'Sere,' he sayde al-so swyþe,
    'Þis lettre ouȝte to make þe blyþe;
        Þer-too þou take good hede:
    Þe kyng wole for þe cuntas sake
    Boþe þy sones knyȝtes make—
        To London I rede þe spede.

19. 'Þe kyng wole for þe cuntas sake
    Boþe þy sones knyȝtys make—
        Þe blyþere þou may be.
    Þy ffayre wyff with þe þou bryng,
    And þer be ryȝt no lettyng,
        Þat syȝte þat sche may see.'
    Þenne sayde þat eerl with herte mylde,
    'My wyff goþ ryȝt gret with chylde,
        And for-þynkes me,
    Sche may nouȝt out off chaumbyr wyn,
    To speke with non ende off here kyn,
        Tyl sche delyveryd be.'

20. But into chaumbyr þey gunne wende
    To rede þe lettrys before þat hende,
        And tydyngys tolde here soone.
    Þenne sayde þe cuntasse, 'So moot I the,
    I wil nouȝt lette tyl I þere be,
        To-morwen or it be noone.

18.2 *wan*, made his way (cf. 31.8, and *wyn* 19.10).
18.3 *hyes*, hastens.
18.4 *fande*, found.
18.5 *took him*, gave him (cf. 67.5) (C).
18.7 *al-so swyþe*, at once.
18.8 *blyþe*, joyful.
18.12 *rede*, advise.   *spede*, hasten.

19.9 *for-þynkes me*, I am sorry.
19.11 'to speak to any member of her family'.

20.1 *gunne*, plural of *gan* (cf. 2.4, etc.).
20.6 *or*, before (cf. 24.6).

ATHELSTON

21. 'To see hem kny3tys, my sones ffre,
     I wole nou3t lette tyl I þere be;
          I schal no lengere dwelle.
     Cryst for-3elde my lord þe kyng
     Þat has grauntyd hem here dubbyng;
          Myn herte is gladyd welle.'

22. Þe eerl hys men bad make hem 3are;
     He and hys wyff fforþ gunne þey fare;
          To Londone ffaste þey wente.
     At Westemynstyr was þe kyngys wone;
     Þere þey mette with Athelstone,
          Þat afftyr hem hadde sente.

23. Þe goode eerl soone was hent,
     And feteryd faste, verrayment,
          And hys sones twoo.
     Ful lowde þe countasse gan to crye,
     And sayde, 'Goode broþir, mercy!
          Why wole 3e us sloo?
     What have we a3ens 3ow done
     Þat 3e wole have us ded so soone?
          Me þynkiþ 3e arn oure ffo!'
     Þe kyng as wood ferde in þat stede;
     He garte hys *sustyr* to presoun lede;
          In herte he was ful woo.

line added in margin, same hand; sone *only visible*

sustyr edd; not legible in MS.

24. Þenne a squyer, was þe countasses ffrende,
     To þe qwene he gan wende
          And tydyngys tolde here soone.
     Gerlondes off chyryes off sche caste;
     Into þe halle sche come at þe laste,
          Longe or it were noone.
     'Sere kyng, I am before þe come

21.3 *dwelle,* delay.
21.4 *for-3elde,* repay (cf. 29.11).
21.5 *dubbyng,* i.e. as knights.
21.6 *gladyd,* delighted.

23.1 *hent,* seized.
23.2 *verrayment,* truly (cf. 26.7).
23.6 *sloo,* kill (cf. 7.12, and past *slow3* 26.11, etc.).
23.9 *þynkiþ,* seems. *arn,* are.
23.10 *as wood,* as if mad (and comp. *wodere* 43.2). *ferde,* behaved. *stede,* place.
23.11 *garte,* caused (ON) (cf. 39.12). *presoun,* prison.

24.4 *gerlondes,* garlands. *chyryes,* cherries (C).

131

Wiþ a chyld, douȝtyr or a sone;
Graunte me my bone,
My broþir and sustyr þat I may borwe
Tyl þe nexte day at morwe
Out off here paynys stronge,

25. 'Þat we mowe wete be comoun sent

In þe playne parlement...

playne *written*
twice
No gap in MS.;
four lines lost

weres

'Dame,' he sayde, 'goo ffro me;
Þy bone schal nouȝt i-grauntyd be,
I doo þe to undyrstande,
For, be hym þat were*d* þe corowne off þorn,
Þey schole be drawen and hangyd to-morn,
Ȝyff I be kyng off lande.'

26. And whenne þe qwene þese wurdes herde,
As sche hadde be beten wiþ ȝerde,
Þe teeres sche leet doun falle.
Sertaynly, as I ȝow telle,
On here bare knees doun sche felle
And prayde ȝit for hem alle.
'A, dame,' he sayde, 'verrayment,
Hast þou broke my comaundement?
Abyyd ful dere þou schalle.'
Wiþ hys ffoot—he wolde nouȝt wonde—
He slowȝ þe chyld ryȝt in here wombe;
Sche swownyd amonges hem alle.

27. Ladyys and maydenys þat þere were
Þe qwene to here chaumbyr bere
And þere was dool inowȝ.
Soone withinne a lytyl spase
A knave-chyld i-born þer wase,

24.9 *bone*, request ('boon') (cf. 39.5).
24.10 *borwe*, stand bail for (cf. 37.7) (and *borewe* 28.9).
24.12 *out off*, (and relieve them) from (*out off* dependent on *borwe* 10).

25.1 'That we may know by general assent' (cf. 41.7).
25.2 *playne*, full.
25.11 *to-morn*, tomorrow morning.

26.2 *ȝerde*, rod.
26.9 *abyyd*, pay for (C).
26.10 *wonde*, hesitate.

27.3 *dool*, sorrow (cf. 34.11).

As bryȝt as blosme on bowȝ.
He was boþe whyt and red;
Off þat dynt was he ded—
　　Hys owne fadyr hym slowȝ.
Þus may a traytour baret rayse
And make manye men ful evele at ayse—
　　Hymselff nouȝt afftyr it lowȝ.

28. But ȝit þe qwene　as ȝe schole here,
Sche callyd upon a messangere,
　　Bad hym a lettre ffonge,
And bad hym wende to Cauntyrbery,
Þere þe clerkys syngen mery
　　Boþe masse and evensonge.
'Þis lettre þou þe bysschop take,
And praye hym for Goddys sake
bande 　　Come borewe hem out off here bonde.
He wole doo more for hym, I wene,
Þanne for me, þouȝ I be qwene,
undyrstande 　　I doo þe to undyrstonde.

29. 'An eerldom in Spayne I have of land;
Al I sese into þyn hand
　　Trewely, as I þe hyȝt;
An hundryd besauntys off gold red—
Þou may save hem from þe ded
　　ȝyff þat þyn hors be wyȝt.'
'Madame, brouke weel þy more-geve
Al-so longe as þou may leve;
　　Þer-to have I no ryȝt;

27.8 *dynt*, blow.
27.10 *baret*, strife, anger.
27.11 *evele at ayse*, miserable, wretched (cf. 'ill at ease').
27.12 'He (Athelston, or possibly Wymound) had no cause to laugh about it afterwards' (C).

28.3 *ffonge*, receive, take.

29.2 *sese*, make over.
29.3 *hyȝt*, promise.
29.4 *besauntys*, gold coins (orig. from *Byzantium*) (cf. 68.5).　　*gold red* (see *SO*, 150).
29.6 *wyȝt*, swift, strong.
29.7 *brouke*, enjoy.　　*more-geve*, endowment (C).
29.8 *leve*, live.

But off þy gold and off þy ffee,
Cryst in hevene ffor-ӡelde it þe;
  I wole be þere to-nyӡt.

30. 'Madame, þrytty myles off hard way
I have reden, siþ it was day;
  Ful sore I gan me swynke;
 And for to ryde now ffyve and twenti þer-too,
An hard þyng it were to doo,
  Forsoþe, ryӡt as me þynke.
Madame, it is ner-hande passyd prime,
And me behoves al for to dyne,
  Boþe wyn and ale to drynke.

fare] re *not visible*

Whenne I have dynyd, þenne wole I fa*re*—
God may covere hem off here care
  Or þat I slepe a wynke.'

way] ay *not visible*

31. Whenne he hadde dynyd, he wente his w*ay*
Al-so faste as þat he may;
  He rod be Charynge-cros,
And entryd into Flete-strete,

hete] te *not visible*

And seþþyn þorwӡ Londone, I ӡow he*te*,
  Upon a noble hors.
Þe messanger, þat noble man,

Over *unclear; perhaps* on

Over Loundone-brygge sone he wan—
  For his travayle he hadde no los—
From Stone into Steppyngebourne
For-soþe his way nolde he nouӡt tourne;
  Sparyd he nouӡt for myre ne mos.

29.10 *ffee*, money.

30.2 *siþ*, since.
30.3 *swynke*, labour, exert.
30.4 *þer-too*, in addition (i.e. a *total* of 55, the distance from London to Canterbury; cf. 33.6) (C).
30.7 *ner-hande*, almost.   *prime*, first part of day, 6–9 a.m. (C).
30.8 *dyne*, breakfast (C).
30.11 *covere*, relieve (cf. 4.5, and *kevere* 35.12).

31.8 *wan*, arrived.
31.9 *travayle*, effort.
31.10 *Steppyngebourne*, Sittingbourne (C).
31.11 *tourne*, turn aside.
31.12 *sparyd*, *sc.* himself or his horse.   *mos* marsh (C).

bysschopryke
as one word

32. And þus hys way wendes he
Fro Osprynge to þe Blee;
  Þenne myʒte he see þe toun
  Off Cauntyrbery, þat noble wyke;
  Þer-in lay þat bysschop ryke,
    Þat lord off gret renoun.

rod *over* was
expunged

33. And whenne þey runggen undern-belle,
He rod in Londone, as I ʒow telle —
  He was non er redy;
  And ʒit to Cauntyrbery he wan
  Longe or evensong began —
    He rod mylys ffyffty.

34. Þe messanger noþyng abod;
Into þe palays forþ he rod,
  Þere þat þe bysschop was inne.
  Ryʒt welcome was þe messanger,
  Þat was come ffrom þe qwene so cleer,
    Was off so noble kynne.
  He took hym a lettre ful good speed,
  And sayde, 'Sere bysschop, have þis and reed',
    And bad hym come wiþ hym.
  Or he þe lettre hadde halff i-redde,
  For dool, hym þouʒte, hys herte bledde —
    Þe teeres ffyl ovyr hys chyn.

35. Þe bysschop bad sadele hys palfray:
'Al-so ffaste as þay may,
  Bydde my men make hem ʒare;
  And wendes before,' þe bysschop dede say,
  'To my maneres in þe way —
    For noþyng þat ʒe spare;
  And loke, at ylke ffyve mylys ende,

32.2 *þe Blee*, the Blean forest.

33.1 *undern*, mid-morning (here 9–10 a.m.?).
33.3 *non er*, not before.

34.1 *abod*, waited (and *bod* 38.1).
34.6 refers to the queen.
34.12 *ffyl*, fell.

35.1 *palfray*, riding horse (C).
35.4 *wendes*, addressed to the messenger.
35.5 *maneres*, manors.

A ffresch hors þat I ffynde,
Schod and noþyng bare;
Blyþe schal I nevere be
Tyl I my weddyd broþer see,
To kevere hym out off care.'

36. On nyne palfrays þe bysschop sprong,
Ar it was day, from evensong,
In romaunce as we rede.
Sertaynly, as I ȝow telle,
On Londone-brygge ded doun felle
Þe messangeres stede.
'Allas,' he sayde, 'þat I was born!
Now is my goode hors for-lorn,
Was good at ylke a nede;
Ȝistyrday upon þe grounde
He was wurþ an hundryd pounde
Ony kyng to lede.'

37. Þenne be-spak þe erchebysschop,
Oure gostly fadyr undyr God,
Unto þe messangere,
'Lat be þy menyng off þy stede,
And þynk upon oure mykyl nede,
Þe whylys þat we ben here;
For ȝiff þat I may my broþer borwe
And bryngen hym out off mekyl sorwe,
Þou may make glad chere;
And þy] *corr. T*   Þy warysoun I schal þe geve,
And God have grauntyd þe to leve
Unto an hundryd ȝere.'

38. Þe bysschop þenne nouȝt ne bod;
He took hys hors, and forþ he rod
Into Westemynstyr so lyȝt;

35.9 *bare,* unsaddled ('bare-back').

36.3 *romaunce,* French book ('romance') (C) (cf. 53.3, 59.3, 73.3).
36.8 *for-lorn,* lost, gone.
36.9 *nede,* necessity.

37.2 *gostly,* spiritual.
37.4 *menyng,* complaining.
37.11 *and,* if (C) (cf. 39.10, 65.10).

38.3 *lyȝt,* swiftly.

Þe messanger on his ffoot al-soo —
Wiþ þe bysschop come no moo,
 Neþer squyer ne kny3t.
Upon þe morwen þe kyng aros,
And takes þe way, to þe kyrke he gos,
 As man off mekyl my3t.
Wiþ hym wente boþe preest and clerk,
Þat mykyl cowde off Goddys werk,
 To praye God for þe ry3t.

39. Whenne þat he to þe kyrke com,
To-ffore þe rode he knelyd anon,
 And on hys knees he ffelle:
'God, þat syt in Trynyté,
A bone þat þou graunte me,
 Lorde, as þou harewyd helle:

þat with a thin stroke through it

Gyltles men 3iff þat þay be,
Þat are in my presoun ffree,
 For-cursyd þere to 3elle,
Off þe gylt and þay be clene,
Leve it moot on hem be sene
 Þat garte hem þere to dwelle.'

40. And whenne he hadde maad his prayer,
He lokyd up into þe qweer;
 Þe erchebysschop saw3 he stande.
He was for-wondryd off þat caas,
And to hym he wente a-pas
 And took hym be þe hande.
'Welcome,' he sayde, 'þou erchebysschop,
Oure gostly fadyr undyr God!'
 He swoor be God levande,

38.7 *morwen*, morning ('morrow').

39.2 *to-ffore*, before. *rode*, rood (C).
39.6 *harewyd*, harrowed.
39.8 *ffree*, strong? (C).
39.9 *for-cursyd*, condemned. *3elle*, howl.
39.10 'If they are free from guilt.'
39.11 *leve*, grant (cf. 75.11). *sene*, visible.

40.2 *qweer*, choir.
40.3 'He saw the archbishop standing there.'
40.4 *for-wondryd*, astonished. *caas*, circumstance.
40.5 *a-pas*, quickly ('apace') (cf. 57.3).
40.9 *levande*, living (Northern or East Anglian form).

'Weddyd broþer, weel moot þou spede,
For I hadde nevere so mekyl nede
Siþ I took cros on hande.

41. 'Goode weddyd broþer, now turne þy rede;
Doo nouȝt þyn owne blood to dede
But ȝiff it wurþy were.

weres For hym þat wered þe corowne off þorn,
Lat me borwe hem tyl to-morn,
Þat we mowe enquere
And weten alle be comoun asent
In þe playne parlement

No gap in MS.;
four lines lost 42. Who is wurþy be schent;
two or eight And, but ȝiff ȝe wole graunte my bone,
lines lost? It schal us rewe boþe or none,
Be God þat alle þyng lent!'

43. Þanne þe kyng wax wroþ as wynde—
A wodere man myȝte no man fynde
Þan he began to bee;
be oþis] corr. Z He swoor *oþis be* sunne and mone:
'Þey schole be drawen and hongyd or

none—

Wiþ eyen þou schalt see.
Lay doun þy cros and þy staff,
Þy mytyr and þy ryng þat I þe gaff;
Out off my land þou fflee!
Hyȝe þe faste out off my syȝt;
Wher I þe mete, þy deþ is dyȝt—
Non oþir þen schal it bee.'

40.10 *spede*, prosper, succeed (cf. 53.12).
40.12 i.e. became archbishop.

41.1 *turne þy rede*, change your mind.
41.2 *doo . . . to dede*, put to death.
41.3 *wurþy*, deserving.
41.6 *enquere*, make enquiry.

42.3 *schent*, punished.
42.4 *but ȝiff*, unless (cf. 48.10, 64.8, 66.12).
42.5 'We shall both regret it before noon.'

43.1 *wax*, became.
43.11 *wher*, wherever. *dyȝt*, appointed.

44. Þenne be-spak þat erchebysschop,
Oure gostly fadyr undyr God,
    Smertly to þe kyng,
'Weel I wot þat þou me gaff
Boþe þe cros and þe staff,
    Þe mytyr and eke þe ryng.
My bysschopryche þou reves me;
And crystyndom for-bede I þe:
    Preest schal þer non syngge;
Neyþer maydyn-chyld ne knave
Crystyndom schal þer non have—
    To care I schal þe brynge.

45. 'I schal gare crye þorwȝ ylke a toun
Þat kyrkys schole be broken doun
    And stoken agayn wiþ þorn;
And þou schalt lygge in an old dyke,
As it were an heretyke.
    Allas, þat þou were born!

46. 'ȝiff þou be ded, þat I may see,
Asoylyd schalt þou nevere bee;
    Þanne is þy soule in sorwe;
And I schal wende in uncouþe *lond*
And gete me stronge men of hond—
    My broþir ȝit schal I borwe.
I schal brynge upon þy lond
Hungyr and þyrst ful strong,
    Cold, drouȝþe and sorwe;
I schal nouȝt leve on þy lond
Wurþ þe gloves on þy hond,
    To begge ne to borwe.'

wende] a dot over second e, *taken by* T *to mean* n. -e lond *not visible*

[44.3] *smertly*, at once.
[44.7] *reves*, deprive (and past *refft* 48.5).
[44.8] *crystyndom*, Christianity (but=specifically 'baptism' in 11) (C).   *for-bede*,ban (excommunicate).

[45.3] *stoken*, blocked (C).
[45.4] *lygge*, lie (cf. 49.9).   *dyke*, ditch (C).

[46.1] *þat I may see*, for all I can do (C).
[46.2] *asoylyd*, absolved.
[46.4] *uncouþe*, foreign.
[46.11] *wurþ*, i.e. the value of...
[46.12] *borwe*, borrow (here only in this sense).

47. Þe bysschop has his leve tan;
 By þat his men were comen ylkan.
     Þey sayden, 'Sere, have good day.'
 He entryd into Flete-strete;
 Wiþ lordys off Yngelond gan he mete
     Upon a nobyl aray.
 On here knees þey kneleden a-doun,
 And prayden hym off hys benysoun;
     He nykkyd hem wiþ 'nay'.
 Neyþer off cros neyþer off ryng
 Hadde þey non kyns wetyng;
     And þanne a knyȝt gan say—

48. A knyȝt þanne spak with mylde voys,
 'Sere, where is þy ryng? Where is þy croys?
     Is it ffro þe tan?'
 Þanne he sayde, 'ȝoure cursyd kyng
 Haþ me refft off al my þyng
     And off al my worldly wan;
 And I have entyrdytyd Yngelond:
 Þer schal no preest synge masse with hond;
non   Chyld schal be crystenyd nan,
 But ȝiff he graunte me þat knyȝt,
 His wyff and chyldryn fayr and bryȝt—
slon   He wolde with wrong hem slan.'

49. Þe knyȝt sayde, 'Bysschop, turne agayn;
 Off þy body we are ful fayn—
     Þy broþir ȝit schole we borwe,
 And, but he graunte us oure bone,
 Hys presoun schal be broken soone,

47.1 *tan*, taken (Northern) (cf. 48.3).
47.2 *by þat*, by then.   *ylkan*, each one (Northern).
47.8 *benysoun*, blessing.
47.9 *nykkyd*, refused.
47.11 'had they awareness of any kind' (i.e. 'they could see neither cross . . .')

48.1 *mylde*, humble (cf. 55.1, etc.).
48.4 *cursyd*, excommunicate (C).
48.5 *þyng*, plural 'goods'; perh. here insignia (of spiritual authority, contrasted with *worldly wan*).
48.6 *wan*, resources.
48.7 *entyrdytyd*, interdicted; see (C) on 44.7.
48.12 *with wrong*, unjustly.

49.2 *þy body*, your presence (cf. 'your person') (C).   *fayn*, glad.
49.5 *broken*, *sc.* broken into.

Hymselff to mekyl sorwe.
We schole drawe doun boþe halle and
                            boures,
Boþe hys castelles and hys toures;
    Þey schole lygge lowe and holewe.
Þouȝ he be kyng and were þe corown,
We scholen hym sette in a deep dunjoun:
    Oure crystyndom we wole folewe.'

50. Þanne, as þey spoken off þis þing,
    Þer comen twoo knyȝtys ffrom þe kyng,
      And sayden, 'Bysschop, abyde,
    And have þy cros and þy ryng,
    And welcome, whyl þat þou wylt lyng—
      It is nouȝt for to hyde.
    Here he grauntys þe þe knyȝt,
    Hys wyff and chyldryn, fayr and bryȝt;
      Agayn I rede þou ryde.
    He prayes þe pur charyté
    Þat he myȝte asoylyd be,
      And Yngelond long and wyde.'

Agayn MS.,
despite T

51. Here-off þe bysschop was ffull ffayn,
    And turnys hys brydyl and wendes agayn—
      Barouns gunne wiþ hym ryde—
    Unto þe Brokene Cros off ston;
    Þedyr com þe kyng ful soone anon,
      And þere he gan abyde.
    Upon hys knees he knelyd a-doun
    And prayde þe bysschop off benysoun;
      And he gaff hym þat tyde:
    Wiþ holy watyr and orysoun
    He asoylyd þe kyng þat weryd þe coroun,
      And Yngelond long and wyde.

49.6 'to his own great discomfiture'.
49.7 *drawe doun*, pull down.
49.12 *crystyndom*, see 44.8 (C).

50.3 *abyde*, wait!
50.5 *lyng*, remain.
50.9 *agayn*, back.   *rede*, advise.

51.10 *orysoun*, prayer.
51.12 *long and wyde*, all over, entirely.

52. Þenne sayde þe kyng anon ryȝt,
    'Here I graunte þe þat knyȝt
        And hys sones ffree,
    And my sustyr hende in halle;
    Þou hast savyd here lyvys alle—
        I-blessyd moot þou bee!'
    Þenne sayde þe bysschop al-so soone,
    'And I schal geven swylke a dome—
        Wiþ eyen þat þou schalt see—
    Ȝiff þay be gylty off þat dede,
    Sorrere þe doome þay may drede
        Þan schewe here schame to me.'

53. Whanne þe bysschop hadde sayd soo,
    A gret ffyr was maad ryȝt þoo,
        In romaunce as we rede.
    It was set, þat men myȝte knawe,
    Nyne plowȝ-lengþe on rawe,
        As red as ony glede.
    Þanne sayde þe kyng, 'What may þis mene?'
    'Sere, off gylt and þay be clene,
        Þis doom hem thar nouȝt drede.'
    Þanne sayde þe good kyng Athelston,
    'An hard doome now is þis on;
        God graunte us alle weel to spede!'

54. Þey fetten forþ sere Egelan—
    A trewere eerl was þer nan—
        Before þe ffyr so bryȝt.
    From hym þey token þe rede scarlet,
    Boþe hosyn and schoon þat weren hym met,
        Þat fel al ffor a knyȝt.
    Nyne syþe þe bysschop halewid þe way

[52.7] *al-so soone*, at once.
[52.8] *dome*, judgment, ordeal (*iudicium dei*) (and *doome* 11).
[52.11] 'they will be more afraid of the ordeal than of confessing their guilt to me'.

[53.5] *rawe*, line ('row').
[53.6] *glede*, coal, ember (C).
[53.9] *hem thar nouȝt*, they need not.
[53.11] *þis on*, this one (cf. *SD* 937).

[54.5] 'The stockings and shoes that were proper for him.'
[54.6] *fel*, were fitting.
[54.7] *halewid*, blessed ('hallowed').

Þat his weddyd broþer scholde goo þat day,
　　To praye God for þe ry3t.
He was unblemeschyd, ffoot and hand;
Þat saw3 þe lordes off þe land,
　　And þankyd God off hys my3t.

55. Þey offeryd hym with mylde chere
Unto Seynt Powlys hey3e awtere
　　Þat mekyl was off my3t.
Doun upon hys knees he felle
And þankyd God þat harewede helle,
　　And hys modyr so bry3t.

56. And 3it þe bysschop þo gan say,
'Now schal þe chyldryn gon þe way
　　Þat þe fadyr 3ede.'

hym] hem *Z*

Fro hem þey tooke þe rede scarlete,
Þe hosen and schoon þat weren hem mete,
　　And al here worldly wede.
Þe ffyr was boþe hydous and red;

ded] ed *not*
visible

Þe chyldryn swownyd as þey were d*ed*;
　　Þe bysschop tyl hem 3ede;
Wiþ careful herte on hem gan look,
Be hys hand he hem up took:
　　'Chyldryn, have 3e no drede.'

57. Þanne þe chyldryn stood and low3:
'Sere, þe fyr is cold inow3.'

he] þey *Z*
hand] d *not*
visible

　　Þorw3-out *þey* wente a-pase.
Þey weren unblemeschyd, foot and han*d*;
Þat saw3 þe lordys off þe land,
　　And þankyd God off his grace.

58. Þey offeryd hem with mylde chere
To seynt Poulys, þat hy3e awtere;

54.8 *scholde*, was to.
54.10 *unblemeschyd*, unharmed (see Introduction, p. 16).

55.2 *awtere*, altar.

56.3 *3ede*, went (and *3ode* 61.9).
56.6 *wede*, clothes ('weeds').
56.10 *careful*, anxious.

57.1 *low3*, laughed.

Þis myracle schewyd was þere;
And ȝit þe bysschop efft gan say,
'Now schal þe countasse goo þe way
Þere þat þe chyldryn were.'

59. Þey fetten forþ þe lady mylde;
Sche was ful gret i-gon with chylde,
In romaunce as we rede.
Before þe fyr when þat sche come,
To Jhesu Cryst he prayde a bone,
Þat leet his woundys blede:
'Now, God, lat nevere þe kyngys ffoo
Quyk out off þe ffyr goo.'
Þer-off hadde sche no drede . . .

No gap in MS.;
three lines lost

60. Whenne sche hadde maad here prayer,
Sche was brouȝt before þe ffeer,
Þat brennyd boþe fayr and lyȝt.
Sche wente ffro þe lengþe into þe þrydde;
Stylle sche stood þe ffyr a-mydde,
And callyd it merye and bryȝt.
Harde schourys þenne took here stronge,
Boþe in bak and eke in wombe;
And siþþen it ffel at syȝt . . .

No gap in MS.;
three lines lost

61. Whenne þat here paynys slakyd was,
And sche hadde passyd þat hydous pas,
Here nose barst on bloode.
Sche was unblemeschyd, ffoot and hand;
Þat sawȝ þe lordys off þe land,
And þankyd God on rode.

58.3 *schewyd*, made manifest? (C).
58.4 *efft*, again.

59.9 *quyk*, alive (C).

60.2 *ffeer*, fire (South-Eastern form).
60.3 *brennyd*, burned.
60.4 *ffro þe lengþe*, lengthwise? (C).
60.6 *merye*, pleasant.
60.7 *schourys*, pains.
60.8 *wombe*, belly.
60.9 'and then it befell for all to see'.

61.1 *slakyd*, abated (cf. 'slack').
61.2 *pas*, path, passage.
61.3 *barst on bloode*, burst out bleeding.

here away

Þey comaundyd men away to drawe,
As it was þe landys lawe,
   And ladyys þanne tyl here ȝode.
Sche knelyd doun upon þe ground,
And þere was born Seynt Edemound—
   I-blessyd be þat ffoode!

62. And, whanne þis chyld i-born was,
It was brouȝt into þe plas;
   It was boþe hool and sound.
Boþe þe kyng and bysschop ffree,
Þey crystnyd þe chyld, þat men myȝt see,
   And callyd it Edemound.
'Halff my land,' he sayde, 'I þe geve,
Al-so longe as I may leve,
   Wiþ markys and with pounde,
And al afftyr my dede,
Yngelond to wysse and rede.'
   Now i-blessyd be þat stounde!

63. Þenne sayde þe bysschop to þe kyng,
'Sere, who made þis grete lesyng,
   And who wrouȝte al þis bale?'
Þanne sayde þe kyng, 'So moot I thee,
Þat schalt þou nevere wete for me,
   In burgh neyþer in sale;
For I have sworn, be Seynt Anne,
Þat I schal nevere be-wreye þat manne
   Þat me gan telle þat tale.
Þey arn savyd þorwȝ þy red—
Now lat al þis be ded,
   And kepe þis counseyl hale.'

[61.7] *drawe*, go ('with*draw*').
[61.8] *lawe*, custom (C).
[61.12] *ffoode*, person, creature.

[62.2] *plas*, square? (F. *place*) (C).
[62.3] *hool*, uninjured ('whole').
[62.9] *markys*, marks (= 160 pence) (C).
[62.11] *wysse*, govern.   *rede*, direct.
[62.12] *stounde*, time, hour (cf. Germ. *Stunde*).

[63.3] *bale*, harm.
[63.5] *for me*, as far as I am concerned.
[63.6] *burgh*, town.   *sale*, hall (i.e. 'nowhere').
[63.10] *red*, advice.
[63.12] i.e. do not let the secret be revealed (*hale*, whole).

64. Þenne swoor þe bysschop, 'So moot I the,
 Now I have power and dignyté
  For to asoyle þe as clene
 As þou were hoven off þe ffount-ston;
 Trustly trowe þou þer-upon,
  And holde it for no wene:
 I swere boþe be book and belle,
 But ȝiff þou me his name telle,
  Þe ryȝt doom schal I deme:
 Þyselff schalt goo þe ryȝte way
 Þat þy broþer wente today,
  Þouȝ it þe evele be-seme.'

65. Þenne sayde þe kyng, 'So moot I the,
 Be schryffte off mouþe telle I it þe;
  Þer-to I am unblyve.
 Sertaynly, it is non oþir
 But Wymound, oure weddyd broþer—
  He wole nevere þryve.'
 'Allas,' sayde þe bysschop þan,
 'I wende he were þe treweste man
  Þat evere ȝit levyd on lyve.
 And he wiþ þis ateynt may bee,
 He schal be hongyd on trees þree
  And drawen with hors ffyve.'

66. And whenne þat þe bysschop þe soþe hade
 Þat þat traytour þat lesyng made,
  He callyd a messangere,
Bad *obscure* Bad hym to Dovere þat he scholde founde
 For to fette þat eerl Wymounde—
  Þat traytour has no pere!
Sere *obscure* 'Sere Egelane and hys sones be slawe,

64.2 *dignyté*, authority.
64.4 *hoven*, lifted.   *ffount-ston*, font (i.e. 'baptised').
64.5 *trustly trowe*, trust faithfully.
64.6 *wene*, doubt, uncertain matter.
64.9 *ryȝt*, just, fitting, proper (? same).
64.10 *ryȝte*, self same.
64.12 'though it ill suit you'.

65.2 *schryffte*, confession (C).
65.3 *þer-to*, at it.   *unblyve*, unhappy (for *unblyþe*).
65.10 *And*, if.   *ateynt*, proved guilty.

66.4 *founde*, hasten.
66.7 *slawe*, slain.

Boþe i-hangyd and to-drawe —
　　Doo as I þe lere —
Þe countasse is in presoun done;
Schal sche nevere out off presoun come
　　But ȝiff it be on bere.'

67. Now wiþ þe messanger was no badde;
　　He took his hors, as þe bysschop radde,
　　　　To Dovere tyl þat he come.
　　Þe eerl in hys halle he ffand;
　　He took hym þe lettre in his hand
　　　　On hyȝ — wolde he nouȝt wone: —
　　'Sere Egelane and his sones be slawe,
　　Boþe i-hangyd and to-drawe;
　　　　Þou getyst þat eerldome.
　　Þe countasse is in presoun done;
　　Schal sche nevere more out come,
　　　　Ne see neyþer sunne ne mone.'

68. Þanne þat eerl made hym glade,
　　And þankyd God þat lesyng was made:
　　　　'It haþ gete me þis eerldome!'
　　He sayde, 'Felawe, ryȝt weel þou bee!
　　Have here besauntys good plenté
　　　　For þyn hedyr-come.'
　　Þanne þe messanger made his mon:
　　'Sere, off ȝoure goode hors lende me on —
　　　　Now graunte me my bone —
　　For ȝystyrday deyde my nobyl stede,
　　On ȝoure arende as I ȝede,
　　　　Be þe way as I come.'

[66.9] *lere,* instruct.
[66.12] *bere,* bier.

[67.1] *badde,* delay.
[67.2] *radde,* commanded.
[67.5] *took,* gave.　　*in,* into (cf. 18.5).
[67.6] *hyȝ,* haste.　　*wone,* hesitate.

[68.6] *hedyr-come,* arrival ('hither-coming').
[68.7] *mon,* complaint.
[68.8] *hors* is plural (cf. 75.2).
[68.11] *ȝoure arende,* your errand (C).

69. 'Myn hors be fatte and corn-fed,
    And off þy lyff I am a-dred,'
        Þat eerl sayde to hym þan;
    'Þanne, ȝiff myn hors scholde þe sloo,
    My lord þe kyng wolde be ful woo
        To lese swylk a man.'

70. Þe messanger ȝit he brouȝte a stede,
    On off þe beste at ylke a nede
        Þat evere on grounde dede gange,
    Sadelyd and brydelyd at þe beste.
    Þe messanger was ful preste;
        Wyȝtly on hym he sprange.
    'Sere,' he sayde, 'have good day;
    Þou schalt come whan þou may;
        I schal make þe kyng at hande.'
    With sporys faste he strook þe stede;
    To Gravysende he come good spede—
        Is ffourty myle to ffande.

71. Þere þe messanger þe traytour a-bood,
    And seþþyn boþe in same þey rod
        To Westemynstyr wone.
    In þe palays þere þay lyȝt;
    Into þe halle þey come ful ryȝt
        And mette wiþ Athelstone.
    He wolde have kyssyd his lord swete.
    He sayde, 'Traytour! nouȝt ȝit! lete!
        Be God and be Seynt Jhon,
    For þy falsnesse and þy lesyng
    I slowȝ myn heyr, scholde have ben kyng
        When my lyf hadde ben gon.'

69.2 *off*, for.
69.6 *lese*, lose (C).

70.3 *gange*, go.
70.5 *preste*, ready (F. *prêt*).
70.6 *wyȝtly*, vigorously (cf. 74.2).
70.9 *at hande*, presently? (C).
70.10 *sporys*, spurs.
70.12 *to ffande*, to experience (rhyme-tag).

71.2 *in same*, together (cf. 72.5).
71.4 *lyȝt*, alighted.

72. Þere he denyyd faste þe kyng
Þat he made nevere þat lesyng,
 Among hys peres alle.
Þe bysschop has hym be þe hand tan;
Forþ in same þey are gan
 Into þe wyde halle.
Myȝte he nevere with crafft ne gynne
Gare hym schryven off hys synne
 For nouȝt þat myȝte be-falle.
Þenne sayde þe goode kyng Athelston,
'Lat hym to þe ffyr gon,
in dede] corr. Ƶ To preve þe treweþe *wiþ alle.*'

73. Whenne þe kyng hadde sayd soo,
A gret ffyr was maad þoo,
 In romaunce as we rede.
It was set, þat men myȝten knawe,
Nyne plowȝ-lenge on rawe,
 As red as ony glede.
Nyne syþis þe bysschop halewes þe way
Þat þat traytour schole goo þat day —
 Þe wers hym gan to spede.
He wente ffro þe lengþe into þe þrydde,
And doun he ffel þe ffyr a-mydde —
 Hys eyen wolde hym nouȝt lede.

74. Þan þe eerlys chyldryn were war ful smerte,
And wyȝtly to þe traytour sterte
 And out off þe ffyr hym hade,
And sworen boþe be book and belle,
'Or þat þou deye, þou schalt telle
 Why þou þat lesyng made.'
'Certayn, I can non oþer red,

72.2 *nevere*, emphatic (= 'ever').
72.7 *gynne*, device, trick ('en*gine*').
72.8 *gare*, make (ON). *schryven*, confess (C).
72.12 *preve*, establish, prove. *wiþ alle*, entirely.

73.9 *hym gan to spede*, things went for him.
73.12 *eyen*, eyes.

74.1 *war*, aware. *smerte*, quickly.
74.2 *sterte*, leapt ('give a *start*').
74.3 *hade*, took.
74.7 *can*, know, have available. *red*, course of action.

Now I wot I am but ded;
    I telle ʒow noþyng gladde:
Certayn, þer was non oþer wyte;
He lovyd hym to mekyl and me to lyte,
    Þer-ffore envye I hadde.'

75. Whenne þat traytour so hadde sayde,
    Fyve goode hors to hym were tayde—
        Alle men myʒten see wiþ yʒe—
    Þey drowen hym þorwʒ ylke a strete,
    And seþþyn to þe Elmes, I ʒow hete,
        And hongyd hym ful hyʒe.
    Was þer nevere man so hardy
    Þat durste ffelle hys ffalse body—
        Þis hadde he ffor hys lye.
    Now Jhesu, þat is hevene-kyng,
    Leve nevere traytour have betere endyng,
        But swyche dome ffor to dye!

74.8 'Now that I know I am a dead man.'
74.10 *wyte*, cause of contention, blame.
74.11 *lyte*, little.

75.2 *tayde*, tied.
75.5 *þe Elmes*, Tyburn? (C).   *hete*, assure, promise.
75.8 *ffelle*, cut down (from gallows).
75.12 'But to die such a death' (lit. (as a result of) such a judgment/punishment).

III

SIR ORFEO

1–24 *restored after Bliss; from Lai le Freine, exc. 13–16*
i-write] *base of letters only visible*

We redeþ oft and findeþ i-write,
And þis clerkes wele it wite,
Layes þat ben in harping
Ben y-founde of ferli þing.
Sum beþe of wer and sum of wo
And sum of joie and mirþe al-so
And sum of trecherie and of gile,
Of old aventours þat fel while,
And sum of bourdes and ribaudy,
And mani þer beþ of fairy;

þingeþ

Of al þinges þat men seþ,
Mest o love for soþe þai beþ.

13–16: *text from AHB* (C)

In Breteyne þis layes were wrouȝt,
First y-founde and forþ y-brouȝt,
Of aventours þat fel bi dayes
Wher-of Bretouns maked her layes;
When kinges miȝt our y-here
Of ani mervailes þat þer were,
Þai token an harp in gle and game
And maked a lay and ȝaf it name.
Now of þis aventours þat weren y-falle
Y can tel sum, ac nouȝt alle.
Ac herkneþ, lordinges þat beþ trewe;
Ichil ȝou telle 'Sir Orfewe'.

25–38: *text from HB*

Orfeo mest of ani þing
Loved þe gle of harping.

2 *clerkes*, scholars. *wite*, know.
3 *ben*, are.
4 *ferli*, marvellous, strange.
5 *beþe*, are. *wer*, war.
8 *fel*, happened. *while*, once.
9 *bourdes*, jokes (cf. 445). *ribaudy*, lewdness.
10 *fairy*, the Otherworld (C).
11 *seþ*, see.
12 *mest*, most. *o*, of.
13 *Breteyne*, Brittany.
15 *bi dayes*, once upon a time.
17 *our*, anywhere. *y-here*, hear.
19 *token*, took. *gle*, minstrelsy, entertainment. *game*, amusement, pleasure.
20 *ȝaf*, gave.
22 *ac*, but.
24 *Ichil*, I will.

Siker was everi gode harpour
Of him to have miche honour.

lerned *B*]
loued *H*

Him-self he lerned for-to harpe
And leyd þer-on his wittes scharpe;   30
He lerned so, þer no-þing was
A better harpour in no plas.

al B] not *in H*

In al þe warld was never man bore
Þat ones Orfeo sat bifore—
And he miȝt of his harping here—   35
Bot he schuld þenche þat he were
In on of þe joies of Paradis,

melodi *B*] joy
and melody *H*

Swiche melodi in his harping is.

39 *A text*
proper begins

Orfeo was a king,
In Inglond an heiȝe lording;   40
A stalworþ man and hardi bo,
Large and curteys he was al-so.
His fader was comen of King Pluto
And his moder of King Juno
Þat sum time were as godes y-hold   45
For aventours þat þai dede and told.
Þis king sojournd in Traciens,
Þat was a cité of noble defens—
For Winchester was cleped þo
Traciens, wiþ-outen no.   50
Þe king hadde a quen of priis
Þat was y-cleped Dame Herodis—
Þe fairest levedi for þe nones

[27] *siker*, sure.
[28] *miche*, great.
[29] *him-self he lerned*, 'he taught himself'.
[30] *leyd þer-on*, 'applied to it'.
[31] *no-þing*, in no way.
[33] *nas*, was not.   *bore*, born.
[34] 'who once sat before Orfeo'.
[35] *and*, if.
[36] *þenche*, think.
[40] *heiȝe*, high.
[41] *hardi*, brave.   *bo*, as well (lit. 'both').
[42] *large*, generous (cf. 451).   *curteys*, courtly (C).
[43] *comen of*, descended from.
[45] *y-hold*, considered.
[46] *dede*, did.
[47] *sojournd*, dwelt.
[49] *cleped*, called.   *þo*, then.
[50] *wiþ-outen no*, 'there is no denying it'.
[51] *priis*, excellence (cf. 64).
[53] *levedi*, lady.   *for þe nones*, untranslatable tag.

Þat miȝt gon on bodi and bones;
Ful of love and of godenisse—   55
Ac no man may telle her fairnise.

Vifel   *B*ifel so in þe comessing of May
When miri and hot is þe day,
And o-way beþ winter schours,
And everi feld is ful of flours,   60
And blosme breme on everi bouȝ
Over-al wexeþ miri anouȝ,
Þis ich quen Dame Heurodis
Tok to maidens of priis
And went in an undren-tide   65
To play bi an orchard side,
To se þe floures sprede and spring
And to here þe foules sing.
Þai sett hem doun al þre
Under a fair ympe-tre,   70
And wel sone þis fair quene
Fel on slepe opon þe grene.
Þe maidens durst hir nouȝt awake
Bot lete hir ligge and rest take.
So sche slepe til after none,   75
Þat under-tide was al y-done.
Ac, as sone as sche gan awake,
Sche crid, and loþli bere gan make.
Sche froted hir honden and hir fet,
And cracched hir visage—it bled wete—   80
rett   Her riche robe hye al to-r*itt*

---

[54] *gon,* go, walk.   *on,* in.
[57] *bifel,* it happened.   *comessing,* beginning.
[58] *miri,* pleasant.
[61] *blosme,* blossom.   *breme,* bright.
[62] *over-al,* everywhere.   *wexeþ,* grows.   *anouȝ,* enough.
[63] *ich,* same (contrast 179).
[64] *to,* two.
[65] *undren-tide,* late morning.
[66] *play,* relax, amuse herself.
[70] *ympe-tre,* grafted tree.
[71] *wel,* very.
[74] *ligge,* lie.
[75] *slepe,* slept (strong preterite).
[77] *gan,* past auxiliary.
[78] *loþli,* hideous.   *bere,* cry.
[79] *froted,* rubbed.
[80] *cracched,* scratched.   *visage,* face.
[81] *hye,* she.   *to-ritt,* tore.

And was reveyd out of hir witt.
Þe tvo maidens hir biside
No durst wiþ hir no leng abide,
Bot ourn to þe palays ful riȝt   85
And told boþe squier and kniȝt
Þat her quen a-wede wold,
And bad hem go and hir at-hold.
Kniȝtes urn and levedis al-so,
Damisels sexti and mo;   90
In þe orchard to þe quen hye come
And her up in her armes nome
And brouȝt hir to bed atte last
And held hir þere fine fast;
Ac ever sche held in o cri   95
And wold up, and o-wy.

When Orfeo herd þat tiding
Never him nas wers for no þing;
He come wiþ kniȝtes tene
To chaumber, riȝt bifor þe quene,   100
And biheld, and seyd wiþ grete pité,
'O lef liif, what is te
Þat ever ȝete hast ben so stille
And now gredest wonder schille?
Þi bodi, þat was so white y-core,   105
Wiþ þine nailes is al to-tore.
Allas! þi rode, þat was so red,

al] *or* as (*MS.*
unclear)

Is al wan as þou were ded,
And al-so þine fingres smale

---

[82] *reveyd*, driven.
[84] *leng*, longer.   *abide*, remain.
[85] *ourn*, ran.   *ful riȝt*, straight.
[87] *a-wede*, go mad.
[88] *at-hold*, seize, restrain.
[89] *urn*, ran.
[90] *sexti* (C).
[91] *hye*, they.   *come*, came.
[92] *nome*, took.
[94] *fine*, very.   *fast*, firmly.
[95] *held*, persisted.   *o*, one, the same.
[96] *wold*, wished (to go . . . .)   *o-wy*, away.
[98] 'Nothing had ever grieved him more.'
[102] *lef liif*, dear life (cf. 406).   *te*, for *þe*; 'what is the matter with you, who, etc.'
[103] *stille*, quiet, calm.
[104] *gredest*, cry.   *schille*, shrilly (cf. 272 (verb)).
[105] *y-core*, excellent (choice, delicate) (cf. 148).
[107] *rode*, face.
[109] *al-so*, likewise.   *smale*, slender.

Beþ al blodi and al pale.   110
Allas! þi lovesom eyȝen to
Lokeþ so man doþ on his fo.
A, dame! Ich beseche, merci!
Lete ben al þis reweful cri,
And tel me what þe is, and hou,   115
And what þing may þe help now.'

Þo lay sche stille atte last
And gan to wepe swiþe fast,
And seyd þus þe king to,
'Allas, mi lord, Sir Orfeo!   120
Seþþen we first to-gider were,
Ones wroþ never we nere;
Bot ever ich have y-loved þe
As mi liif, and so þou me;
Ac now we mot delen a-to—   125
Do þi best, for Y mot go.'
'Allas!' quaþ he, 'for-lorn Icham!
Whider wiltow go, and to wham?
Whider þou gost Ichil wiþ þe,
And whider Y go þou schalt wiþ me.'   130
'Nay, nay, Sir, þat nouȝt nis!
Ichil þe telle al hou it is.
As Ich lay þis under-tide
And slepe under our orchard side.
Þer come to me to fair kniȝtes,   135
Wel y-armed al to riȝtes,
And bad me comen an heiȝing
And speke wiþ her lord þe king;
And Ich answerd at wordes bold,
Y no durst nouȝt, no Y nold.   140

111 *eyȝen*, eyes.
112 *so*, as.   *fo*, enemy.
114 *lete ben*, leave.   *reweful*, pitiful.
118 *swiþe*, very.   *fast*, bitterly.
121 *seþþen*, since.
122 *wroþ*, angry.   *nere*, were not.
125 *delen*, part.   *mot*, must (*sc.* go).   *a-to*, our separate ways; apart.
127 *for-lorn*, lost.
128 *wham*, whom.
131 *þat nouȝt nis*, that cannot be.
136 *al to riȝtes*, properly.
137 *an heiȝing*, in haste.
139 *at*, with.
140 *no . . . no*, neither . . . nor.   *nold*, would not, did not wish (=*ne*+*wold*; cf.
nas, *nil*=*he ne was*, *he ne wil*).

Þai priked oȝain as þai miȝt drive;
Þo com her king al-so blive
Wiþ an hundred kniȝtes and mo
And damissels an hundred al-so,
Al on snowe white stedes —   145
As white as milke were her wedes.
Y no seiȝe never ȝete bifore
So fair creatours y-core.
Þe king hadde a croun on hed;
It nas of silver, no of gold red,   150
Ac it was of a precious ston —
As briȝt as þe sonne it schon,
And as son as he to me cam,
Wold Ich, nold Ich, he me nam,
And made me wiþ him ride   155
Opon a palfray bi his side,
And brouȝt me to his palays
Wele atird in ich ways,
And schewed me castels and tours,
Rivers, forestes, friþ wiþ flours   160
And his riche stedes ichon,
And seþþen me brouȝt oȝain hom
Into our owhen orchard,
And said to me þus after-ward,
"Loke, dame, to-morwe þatow be   165
Riȝt here, under þis ympe-tre,
And þan þou schalt wiþ ous go
And live wiþ ous ever-mo;
And ȝif þou makest ous y-let,
Whar þou be, þou worst y-fet,   170
And to-tore þine limes al
Þat no þing help þe no schal;

---

141 *priked*, spurred.   *oȝain*, back.   *as þai miȝt drive*, with all speed.
142 *al-so blive*, quickly.
154 'Whether I liked it or not' (C).   *nam*, took.
156 *palfray*, riding horse (C).
158 *atird*, furnished, adorned.   *ich ways*, every way.
160 *friþ*, wood.
161 *ichon*, every one.
162 *seþþen*, then.   *hom*, home.
163 *owhen*, own (C).
165 *loke*, be sure.   *þatow*, for þat þou.
169 'if you cause us to be hindered'.
170 *whar*, wherever.   *worst*, shall be.   *y-fet*, fetched.
171 *to-tore*, torn apart.   *limes*, limbs.

And, þei þou best so to-torn,
3ete þou worst wiþ ous y-born." '

When King Orfeo herd þis cas,   175
'O we!' quaþ he, 'Allas, allas!
Lever me were to lete mi liif
Þan þus to lese þe quen mi wiif!'
He asked conseyl at ich man,
Ac no man him help no can.   180
A-morwe þe under-tide is come
And Orfeo haþ his armes y-nome,
And wele ten hundred kni3tes wiþ him,
Ich y-armed, stout and grim,
And wiþ þe quen wenten he   185
Ri3t unto þat ympe-tre.
Þai made scheltrom in ich a side
And sayd þai wold þere abide
And dye þer everichon
Er þe quen schuld fram hem gon;   190
Ac 3ete amiddes hem ful ri3t
Þe quen was o-way y-tvi3t—
Wiþ fairi forþ y-nome—
Men wist never wher sche was bi-come.
Þo was þer criing, wepe and wo;   195
Þe king into his chaumber is go,
And oft swoned opon þe ston,
And made swiche diol and swiche mon
Þat nei3e his liif was y-spent;

---

¹⁷³ *þei*, though.   *best*, be.
¹⁷⁴ *y-born*, carried off.
¹⁷⁵ *cas*, matter, situation.
¹⁷⁶ *o we*, exclamation of sorrow (and *o way* 234).
¹⁷⁷ *lever*, preferable.   *were*, it would be.   *lete*, give up.
¹⁷⁸ *lese*, lose.
¹⁷⁹ *conseyl*, advice.   *at*, from.
¹⁸¹ *a-morwe*, the next day.
¹⁸² *y-nome*, taken.
¹⁸³ *wele*, 'a good'.
¹⁸⁴ *stout*, firm, vigorous.   *grim*, fierce.
¹⁸⁵ *he*, they.
¹⁸⁷ *scheltrom*, shield-wall (C).
¹⁹² *y-tvi3t*, snatched.
¹⁹³ 'By fairies,' 'by supernatural means' (C).
¹⁹⁴ *bi-come*, gone (cf. 288).
¹⁹⁶ *is go*, has gone.
¹⁹⁷ *ston*, i.e. the floor.
¹⁹⁸ *diol*, grief ('dole').   *mon*, moan.
¹⁹⁹ *nei3e*, almost.   *y-spent*, ended (cf. 215).

Þer was non amendement.   200
He cleped to-gider his barouns,
Erls, lordes of renouns,
And when þai al y-comen were,
'Lordinges,' he said, 'bifor ʒou here
Ich ordainy min heiʒe steward   205
To wite mi kingdom after-ward;
In mi stede ben he schal
To kepe mi londes over-al.
For now Ichave mi quen y-lore,
Þe fairest levedi þat ever was bore,   210
Never eft Y nil no woman se;
Into wildernes Ichil te
And live þer ever-more
Wiþ wilde bestes in holtes hore.
And when ʒe understond þat Y be spent,   215
Make ʒou þan a parlement
And chese ʒou a newe king;
Now doþ ʒour best wiþ al mi þing.'

Lo, was þer wepeing in þe halle
And grete cri among hem alle!   220
Unneþe miʒt old or ʒong
For wepeing speke a word wiþ tong.
Þai kneled a-doun al y-fere
And praid him, ʒif his wille were,
Þat he no schuld nouʒt fram hem go;   225
'Do way!' quaþ he, 'it schal be so!'
Al his kingdom he for-soke;
Bot a sclavin on him he toke.
He no hadde kirtel no hode,

200 'There was no help for it.'
201 *cleped*, summoned.
206 *wite*, look after.   *after-ward*, henceforth.
207 *stede*, place.
209 *y-lore*, lost.
211 *eft*, again.
212 *te*, go (also 290, 318, etc.).
214 *holtes*, woods.   *hore*, grey.
215 *spent*, dead (cf. 199).
217 *chese*, choose.
218 *þing*, affairs.
221 *unneþe*, hardly, with difficulty.
223 *y-fere*, together.
226 *do way!* enough! no more!
228 *sclavin*, pilgrim's mantle, cloak.
229 *kirtel*, tunic (C).

Edd. add no;
cf. ne *B*

Schert, *no* no noþer gode;   230
Bot his harp he tok algate
And dede him barfot out atte ȝate.
No man most wiþ him go—
O way! what þer was wepe and wo,
When he, þat hadde ben king wiþ croun,   235
Went so poverlich out of toun!
Þurth wode and over heþ
Into þe wildernes he geþ.
Noþing he fint þat him is ays,
Bot ever he liveþ in gret malais.   240
He þat hadde y-werd þe fowe and griis,
And on bed þe purper biis,
Now on hard heþe he liþ—
Wiþ leves and gresse he him wriþ.
He þat hadde had castels and tours,   245
River, forest, friþ wiþ flours,
Now, þei it comenci to snewe and frese,
Þis king mot make his bed in mese.
He þat had y-had kniȝtes of priis
Bifor him kneland, and levedis,   250
Now seþ he no þing þat him likeþ
Bot wilde wormes bi him strikeþ.
He þat had y-had plenté
Of mete and drink, of ich deynté,
Now may he al-day digge and wrote   255
Er he finde his fille of rote.
In somer he liveþ bi wild frut
And berien bot gode lite;

230 'nor any other possession'.
231 *algate*, anyway, at any rate.
232 *dede him*, passed.
233 *most*, might.
236 *so poverlich*, in such poverty.
237 *þurth*, through.
238 *geþ*, goes.
239 *fint*, finds.   *ays*, comfort.
240 *malais*, discomfort.
241 *y-werd*, worn.   *fowe*, parti-coloured fur (C).   *griis*, grey fur.
242 *purper*, purple (material).   *biis*, deep-coloured? fine linen? (C).
244 *wriþ*, covers.
248 *mese*, moss.
250 *kneland*, kneeling.
251 *likeþ*, pleases.
252 *wormes*, snakes.   *strikeþ*, slither.
254 *deynté*, delicacy.
255 *wrote*, grub.
258 'And berries, of little worth.'

In winter may he no þing finde
Bot rote, grases and þe rinde.   260
Al his bodi was o-way duine
For missays, and al to-chine—
Lord! who may telle þe sore
Þis king sufferd ten ȝere and more?
His here of his berd, blac and rowe,   265
To his girdel-stede was growe.
His harp, where-on was al his gle,
He hidde in an holwe tre,
And when þe weder was clere and briȝt
He toke his harp to him wel riȝt   270
And harped at his owhen wille—
Into alle þe wode þe soun gan schille,
Þat alle þe wilde bestes þat þer beþ
For joie abouten him þai teþ,
And alle þe foules þat þer were   275
Come and sete on ich a brere
To here his harping a-fine,
So miche melody was þer-in;
And, when he his harping lete wold,
No best bi him abide nold.   280

He miȝt se him bi-sides,
Oft in hot under-tides,
Þe king of fairy wiþ his rout
Com to hunt him al about
Wiþ dim cri and bloweing   285
And houndes also wiþ him berking;
Ac no best þai no nome,
No never he nist whider þai bi-come.

260 *rinde*, bark.
261 *duine*, shrunken, wasted.   *to-chine*, split.
265 *rowe*, rough.
266 *girdel-stede*, waist.
267 *gle*, pleasure.
268 *holwe*, hollow.
272 *schille*, resound.
274 *teþ*, go.
276 *sete*, sat (cf. 395, 413).   *brere*, briar.
277 *a-fine*, to the end.
279 *lete*, leave off.
281 *him bi-sides*, near by.
283 *rout*, company.
284 *him al about*, 'all around him'.
285 *dim*, faint (C).
286 *berking*, barking.
287 *nome*, took.

And oþer while he miȝt him se
As a gret ost bi him te,   290
Wele atourned, ten hundred kniȝtes,
Ich y-armed to his riȝtes,
Of cuntenaunce stout and fers
Wiþ mani desplaid baners,
And ich his swerd y-drawe hold—   295
Ac never he nist whider þai wold.
And oþer while he seiȝe oþer þing:
Kniȝtes and levedis com daunceing
In queynt atire, gisely,
Queynt pas and softly.   300
Tabours and trunpes ȝede hem bi
And al maner menstraci.

And on a day he seiȝe him bi-side
Sexti levedis on hors ride,
Gentil and jolif as brid on ris—   305
Nouȝt o man amonges hem þer nis—
And ich a faucoun on hond bere
And riden on haukin bi o rivere.
Of game þai founde wel gode haunt,
Maulardes, hayroun and cormeraunt.   310
Þe foules of þe water ariseþ;
Þe faucouns hem wele deviseþ.
Ich faucoun his pray slouȝ—
Þat seiȝe Orfeo, and louȝ.
'Parfay!' quaþ he, 'þer is fair game;   315
Þider Ichil, bi godes name!

---

290 *ost*, army, host.
291 *atourned*, equipped.
292 *to his riȝtes*, properly.
293 *cuntenaunce*, appearance.   *fers*, fierce.
294 *desplaid*, unfurled.
299 *queynt*, elegant, curious.   *gisely*, skilfully.
300 *pas*, steps.
301 *tabours*, small drums.   *trunpes*, trumpets.   *ȝede*, went.
302 *menstraci*, minstrelsy.
305 *jolif*, lively.   *brid*, bird.   *ris*, twig.
307 *faucoun*, falcon.
308 *on haukin*, a-hawking.
309 *haunt*, profusion.
310 *maulardes*, mallard.   *hayroun*, heron.   *cormeraunt*, cormorant?
312 *deviseþ*, observe.
313 *slouȝ*, killed.
314 *louȝ*, laughed.
315 *parfay*, 'by my faith'; truly.

Ich was y-won swiche werk to se!'
He aros and þider gan te.
To a levedi he was y-come;
Bi-held, and haþ wele under-nome   320
And seþ bi al þing þat it is
His owhen quen, Dam Heurodis.
ȝern he bi-held hir and sche him eke,
Ac noiþer to oþer a word no speke.
For messais þat sche on him seiȝe,   325
Þat had ben so riche and so heiȝe,
Þe teres fel out of her eiȝe.
Þe oþer levedis þis y-seiȝe
And maked her o-way to ride—
Sche most wiþ him no lenger abide.   330

'Allas!' quaþ he, 'now me is wo!
Whi nil deþ now me slo?
Allas, wroche, þat Y no miȝt
Dye now after þis siȝt!
Allas! to long last mi liif   335
When Y no dar nouȝt wiþ mi wiif,
No hye to me, o word speke.
Allas! whi nil min hert breke?
Parfay,' quaþ he, 'tide wat bitide,
Whider so þis levedis ride   340
Þe selve way Ichil streche—
Of liif no deþ me no reche.'
His sclavain he dede on al-so spac
And henge his harp opon his bac
And had wel gode wil to gon—   345
He no spard noiþer stub no ston.

---

317 *y-won*, accustomed.   *werk*, activity.
320 *under-nome*, understood.
323 *ȝern*, eagerly.   *eke*, also.
324 *speke*, spoke.
330 *most*, was (not) allowed.
332 *slo*, slay.
333 *wroche*, wretch.
335 *last*, lasts.
337 *No hye*, nor she.   *o*, any.
339 *tide what bitide*, come what may.
340 *whider so*, wherever.
341 *selve*, same.   *streche*, hasten.
342 *me no reche*, 'I care not (for myself)'.
343 *dede on*, put on; cf. our 'don', 'doff' (='do on', 'do off').   *spac*, quickly.
344 *henge*, hung.
346 *spard*, 'spared', avoided.   *stub*, stump.

In at a roche þe levedis rideþ,
And he after, and nouȝt abideþ.
When he was in þe roche y-go
Wele þre mile oþer mo,   350
He com into a fair cuntray
As briȝt so sonne on somers day,
Smoþe and plain and al grene—
Hille no dale nas þer non y-sene.

lond *A*] Amidde þe lond a castel he *se*iȝe   355
launde *H* Riche and real and wonder heiȝe.
Al þe ut-mast wal
Was clere and schine as cristal.
An hundred tours þer were about,
Degiselich and bataild stout.   360
Þe butras com out of þe diche
Of rede gold y-arched riche.
Þe vousour was avowed al
Of ich maner divers aumal.
Wiþ-in þer wer wide wones   365
Al of precious stones;
Þe werst piler on to biholde
Was al of burnist gold;
Al þat lond was ever liȝt,
For when it schuld be þerk and niȝt   370
Þe riche stones liȝt gonne
As briȝt as doþ at none þe sonne.
No man may telle, no þenche in þouȝt,
Þe riche werk þat þer was wrouȝt;
Bi al þing him þinkeþ þat it is   375
Þe proude court of Paradis.

347 *in at*, into.
352 *so*, as.
353 *plain*, level.
355 *lond*, land? clearing? (C).
356 *real*, royal.
357 *ut-mast*, outermost.
358 *schine*, bright.
360 *degiselich*, remarkable.   *bataild*, embattled.   *stout*, strongly.
363 *vousour*, vault (C).   *avowed*, decorated, coloured.
364 *maner*, kind.   *aumal*, enamel.
365 *wide*, spacious.   *wones*, dwellings.
367 'even the worst pillar you could see'.
370 *þerk*, dark.
371 *liȝt gonne*, shone.
373 *þenche in þouȝt*, think, conceive.
375 *þinkeþ*, seems.

New para MS   In þe castel þe levedis aliʒt;
He wold in after ʒif he miʒt.
Orfeo knokkeþ atte gate;
Þe porter was redi þer-ate   380
And asked what he wold have y-do.
'Parfay!' quaþ he, 'icham a minstrel, lo!
To solas þi lord wiþ mi gle
ʒif his swete wille be.'
Þe porter undede þe gate anon   385
And lete him into þe castel gon.
Þan he gan bihold about al,
And seiʒe ful liggeand wiþ-in þe wal
Of folk þat were þider y-brouʒt,
And þouʒt dede, and nare nouʒt.   390
Sum stode wiþ-outen hade
And sum non armes nade
And sum þurth þe bodi hadde wounde
And sum lay wode y-bounde
And sum armed on hors sete   395
And sum a-strangled as þai ete
And sum were in water a-dreynt
And sum wiþ fire al for-schreynt.
Wives þer lay on child-bedde,
Sum ded and sum a-wedde,   400
And wonder fele þer lay bi-sides
Riʒt as þai slepe her under-tides—
Eche was þus in þis warld y-nome,
Wiþ fairi þider y-come.

Þer he seiʒe his owhen wiif,   405
liif] lef *edd.*   Dame Heurodis, his *lef* liif,
Slepe under an ympe-tre—

378 *wold in*, wished (or intended) to enter.
381 *y-do*, done.
383 *solas*, entertain.
388 *ful*, indeed.   *liggeand*, lying.
390 *þouʒt*, seemed.   *nare*, were not.
391 *hade*, head.
392 *nade*, had not.
393 *þurth*, through.
394 *wode*, mad.
396 *a-strangled*, choked.
397 *a-dreynt*, drowned.
398 *for-schreynt*, shrivelled.
400 *a-wedde*, driven mad.
401 *wonder fele*, an amazing number.
402 *her under-tides*, 'their mornings', in the morning.

Bi her cloþes he knewe þat it was he.
And whan he hadde bihold þis mervails alle
He went into þe kinges halle;   410
Þan seiȝe he þer a semly siȝt,
A tabernacle blisseful and briȝt,
Þer-in her maister king sete
And her quen fair and swete.
Her crounes, her cloþes schine so briȝt   415
he hem   Þat unneþe bihold *hem he* miȝt.
When he hadde biholden al þat þing
He kneled a-doun bifor þe king.
'O lord,' he seyd, 'ȝif it þi wille were,
Mi menstraci þou schust y-here.   420
Þe king answerd, 'What man artow
Þat art hider y-comen now?
Ic, no non þat is wiþ me,
No sent never after þe.
Seþþen þat Ich here regni gan   425
Y no fond never so fole-hardi man
Þat hider to ous durst wende
Bot þat Ichim wald of-sende.'
'Lord,' quaþ he, 'trowe ful wel,
Y nam bot a pover menstrel;   430
And, sir, it is þe maner of ous
To seche mani a lordes hous —
Þei we nouȝt welcom no be,
Ȝete we mot proferi forþ our gle.'

Bifor þe king he sat a-doun   435
And tok his harp so miri of soun
his harp *A*] yt *B*   And trempeþ *it* as he wele can
And blisseful notes he þer gan,
Þat al þat in þe palays were

---

408 *he*, she.
411 *semly*, pleasant.
412 *blisseful*, beautiful (cf. 438) (C)).   *tabernacle*, canopied structure.
413 *maister*, lord.
415 *schine*, shone.
420 *schust* = *schuldest*.
421 *artow* = *art þow* (cf. 452, 454).
425 *regni*, reign.   *gan*, began.
428 *Bot that*, unless.   *Ichim* = *Ich him*.   *wald*, wished.   *of-sende*, send for.
429 *trowe*, believe.
431 *maner*, custom.
434 *proferi*, offer.
437 *trempeþ*, tunes.   *wele can*, knows well how to.

Com to him for-to here   440
And liggeþ a-doun to his fete—
Hem þenkeþ his melody so swete.
Þe king herkneþ and sitt ful stille;
To here his gle he haþ gode wille.
Gode bourde he hadde of his gle;   445
Þe riche quen al-so hadde he.
When he hadde stint his harping,
Þan seyd to him þe king,
'Menstrel, me likeþ wele þi gle;
Now aske of me what it be.   450
Largelich Ichil þe pay;
Now speke, ant tow miȝt asay.'
'Sir,' he seyd, 'Ich biseche þe
Þatow woldest ȝive me
Þat ich levedi briȝt on ble   455
Þat slepeþ under þe ympe-tre.'
'Nay!' quaþ þe king, 'þat nouȝt nere.
A sori couple of ȝou it were,
For þou art lene, rowe and blac,
And sche is lovesum, wiþ-outen lac.   460
A loþlich þing it were for-þi
To sen hir in þi compayni.'
'O sir,' he seyd, 'gentil king,
Ȝete were it a wele fouler þing
To here a lesing of þi mouþe;   465
So, sir, as ȝe seyd nouþe,
What Ich wold aski, have Y schold,
And nedes þou most þi word hold.'
Þe king seyd, 'Seþþen it is so,

441 *liggeþ*, lie.
442 *þenkeþ*, seems.
443 *sitt*, sits.
445 *bourde*, pleasure (contrast 9).
446 'so did she'.
447 *stint*, ended.
450 *what it be*, anything.
451 *largelich*, generously.
452 *asay*, make trial.
455 *on ble*, of complexion.
457 'that could never be'.
458 'an ill-matched pair you'd make'.
460 *lac*, blemish.
461 *loþlich*, distasteful.   *for-þi*, therefore.
465 *lesing*, lie.
466 *nouþe*, just now.
467 'Whatever I asked, I ought to have' (C).
468 *nedes*, of necessity (='thou needs must').   *hold*, keep.

Take hir bi þe hond and go.   470
Of hir Ichil þatow be bliþe.'
He kneled a-doun and þonked him swiþe.

His wiif he tok bi þe hond
And dede him swiþe out of þat lond
out of þat] in- And went him out of þat þede —   475
to his owhen? Riȝt as he come þe way he ȝede.
(C) So long he haþ þe way y-nome,
W.] Trasyens To Winchester he is y-come,
B (cf. 47) Þat was his owhen cite,
Ac no man knewe þat it was he.   480
No forþer þan þe tounes ende
he *not in MS.* For knoweleche no durst *he* wende,
Bot wiþ a begger, y-bilt ful narwe,
Þer he tok his herbarwe,
To him and to his owhen wiif   485
As a minstrel of pover liif,
And asked tidinges of þat lond,
And who þe kingdom held in hond.
Þe pover begger in his cote
Told him, everich a grot,   490
Hou her quen was stole o-wy
Ten ȝer gon wiþ fairy,
And hou her king en exile ȝede —
Bot no man nist in wiche þede —
And hou þe steward þe lond gan hold,   495
And oþer mani þinges him told.

A-morewe oȝain none tide
He maked his wiif þer abide.
Þe beggers cloþes he borwed anon

---

471 'I wish you joy of her'.
474 *swiþe*, quickly.
475 *þede*, country.
481 *forþer*, further.
482 *for knoweleche*, for fear of recognition.
483 'in a beggar's house, very narrowly built'.
484 *herbarwe*, lodging.
485 *to him*, for himself.
489 *cote*, cottage, hovel.
490 *grot*, scrap; detail.
492 *gon*, ago, past.
493 *en exile*, into exile.
495 *gan*, past auxiliary (cf. 511, plural *gun* 504, etc.).
497 *oȝain*, towards.

And heng his harp his rigge opon,   500
And went him into þat cité
Þat men miʒt him bihold and se.
Erls and barouns bold,
Burjays and levedis him gun bihold.
'Lo!' þai seyd, 'swiche a man!   505
Hou long þe here hongeþ him opan!
Lo, hou his berd hongeþ to his kne!
He is y-clongen al-so a tre!'
And, as he ʒede in þe strete,
Wiþ his steward he gan mete,   510
And loude he sett on him a crie:
'Sir steward,' he seyd, 'merci!
Icham an harpour of heþenisse;
Help me now in þis destresse!'
Þe steward seyd, 'Com wiþ me, come;   515
Of þat Ichave þou schalt have some.
Everich gode harpour is welcome me to
For mi lordes love, Sir Orfeo.'
In þe castel þe steward sat atte mete,
And mani lording was bi him sete.   520
Þer were trompours and tabourers,
Harpours fele, and crouders.
Miche melody þai maked alle,
And Orfeo sat stille in þe halle
And herkneþ when þai ben al stille;   525
He toke his harp and tempred schille.
Þe blisfulest notes he harped þere
Þat ever ani man y-herd wiþ ere.
Ich man liked wele his gle;
Þe steward biheld and gan y-se   530
And knewe þe harp als blive.
'Menstrel,' he seyd, 'so mot þou þrive,
Where hadestow þis harp and hou?

---

500 *rigge*, back.
504 *burjays*, citizens.
505 'Look at that man!'
506 *opan*, upon.
508 *y-clongen*, withered.   *al-so*, like.
511 *sett . . . crie*, called to him.
513 *of heþenisse*, from foreign lands.
521 *trompours*, trumpeters.   *tabourers*, drummers.
522 *fele*, many.   *crouders*, fiddlers (C).
525 *herkneþ when*, listens until.   *stille*, quiet.
531 *als blive*, at once (and 583).
532 *so mot þou þrive*, as you wish to prosper.

Y pray þat þou me telle now.'
'Lord,' quaþ he, 'in uncouþe þede,   535
Þurth a wildernes as Y ȝede,
Þer Y founde in a dale
Wiþ lyouns a man to-torn smale—
And wolves him frete wiþ teþ so scharp.
Bi him Y fond þis ich harp.   540
Wele ten ȝere it is y-go.'
'O!' quaþ þe steward, 'now me is wo!
Þat was mi lord, Sir Orfeo!
Allas, wreche, what schal Y do
Þat have swiche a lord y-lore?   545
A way! þat Ich was y-bore,
Þat him was so hard grace y-ȝarked
And so vile deþ y-marked!'
A-doun he fel a-swon to grounde.
His barouns him tok up in þat stounde   550
And telleþ him hou it geþ:
'It nis no bot of mannes deþ'.

King Orfeo knewe wele bi þan
His steward was a trewe man
And loved him as he auȝt to do,   555
And stont up, and seyt þus, 'Lo!
Steward, herkne now þis þing:
Ȝif Ich were Orfeo þe king,
And hadde y-suffred ful ȝore
In wildernisse miche sore,   560
And hadde y-won mi quen o-wy
Out of þe lond of fairy,
And hadde y-brouȝt þe levedi hende
Riȝt here to þe tounes ende,

[535] *uncouþe*, unknown.
[538] *smale*, in small pieces.
[539] *frete*, had eaten.
[540] *ich*, same.
[547] *grace*, fortune.   *y-ȝarked*, ordained.
[548] *y-marked*, allotted.
[549] *a-swon*, in a swoon.
[550] *stounde*, time.
[551] *hou it geþ*, how the world goes.
[552] 'There is no help for a man's death.'
[554] *trewe*, loyal.
[556] *stont*, stands.   *seyt*, says.
[559] *ȝore*, long.
[560] *sore*, sorrow, misfortune.
[563] *hende*, pleasant (see on *SD* 277).

And wiþ a begger her in y-nome, 565
And were mi-self hider y-come
Poverlich to þe þus stille
For to asay þi gode wille,
And ich founde þe þus trewe
Þou no schust it never rewe; 570
Sikerlich, for love or ay,
Þou schust be king after mi day;
And ȝif þou of mi deþ hadest ben bliþe,
Þou schust have voided, al-so swiþe.'

Þo al þo þat þer-in sete 575
Þat it was King Orfeo underȝete,
And þe steward him wele knewe—
Over and over þe bord he þrewe
And fel a-doun to his fet;
So dede everich lord þat þer sete, 580
And al þai seyd at o criing
'Ȝe beþ our lord, sir, and our king!'
Glad þai were of his live;
To chaumber þai ladde him als bilive
And baþed him and schaved his berd 585
And tired him as a king apert,
And seþþen wiþ gret processioun
Þai brouȝt þe quen into þe toun
Wiþ al maner menstraci—
Lord! þer was grete melody! 590
For joie þai wepe wiþ her eiȝe
Þat hem so sounde y-comen seiȝe.
Now King Orfeo newe coround is,
And his quen, Dame Heurodis,
And lived long after-ward, 595
And seþþen was king þe steward.

---

565 *her*, here. *in*, lodging.
568 *asay*, test.
570 'you would never have cause to regret it'.
571 *sikerlich*, assuredly. *ay*, fear.
574 *voided*, been banished. *al-so swiþe*, at once.
576 *underȝete*, realised.
578 *bord*, table.
581 'with one voice'.
583 *live*, life.
586 *tired*, clothed (='attired'). *apert*, openly.
592 *sounde*, safe.
596 'and after [them], the steward became king'.

New para MS	Harpours in Bretaine after þan
	Herd hou þis mervaile bigan,
	And made her-of a lay of gode likeing,
	And nempned it after þe king. 600
	Þat lay 'Orfeo' is y-hote;
	Gode is þe lay, swete is þe note.

Þus com Sir Orfeo out of his care;
God graunt ous alle wele to fare! Amen.

599 *likeing*, pleasure.
600 *nempned*, named.
601 *y-hote*, called.

Commentary

Havelok

Havelok is preserved in MS. Laud Misc. 108 in the Bodleian Library, Oxford, in which it occupied ff. 204–219v (col. 1). A leaf has been lost between ff. 211 and 212; otherwise the text of *Havelok* is complete but for a few lines omitted by the scribe. The manuscript is generally considered to date from the early fourteenth century. In addition, a few lines are preserved on a number of scraps of paper kept in the Cambridge University Library under the number 4407 (19). These lines represent a corrupt version of the text, copied probably at the end of the fourteenth century, and recourse has been had to them in only one reading.

The first generally accessible edition of the Laud text is that of W. W. Skeat under the title *The Lay of Havelok the Dane* (Early English Text Society, Extra Series iv, London, 1868). Skeat's second edition (Oxford, 1902) is much revised, generally though not always for the better; this second edition, as revised by Kenneth Sisam in 1915 and 1956, remains indispensable for the detailed study of the poem, though for lines 735–928 and 1771–1924 of the present edition it has been superseded by G. V. Smithers' text in *Early Middle English Verse and Prose*, ed. J. A. W. Bennett and G. V. Smithers, Oxford, 1966, no. 4. Important textual notes by Smithers are also to be found in *English and Germanic Studies*, ii (1948–9), 1–9; iii (1949–50), 65–70. The edition of F. Holthausen (London, 1901, revised 1928) is also useful.

The Skeat-Sisam edition is heavily emended in comparison with that of Smithers, and in particular has been much altered in the interests of metrical regularity. Though the emendations are faithfully recorded at the foot of the page, the printed text gives an impression of metrical smoothness which is not characteristic of the manuscript. Modern editors have as a rule ceased to expect metrical regularity of this kind in Middle English romances, and the present editors have in general relegated possible emendations on metrical grounds to the textual notes, at the cost of leaving a number of broken-backed lines in the text. Apart from such instances the incidence of obvious corruption is not great, though it should be remembered that we have here only one version of a poem which may well have been orally transmitted. The scribe frequently omits, less often adds, letters for no apparent reason, and these cases, whether the result of carelessness or of caprice, have generally been normalised. We have kept some of the manuscript spellings rejected by Skeat, such as *an* for *and*, *il* for *ilk*, since these may represent current speech, and others, such as *hw* for *hu*, which seem to be genuine orthographical conventions. The scribe's practice of writing *th* and *cth* for *ht* and of arbitrarily dropping

172

or adding *h*, both initially and elsewhere, seemed, on the other hand, to invite confusion; and *ht*, *cht* respectively have been printed for *th* and *cth* where appropriate, and the use of *h* normalised. (Recently Angus McIntosh has argued that the MS. was written by a scribe from West Norfolk; see 'The Language of the Extant Versions of *Havelok the Dane*' in *MÆ* XLV (1976), 36–49.)

Title. The Latin heading of the poem in the MS. is *Incipit Vita Hauelok quondam Rex Anglie et Denemarchie*, of which the first three words have been almost entirely cut away. 'Vita' was the name given to a saint's life, and although some English romances (e.g. *Ipomadon B* in MS. Harl. 2252) are called 'The Life of (*x*) . . .', 'Vita' had religious associations (cf. the 'Vita de Dowel' headings in the *Piers Plowman* MSS.). If the Latin title is the author's, this fact would suggest that he was a cleric, a view supported by many details as well as by the general tone of the poem. Other terms used to describe the poem's genre are *gest* (2989, with which cf. 2332 (C)), *rime* (21, 23, 3000, 3003), *storie* (1646, 1739), *tale* (3, 5, etc.). On genre-terms in ME narrative poetry, see the articles by Paul Strohm, '*Storie, Spelle, Geste, Romaunce, Tragedie*: Generic Distinctions in the ME Troy Narratives' (*Spec.* 46 (1971), 348–59) and 'Some Generic Distinctions in the *Canterbury Tales*' (*MP* 68 (1971), 321–28), which deals with *tale, storie, fable*, and so on.

1–26. *Prologue.* The poet draws the attention of his mixed audience (1–2) and asks for a drink (14–15). The setting could be a tavern or a hall in a manor-house, but the lines are plainly adaptable to any occasion on which the poem might be read aloud. The conventional 'minstrel' opening of this type has three elements: a call for attention, a call for a drink, and a call for a blessing, the last recurring at the end (see *Epilogue* (C) below). But the invocation of Christ here is unusually solemn (cf. also 2999–3006) and strengthens the likelihood of clerical authorship (see note on Title above). Cf. H. L. Creek, 'The Author of *Havelok the Dane*' (*Englische Studien* 48 (1914–15), 193–212).

25–6. The repetition of 9–10 (a common feature in poems designed for oral delivery) stresses the hero's altruism. The importance of *strength* as necessary for kingship is brought out by R. W. Hanning in '*Havelok the Dane*: Structure, Symbols, Meaning' (*SP* 64 (1967), 586–605). In this and other respects Havelok recalls the Old English epic hero Beowulf.

27ff. The portrait of the ideal king or *rex justus*, which is not parallel-ed in the French versions of the story (the *Lai d'Havelok* and Geffrei Gaimar's *L'Estorie des Engles*, both twelfth century), may owe something to the classical rhetorical tradition of ancestor-praise. Schelp notes that the use of the good times past as an exemplary critique of the present is unique in romances (*Hav.* is covered in pp. 31–53 of H. Schelp, *Exemplarische Romanzen im Mittelenglischen* (Göttingen, 1967)). The presentation of Havelok himself as a king belongs to the type called 'primitive' by W. W. Comfort, though somewhat modified by popular and human traits which make him a convincing, if idealised, creation ('Character Types in the *Chansons de Geste*', *PMLA* 21 (1906), 279–434).

31–2. *dreng, bondeman* and *swain* are among the more important of the numerous words testifying to Scandinavian influence on *Hav. dreng:* 'a free tenant . . . holding by a tenure older than the Norman conquest . . . partly military, partly servile' (*OED*) *bondeman*: not a slave, as subsequent developments of meaning might suggest. *swain* (1) 'a young man attending on a knight'; (2) 'a male . . . serving-man' (*OED*). (It could be either here.) The list of ranks in 31 is a formula which recurs at 1331 and also at 2188–9 and 2199, as does that in 32 at 1332 (somewhat changed). The list also includes Old English social terms (*thayn, kniht*) and Norman ones (*barun*). The OE *þegn* was originally a military retainer of a king or great lord, virtually later 'knight'.

33. *clerkes* as distinguished from *prestes* must refer to the lower orders, specifically those of deacon, subdeacon, acolyte, exorcist, reader and *ostiarius* (door-keeper).

40. For phrasing, cf. *SO* 112. Perhaps echoing the belief that a serpent produced poison in its gall (see *OED s.v.* II.5).

47. On 'red gold' see *SO* 150 (C), p. 200 below.

51–8. With the happy condition of merchants travelling in Athelwold's England, compare that of Havelok in Godard's Denmark (1771ff.).

87–105. Ten couplets rhyming on *-ede*, the last being incomplete. On the metre, see Bruce Mitchell, 'The Couplet System in *Havelok the Dane*' (*N & Q* 208 (1963), 405–6).

97. On *largesse*, cf. *SO* 42 (C), p. 199 below.

132–3. Literally, 'I should never be displeased/Even if I were in heaven', a way of saying 'even though I were dead, I should have no cause to complain (of *her* situation)'.

158. The ancient capital of Wessex. Cf. *SO*, 47–50 (C), p. 199 below.

160. The semantic development of this idiomatic use of *can* is from its original sense 'know' > 'acknowledge' > 'express'.

181. Godard's power and authority are a strong recommendation —*if* he is also 'trewe man' (179). Contrast the authoritative figure of Ubbe later in the poem, and see 2205ff. (C).

186–8. The use of the sacramental vessels and so on is a measure of the extreme solemnity of the oath, to break which will constitute not just sacrilege but blasphemy.

192. The earliest age at which the princess could marry.

195. MS. *Gon* may mean 'walk' (cf. 2781), a sense inappropriate here.

199. The precise wording of the oath is significant, as Godrich's contemptuously literalistic behaviour later is to bring out. (The use of

174

hexte at 1082 confirms Skeat's emendation; *beste* has come in from the following line.)

210–31. The king's self-mortification in his last moments underlines his exemplary piety. His purpose is to unite himself with the suffering Christ, whose last words on the cross (in Luke 22, 46) are 'In manus tuas commendo animam meam', 'Into your hands I commit my spirit'.

244. Psalms were customarily sung for the repose of a person's soul.

245–7. We must understand either (a) *soule* as the subject of *wone* in 247, or (b) *leve* or *late* ('allow', 'let') before *wone* (as in 406 below).

251. See *SD* 608 (C); here he puts *himself* in legal possession.

257. I.e. for as long as they lived (cf. 1409 (C), 2215).

260ff. Having assumed power, the Earl makes it sure in two stages: by exacting a universal oath of allegiance (254–5) and by placing his supporters in positions of authority throughout the land (260–73). With the list of ranks in descending order (261–2), cf. 31–2 (C) above.

277. Literally, 'there was fear of him on all England'.

302. A fine piece of realistic psychology: the villain attributes his own 'pride' to his victim (but contrast 855–7 (C)).

311. A typical idiomatic asseveration; cf. 1748.

335. An allusion to the death of the 'wicke traytur Judas', to whom Godrich has been compared (319).

328–37. A prayer for the heroine in distress rounds off the first movement of the poem. *shul we nou laten* (328) and *Say we nou forth* (338) are formulas marking narrative transitions of a type very common in poetry designed for oral delivery. This is the first of many such prayers and execrations interjected by the author on behalf of his virtuous and against his villainous characters (cf. 403–7, if it is authorial; 426–7, 543–5).

339. The close parallel between the Danish and English situations is brought out by phrases like 'was þe trewest' (374), echoing 'was trewe man' (179), and the similar-sounding names of the villains. (Cf. 485 (C).)

393. Literally, 'that it may be very well pleasing to their kin', perhaps to be paraphrased: 'in such a manner as may be fitting to their (royal) birth'. The sense is odd, but no improvement has been proposed.

408ff. Godard's villainy operates instantly (*sone*), unlike Godrich's, and is more extreme.

410. MS. *eir* (for *heir*) remains unexplained; Sisam's emendation seems inevitable.

426–37. A formal malediction (*malisun*). The ritual quality is apt, since Godard has broken an oath of the utmost solemnity (cf. the formal litany-like speech of Ubbe at 2173–92 (C) and contrast the more colloquial curse at 447).

457ff. Havelok is a medieval Oliver Twist; but the response he meets surpasses in cruelty anything in Dickens. The concern with *hunger* here as later (see 826ff.) is one of many touches bringing the poem close to everyday reality and the experience of 'Wives, maydnes, and alle men' (2). On 465 see Skeat's note.

478. *seli knaue*. Havelok, the child born to be king (cf. also 977–80) survives Godard's Herod-like slaughter of the innocents by a wise strategem that appeals to the tyrant's latent sense of insecurity. God-ard's unexpectedly sudden pity is explicitly acknowledged as a 'miracle' (501). The only explanation for his irrational resolve not to kill Havelok on the spot is superstitious fear of murdering the true heir with his own hands. As in *King Horn* and the Constance-saga (versions of which occur in *Emaré* and Chaucer's *Man of Law's Tale*) the expedient of sending a royal innocent to drown at sea fatally misfires.

485. A line directly echoed at 2177, see (C), where Ubbe offers Havelok his allegiance. (On structural duplication in the poem generally, see Hanning, *art. cit.*)

548. For the text of the fragments, the additional lines of which in general add nothing to the sense, see Skeat-Sisam, pp. 103ff. For an odd number of rhyming lines, cf. the nineteen in 87–105 and see (C).

561. *þis knaue*. The cruelty of Grim and his wife is hardly excused by their not knowing who Havelok is. Like St Paul (Acts 9, 3) they are sinners who (quite literally) see the light. In being 'saved', they save the king-to-be and win for their children greatness and for themselves an honoured remembrance 'til domesday' (2525–30).

572ff. *Weilawei* goes with the two exclamations: 'alas that I was born' and 'alas that no vulture [etc.] might seize him!' (i.e. 'would that they did!'). *Him* refers to Grim; the past tense may suggest that the poet or scribe is thinking in terms of indirect speech in 573ff.

586. *binne* refers to the inner room of a two-roomed cottage whose entrance was through the kitchen or outer room (cf. 'but and ben').

606. The *kyne-merk* is more fully described at 1264–5 and 2144–52. The 'miracle fair and god' of 501 here receives dramatic confirmation. Grim's whole speech of homage has quasi-allegorical overtones (see especially 629–33 with its repetition of the word *fre*). On the tradition of the royal birthmark in the form of a cross, see Marc Bloch, *Les Rois Thaumaturges* (Paris, Colin (1961), pp. 245–56).

664. Virtually the formula for the genre of romance, which has the basic structure of comedy. Schelp (*op. cit.*, p. 45) points to the under-lying fairytale pattern of *Hav.* revealed by this line.

674. *Dramatic irony:* Havelok *had* eaten no bread until he was entrusted to Grim. For other examples of this device, which is a favourite with the poet, see 1075, 1115–18, 1124, 1671, 2036, 2101–10, 2170ff. and (C) on all these.

683. The ingratitude of *swikes* is a common romance convention, as is their hypocrisy (690). Contrast 2861ff. (C) on Havelok.

695f. For a discussion of the rhyme, see Sisam's notes.

728–34. Another transitional passage: we are told what is in store
and invited to continue listening. The pauses seem to occur after sec-
tions of between 300 and 600 lines, which may indicate suitable points
for actual breaks in the reading out of the poem. Similar pausing-
places may be at lines 1182, 1646, 2270, 2516 (cf. also 2398 (C) and
2487–90).

732. MS. *prie* is inexplicable, and Skeat's *yete* the best suggestion so
far.

736. Lindsey, the part of north-east Lincolnshire now called
Humberside.

741f. *erde* 'dwell' is the word required by the sense here, but it re-
duces the homophonic rhyme, which is perfectly permissible in ME
poetry, to an assonance. Smithers (*op. cit.*, p. 291) suggests that *erþe*
may be a genuine phonetic variant of *erde*.

743–8. These lines make sense, but the amount of repetition in them
suggests a scribe's attempt to restore a partly illegible exemplar, or else
a lapse of memory in oral transmission. On 747ff. see Smithers, *op.
cit.*, pp. 291ff.

751–86. A passage unusual in ME romance not because of its
realistic detail but because of its accurate description of a social world
notable by its absence from most romances. Schelp aptly notes in *Hav.*
the far greater detail in the description of popular than of courtly
milieux (*op. cit.*, pp. 33–4).

745. The Great Seal of Grimsby (late 13th century to early 14th
century) represents the gigantic figure of 'Gryem' with, on his right,
'Habloc' and on his left 'Goldeburgh' (photograph in Skeat-Sisam).

755. *qual* is quite obscure; it may be a form of 'whale', but see
Smithers, *loc. cit.*

757. *hwel* is adequately explained by Skeat-Sisam as a mistake for
hel, itself a possible spelling of *el*. Smithers' objection to the emendation
as 'palaeographically improbable' seems nugatory.

775. Lincoln was one of the greatest towns in England at this time.
On the strong local associations of the Havelok-Grim story, Sisam
writes: 'The earliest French version is that of Gaimar, whose patroness,
Constance Fitzgilbert, was a Lincolnshire lady. Robert Manning, who
first mentions the English story . . . lived at Brunne (Bourne) in Lincs.'
(For echoes of the poem in Mannyng, compare *Hav.* 681–2 with
Handlyng Synne 5613–14 and 5811–12 respectively.) A further Lincolnshire connection is suggested by Judith Weiss, who posits the influence
on *Hav.* of an *abbreviationem . . . de principatu regni et tyrannidis* (wrongly
translated by her, following Stevenson, as *The Principles of Kingship and
Tyranny*). This was written by the philosopher and theologian Robert
Grosseteste (b. *c.* 1175), who was Bishop of Lincoln from 1235 until his
death in 1253 (see her valuable article, 'Structure and Characterization
in *Havelok the Dane*', *Spec.* 44 (1969), 247–57). W. A. Pantin uncon-
vincingly identifies this with one of Grosseteste's Lyons memoranda,

noting that it 'does not deal with secular politics, but with the alleged "tyranny" of the Archbishop of Canterbury in demanding excessive procurations' (in D. A. Callus (ed.), *Robert Grosseteste: Scholar and Bishop* (Oxford, 1953), p. 202). But if Adam Marsh's quoted title is correct, such an identification is highly improbable, and the treatise must be presumed lost, as Miss Weiss supposes. (We are grateful to Dr M. H. Keen for help with this point.)

786. On the word see Smithers, *loc. cit.*

797f. MS. *longe* rhyming with *gange*. Skeat emends *þe gange* to *hem gange* so as to make *gange* into a verb. Smithers keeps *þe* and takes it as 'thee'. But Havelok is not here addressing Grim; it is easier to take *gange* as for *genge* (cf. 788). The rhyme may then be restored by emending to *lenge* in 797 with the sense 'longer'.

800–4. Not a 'working-class' (let alone a 'revolutionary') but an orthodox Christian sentiment (cf. II Thess. 3, 8–11). Translate 803 'Ought not to have that [*sc.* food and drink] except as a result of working [*long on swink*]'.

855–8. An unrealistic touch, heightening our sense of the extreme poverty of the future king (cf. also 885–6 below, where the requirements of the *plot* unrealistically have the Earl of Cornwall living in Lincoln).

871, 876. Skeat supplies *Poure þat on fote yede* (cf. 101), and *þer þe erles mete he tok.*

914–22. Havelok's mastery of all these humble skills exemplifies his own belief that 'It is no shame for to swinken' (801). It is not Havelok who is degraded by *swink* but labour that is ennobled by his doing it. The treatment of Havelok's education for greatness recalls the *enfances* of such heroes of romance as Perceval, but is novel in making him a penniless hired labourer and not just an uncouth country swain. Havelok's claim to kingship is thus doubly founded, on royal birth (divinely sanctioned) and on personal merit, both being necessary for the ideal king. Cf. the description of his character at 947–60, also 977–9, and the combination of strength and gentleness noted at 993.

941. *star* is apparently dried sedge used for kindling.

944. The MS. has always been read as *citte*, of which Skeat's *kitte* is the natural emendation. But the reading may be *titte* 'dragged'. For pairs of synonymous phrases, cf. 952, 989, etc.

951–3. 'There was no boy so little, when it came to sporting and romping, that Havelok was not willing to play with him.' The assonance in 951–2 is probably genuine; cf. 2681ff.

957–60. A better basis for successful rule than that enjoyed by Godrich (277–9) or Godard (439–40).

983. For plural *al* cf. 1301; but Skeat may be right to emend.

989f. MS. *al he was long* should mean 'just so he was long', but as *heye* and *long* are effectively synonymous the comparison makes little sense. Transposition (with Holthausen) of *long* and *strong* breaks up the alliterative phrase in 990; we therefore read *als* with Skeat.

998–9. *layke on grene* 'indulge in wanton amorous play'. See the note by Angus McIntosh in *RES* 16 (1940), pp. 189–93.

1017. *Champiouns* were professional fighters, presumably possessed of outstanding physical strength.

1025ff. Putting the shot ('stone-casting') was one of the most popular medieval games.

1061. Havelok's achievement at putting is a *selkouth* 'marvel', 'wonder' not a *miracle* (cf. 501 and John Stevens, *Medieval Romance* (London, 1973), pp. 100–2).

1074. *strong* may have come in from the previous line; Holthausen emends to *fayr*.

1075–8. Dramatic irony. Godrich's marrying of Havelok to Golde-burh enables the latter to overthrow the usurper and regain her in-heritance, whilst Godrich's children are disinherited (2838–42). Cf. 674 (C) above.

1082, 1085–6. With Godrich's frivolity over the meaning of *hexte*, compare the behaviour of Wymound over his oath in *Ath.* 68.1–3.

1087. India proverbially stood for 'the end of the world'; cf. the Wife in Chaucer's *Wife of Bath's Tale* (D 823–4) who was as faithful 'As any wyf from Denmark unto Ynde'.

1094, 1099. *cherl* (< OE *ceorl*), roughly 'yeoman'. *þral* (< ON *þræll*) 'slave, thrall'. Used as a term of insult, 1160 below, like 'peasant-slave' in *Hamlet* II.ii.523. For an interesting discussion of social ranks in the Scandinavian community, see Gwyn Jones, *A History of the Vikings* (London, 1968), p. 145ff., especially 147–9, on the thrall.

1102f. We should probably emend *shop* 'created' to *swoc* 'betrayed' for the sake of the rhyme on *hok* (for the phonology, OE *ā* after *w* rhyming on OE *ō*, see Skeat-Sisam, Introduction, 20 (1)); but, if so, *Satanas* looks like a slip for *Judas*.

1106. on *hende*, see *SD* 277 (C).

1115–18, 1163–4, 1178–80. Note the dramatic ironies: Goldeburh does obtain a king for husband; Godrich is burnt alive; Goldeburh and Havelok are worthily married by an archbishop, showing God's providence at work (1182).

1130. Literally, 'in your despite'; from F. *malgré*, Lat. *mala gratia* (cf. 'With an ill grace').

1149. Skeat supplies *With dintes swipe hard and strong*.

1155. *one* 'alone' is the likely reading and makes good sense. Alter-natively, the MS. reading may be *oue*, a possible spelling for *awe* 'fear', in which case the sense would be 'Havelok was afraid' (literally 'fear was to Havelok').

1174–5. A medieval marriage-custom, now largely supplanted by the giving of presents (though something similar is kept up in Greek communities).

1190. We should probably read *awe* 'possess' for MS. *hawe*. For the latter as a form of *have*, cf. *SD* 30; for long and short *a* rhyming before *w*, cf. 1183f.

1193. The vocabulary of love, which is generally kept well out of this down-to-earth romance, here makes a brief appearance.

1207–48. The reception Grim's children give to Havelok and Goldeburh demonstrates their loyalty, anticipating Havelok's successful reception in Denmark. 1223ff. show that Grim's family have prospered since the days of their poverty during the 'strong dere' (826ff.).

1209f. The forms *neme, keme* for *nome, come* are unexplained.

1252. *kynde*='nature'; 'unkind' behaviour is *unnatural*, as in the complex word-play of Hamlet's 'A little more than kin, and less than kind'. Here, however, *kynde* involves social rank, and such a marriage is seen as being against nature; cf. *SO* 457ff., *Reeve's Tale*, A 4271–2.

1299f. Cf. 1189f. on the rhyme; here *drawe* has a short, *awe* a long vowel, so that emendation to *hawe* would be defensible here. *Hom* in this dialect can hardly be 3rd person plural and the sense, if the MS. reading is to be kept, must be 'to have my home there'. Holthausen adds *pouhte* before *hom*, apparently to avoid the awkwardness of *for-to* after *wolde* (which as a modal auxiliary should be followed by a simple infinitive; see however T. Mustanoja, *Middle English Syntax* (Helsinki, 1960), p. 522), and both he and Skeat emend *hom* to *hem*. But certainty seems impossible here.

1306. *ek* should probably be emended, with Holthausen, to *yet*, for the sake of the rhyme.

1333. The scribe has mistaken the syntax after the long catalogue of the inhabitants of Denmark. Skeat's emendation makes good sense and could have been misread as *makede*, copied as *mad*.

1340. If Zupitza's reconstruction is correct, the uncommon dual pronoun *wit* will have confused the scribe. But Holthausen's *Nim me with þe* may be thought palaeographically more likely.

1409. This expression appears to be an echo of the old formulaic phrase *die . . . qua . . . rex fuit vivus et mortuus,* as used in, e.g., King Stephen's Charter of Liberties, in W. Stubbs, *Select Charters,* ed. H. W. C. Davis (Oxford, 1913), p. 143. The phrase was apparently passing out of use in the thirteenth century. (We are grateful for this reference to Dr Maurice Keen of Balliol College, Oxford.)

1425–8. Havelok is being tactful as well as charitable: his account of events in 1415–18 accords with what he was described as 'seeing' (466–77), but the favourable interpretation of Grim's motive does not fit the facts. Until Grim discovered that the boy was Birkabeyn's heir, he was willing enough to kill in order to gain his freedom (561–6), even though he should 'shende his soule'.

1633. Holthausen restores the polite *you* appropriate to Havelok's position.

1640. The shrewd worldly wisdom of this gnomic utterance sounds odd in context; Havelok's proffer of what is virtually a bribe is presumably justified by his overriding claims as king of Denmark (cf. also 1698 (C), which seems to be praising Grim's son(s) on prudential rather than moral grounds).

1645–6. Another pausing-place in the poem, reminding us of its being composed for oral delivery (cf. 728 (C) above).

1671. Dramatic irony: Ubbe is unaware that Havelok is his King (cf. 2035 (C)).

1698. This exclamation presumably refers to Havelok's having been brought up ('fed') by Grim (the 'good man'), whose worthy offspring are now proving stalwart supporters to the hero.

1700–18. This whole passage somewhat overstates the obvious—that Havelok and Goldeburh are extremely attractive and readily win love and admiration; but perhaps its main point is that their royalty manifests itself in their looks, and Ubbe's merit is to be able to respond even before he realises what he is responding to.

1725. *nis* for *is*. Skeat's emendation (1868 ed.) is much preferable to his later version *is wimman non*, which represents a larger change. In any case *nan* ought to be read for the rhyme.

1736. *bite* is not a forcing of the sense for the sake of the rhyme but a meaning common in the 13th century, when 'bite' could cover the consuming of liquid as well as solid food (cf. 'taste', which also bore the general sense 'touch', as in *Piers Plowman*, B, XVII, 149, cf. also C, VI, 179).

1741. On *kil-þing*, see Smithers, *EGS* iii (1949–50), 67–8; but Skeat's emendation of *þe kilþing* to *ilk þing* may still be the safer reading.

1761. *Bernard was trewe*. The need for loyalty in knights and retainers is fundamental in this poem, as in much literature of the period (cf. *SO* and *Ath.* in this vol.). The failure of the regents to be 'trewe' to their respective lords is the root cause of Havelok's and Goldeburh's sufferings. Godrich is 'wiht' and 'of [his] bodi so god kniht', as Havelok recognises (2725–6), but he is not 'trewe'. Birkabeyn also had (mistakenly) chosen Godard for regent because he *thought* him 'under mone . . ./þe trewest . . .' (373–4).

1768. Generosity is rarely found in romances except in company with the other virtues (see also 2946).

1772. *ladde*, like *boye* (1904) here has the sense of 'low ruffian'. Contrast 2261, where it refers to 'ordinary people (of low social rank)', also 2329.

1771–2056. The scene is reminiscent of the attempt on Lot's guests in Gen. 19. 1963–4 and 2021–4, however, make it plain that the motive for the attack is to rob Bernard's house and guests, not specifically to rape Goldeburh, as Ubbe had feared (1749–50). The whole incident of the fight by moonlight graphically illustrates the lawlessness that prevails in Godard's Denmark. The detail of clothing at 1961–2 is suggestive of the contemporary abuse of 'maintenance', whereby armed retainers of great landowners wearing their masters' livery oppressed and intimidated defenceless people (1933–4 shows with ironic force that the 'sergaunz' are Ubbe's own retainers!—on the question of Ubbe's position, see the article 'Havelok's Return' by Maldwyn Mills in *MÆ* XLV (1976), 20–33). Havelok's rôle in the fight is not simply that of the martial hero of a 'gest' but that of the 'riht eir' quelling disorder in his kingdom (cf. 2157–81, on Havelok's father). Lines such as 1811–14, 1850–6, 1863–4, 1898, 1982–92 illustrate the unrealism characteristic of romance.

1788. The rhyme requires the participle *dropen*. The sense of the perfect may be understood by paraphrasing, 'I will see some of you dead' (cf. also 1810).

1824. *u* and *n* are not always easily distinguished in the MS. If Smithers' *speu* is not the MS. reading, it is an almost sure emendation.

1830. Dobson's emendation (see *EGS* i (1947–8), 58f.) restores the rhyme. The following line suggested *swerd* to the scribe, but there is no need for 1830 to refer to an offensive weapon.

1844. The cowardly 'dogges' (cf. also 1888, 1972) who assail their fierce quarry in a pack, end up appropriately in ditches (1927–8). In 1999 Havelok is compared to a 'hund', here a hunting-dog, a sense to which 'hound' was later to become restricted (but note 2440).

1854. *ferlik* anticipates *selcuth* at 2124 (cf. also *ferlike* at 1260, *selkouth* at 1061).

1869. Holthausen's suggestion of *glebes* 'clods' for *gleyves* 'swords, spears' is not strictly necessary; 1842f. may confirm the sense here, though 1843ff. suggest that *shoten*='rush'.

1887. The syntax is confused: Huwe means either 'Both of you seize' (*gripeth eyþer inker*) or 'Let each of us two seize' (*gripe eyþer unker*). The mixture may stand as realistic colloquialism (but *unker* was probably used as 'you two' in ME).

1922. See Smithers (*Early Middle English Verse and Prose*, 296f.) for an explanation of the phrase.

1976. *OED* gives *ride* as a transitive verb (sense IV) from *c*. 1225. But *riden on stede* is normal in this text, and the reading should probably be emended.

2014. For the phrase *leye oth* 'perjure oneself', see Smithers (*EGS* ii (1948–9), 2ff.).

2036. The senses 'someone like this man . . . who has slain them' or, without the comma, 'except as this man . . . has slain them' are unsatisfactory; we would expect either 'who . . . but this man . . .' or 'who . . . like this man . . .' But cf. 1887 (C) above, and cf. 2027. Note the dramatic irony: Havelok, unlike (say) the hero of *Beowulf*, is not really a 'man of ferne londe' in the sense of 'a complete foreigner'. Cf. 1671 above.

2041. Cf. 1698 (C) above.

2042. For the palaeographical causes of the corruption here, see Sisam's note.

2047. The latent prowess Ubbe thought he detected at 1655–6 has now been demonstrated, and he now wishes to ratify Havelok's status. The quasi-formulaic rhyme *kniht/wiht*, which occurs six times in the poem (see 344–5, 2191–2, 2249–50, 2351–2, 2725–6), emphasises that to be doughty was the basic requirement of a chivalric hero.

2050. Cain: the first murderer, from whom the *laddes* could be aptly said to be descended. 'Eves' is superfluous.

2065. On *palefrey*, see *SD* 413 (C) in Part Two.

2101–10. More dramatic irony. The audience is by now alert to the meaning of the light: the fact that Ubbe should wonder whether his unusual guests are involved in 'sotshipe' (? alluding to 'unlawful practices', 'witchcraft') intensifies the audience's pleasurable anticipation of the discovery he is to make. The question of 2119 (cf. 2101) heightens the *tension* in spite of the fact that there is no *suspense*, the cross-symbol's meaning at 2147–8 being immediately clear.

2131. Holthausen substitutes *torches* for *serges* to avoid the repetition; but, though *serges* may well be wrong, there is no certainty that *torches* is right. The lines as they stand give a good (if prosaic) meaning: 'a hundred and seven tapers' (the number seems without significance).

2140. The innocent word *gamen* (cf. also 1721) signalises a contrast with the *sotshipe* Ubbe had apprehended at 2104.

2150. The *carbuncle* or ruby was described in medieval tradition as 'the lord of all precious stones', which 'burnt like a red-hot coal, shone in dark places like a fire, won worship and honour for its wearer, and symbolised Christ'. Its appropriateness to Havelok needs no arguing. (See the refs. under 'carbunculus' in *English Medieval Lapidaries*, ed. Joan Evans and Mary S. Serjeantson (*EETS*, Original Series 190 (1933).)

2166. A moving and memorable image.

2170ff. Another touch of dramatic irony: Havelok thinks further trouble lies in store, but he has reached his journey's end. The poet finely brings out the tender concern of Ubbe, who hovers between seeing Havelok as his sovereign and as his 'son', and even in offering homage (*manred*) uses the intimate pronouns *þu* and *þe*. His speech concluding this fairytale-like scene, itself the climax of Havelok's story, possesses the quality almost of a litany.

2205ff. The exact nature of the *justise*'s authority in Denmark (cf. also 2280ff.) is unspecified, but its reality is not in question (see 2294). He has presumably sworn loyalty to Godard with the rest of the Danes (cf. 440–3), and line 2178 may be a way of excusing his fault. At any rate, his offer of *manred* may be seen as symbolically 'cancelling' the yielding of *manred* to Godard under duress (484–96) which had marked the lowest point of Havelok's fortunes. Ubbe's very words at 2179, 'For þu art comen of Birkabeyn', seem to reverse Havelok's 'Birkabein/

Nevere yete me ne gat' (495–6).

2249. Cf. OE *middangeard* 'middle enclosure' (i.e. between heaven and hell; so 'earth'); it was subsequently reformed as 'middle earth' on the basis of a false etymology.

2254. In this line, *þe* may have been lost by haplography after *boþe*.

2278. *lef and loth* is a proverbial phrase; it is rather clumsily used here, as at 2318 below (contrast 441, where the line is identical) since it *seems* to contradict 2276–7.

2321–4. Havelok appears to be 'elected' king in the customary manner of the Danes. His claim derives from Birkabeyn, but is ratified by popular assent (cf. the situation in Denmark alluded to when Hamlet speaks of Claudius as 'Popp'd in between the election and my hopes' (*Hamlet* V.ii.65)).

2332ff. In these often-quoted lines, the contrast seems to be one between works *read* out aloud (courtly 'romances' in French) and works *sung*, perhaps by the gleemen who strike the tabor ('gestes' in the language of the ordinary people). The *Havelok*-poet has called his own work a 'gest' (2989) not a 'romanz' (which is probably what he would have called his French source, if he had one), but he can hardly have intended it to be 'sung'.

2387. There is a grim appropriateness in having Godard hunted down while he is engaged in hunting.

2398–2402, 2458–2464. Passages of recapitulation, perhaps suggesting that the poem was read out in two or more 'sessions', between which the audience might have forgotten some of the relevant details of Godard's crimes (cf. also 726–32 (C) above and 2487–90 below).

2426. *Helpe* may be a subjunctive, 'if you help me', which would give a better sense than the imperative. But in that case we should probably restore *ye* after it.

2463. The loss of *with* may be suggested on non-metrical grounds by the occurrence of the letters *wiþ* in the following words, and the possibility of a haplographic error; the repetition of *with* in the preceding lines supports it here.

2481–90. The horrific judgment passed on Godard fulfils the prophetic words of Grim at 613–14. The nature of the punishment (see 2498ff.) sufficiently conveys the poet's intense abhorrence of treachery (cf. also the death of Wymound in *Ath.*): *he was fals*. The poet can afford no Christian pity for a 'Sathanas' (2517). Cf. also the reaction of the queen after the burning of Godrich (2847) below: *Þo was Goldeboru ful bliþe*, etc.

2501–2. See Smithers (*EGS* iii (1949–50), 69–72) for a discussion of this couplet.

2515. *henge* is inappropriate here, since we require a transitive verb. But for the reverse confusion, see perhaps 2703.

2522. The staff symbolises Ubbe's authority in Denmark, as that of a sort of deputy or first minister to the king (cf. 2963–6 below).

2525ff. Although there is no break in the MS. here, there is a gap in the story, part of which the poet seems to have omitted. Havelok is now back in England for the last stage of the story, the settling of the score with the other usurper, Godrich. Skeat here assumes the loss of a passage describing Havelok's return to England; but the journey is implied in the account of the founding of the priory, and the passage as it stands provides an adequate transition: we may not assume that the poet intended otherwise.

2529. MS. *haveden* is defensible as referring to Grim's whole family, but the point is not to be pressed.

2557f. The repetition of the rhyme-words from 2555f. suggests corruption. *Welde* in 2557 and *shelde* in 2558 constitute a possible emendation, though a shield is not usually thought of as a weapon; cf. however the OE *Battle of Maldon* 130f.: *wæpen up ahof/bord to gebeorge* 'he raised his weapon, his shield for protection'. In order to have the dative *shelde* we need a further emendation such as *gisarm with shelde*; and 2556 *sheld* would probably have to be taken as a mistake for *swerd*. These consequential emendations probably rule out the suggestion. Holthausen reads *wepne of ferd . . . gisarm or swerd*.

2562. Skeat emends to *y-boren so*, which still leaves a weak sense, while the prefix *y-* is very rare in this text. Dobson (*EGS* i (1947–8), 59) would read *ye bere so* and translate 'you may say so', 'you may be sure'. Neither emendation seems convincing.

2581ff. Godrich's speech blends scaremongering, appeals to patriotism, and sheer lies, but it certainly succeeds in its aim of rousing the English to resist the invading *uten-laddes* (see 2686–92). As a reminiscence of the historical Danish invasions, it seems accurate enough (see Gwyn Jones, *op. cit.*, pp. 354–86), but of course inappropriate to the situation represented in the poem.

2625ff. As in OE heroic poems (e.g. *The Battle of Maldon*) the *Havelok*-poet makes no attempt to evoke a general mêlée, but concentrates on the individual exploits of his five heroes. The initial duel of Ubbe and Godrich serves as preparation for the climactic one between the latter and Havelok, but it has the effect possibly of diminishing the hero's prowess and inadvertently enhancing the villain's, since Godrich must be seriously worn out by the time he encounters Havelok (see 2674–6).

2663. Dobson's emendation (see *EGS* i (1947–8), 59) removes a rhyme false in both consonant and vowel, for *boþe* takes its vowel from OE *bā*, and thus has an open $\bar{\varrho}$ in ME, whereas *drowe*, from OE *drōgon*, has close $\bar{\varrho}$; *lowe* has $\bar{\varrho}$ from early ME *ā*. $\bar{\varrho}w$ and $\bar{\varrho}w$ certainly became the same sound later in ME, and Dobson suggests that they had already coalesced in the dialect of the author of *Hav.*

2681f. On the rhyme, cf. 951f.

2695. Holthausen emends *levin* 'lightning' to *leun* 'lion', which is perhaps supported by the reference to beasts in 2696 and would fit well with the animal imagery common in the poem (cf. e.g. 2440–53 above). The lion symbolised courage (cf. Ywain's lion in *YG*, in Part Two), a quality Godrich undeniably possesses.

2703. The sense 'there was none who could withstand his strokes . . . so that (the enemy) fell' is defensible but unidiomatic, and Skeat's addition of *ne* should probably be accepted. Against taking *felden* as a rare form for 'fell' (see *OED s.v. fall*, 'Forms') is the MS. reading *feldem*, which could be for *felde hem* as 716 *havedet* is for *havede it*; if so, it would be necessary to omit *dos*. It is improbable, though, that the same scribe would miss the transitive sense of *felde* and yet retain the final *m* which depends on that sense. For *feldem* as an error for *felden*, cf. 2751, MS. *drawem*.

2709ff. Havelok's speech and behaviour here are wholly in character, recalling the description in 993–6: 'Als he was strong, so was he softe', etc. The hero's knightly generosity to his foe illustrates his fitness to rule and justifies him when Godrich, having rejected the offer of amnesty, persists in a wrong cause and duly meets his 'doom'. Throughout, Havelok's scrupulously correct behaviour discloses that respect for 'lawe of londe' (2820) which had been the ordinary man's guarantee against arbitrary power during the reign of the ideal king Athelwold (see especially 28–9). Havelok does not forget that he is acting on behalf of the queen, against whom Godrich has offended (cf. 2768–70, 2805–11) and becomes ruler of England only with the people's consent (2822), not by his own claim. The degradation of Godrich takes place only after he has been tried and condemned by his peers with due process of law ('Lokes þat ye demen him riht', 2817).

2724. MS. *mi dede* makes no sense. Holthausen's *mi deole* 'my sorrow' is an easier emendation and gives better sense than Zupitza's, but *deole* is a Southern and Western spelling not typical of the dialect or scribal practice of the poem as we have it.

2808. Stratmann emends *we* to *he*; in strict logic this is correct, but the MS. reading is comprehensible and may reflect the idiom of spoken English; for *wot* plural, see *OED s.v. wot* 2.

2861ff. The spate of marriages that follows upon the recovery of the kingdom opens the conclusion of the tale in the classic 'comic' mode appropriate to romance as a genre. There is a marked 'fairytale' flavour to the ennobling of Grim's family and humble characters like Bertram the cook (for their services to the royal pair) which must have enhanced the poem's appeal to an audience of common folk (cf. Shakespeare's *The Winter's Tale*). Havelok's gratitude is not the least endearing of his qualities and serves to contrast him strongly with the two dead tyrants (see 2876–8, 2907–8, also 2943–6).

2954. *Laste* is a genuine past form, but this may be a case where metrical considerations may be allowed to weigh in favour of Skeat's emendation *lastede*.

2989–end. *Epilogue.* A summary which pleasingly brings to mind the whole sequence of events that have made up the 'gest' and enables the poet more effectively to solicit the good will of his audience by reminding them of the enjoyment he has given them through his work.

Athelston

Athelston occupies ff. 120–131 in MS. 175 of Gonville and Caius College, Cambridge. The text, apart from some apparent scribal omissions, is complete; the MS. contains 812 lines.

The poem was edited by C. H. Hartshorne in *Ancient Metrical Tales* (London, 1829) and by T. Wright and J. O. Halliwell in *Reliquiae Antiquae* (London, 1841–3); the important editions, however, are those by J. Zupitza, 'Die Romanze von Athelston', *Englische Studien* xiii (1889), 331–414, xiv (1890), 321–44 (Z), and A. McI. Trounce (*EETS*, 224, 1951 for 1946, previously issued in the Publications of the Philological Society, no. xi, 1933) (T). Trounce's careful, thorough edition may be considered the standard text. The manuscript is generally clearly written, though a few line-endings in the second column of the verso side are obscured by the binding; in these cases the supplements of previous editors have been accepted.

The MS. has an admixture of Northern spellings and forms (see C on *Ywain and Gawain*), some of which the rhymes show to be original (e.g. 40.9ff., 47.1f.). The only problem is the scribe's use of double *f*: at the beginning of the line this has its usual significance of capital *F*, but within the line it is often used initially as well as within the word in such a way as to suggest that no capital is intended. Contrary to the practice of Zupitza and Trounce we have preserved these spellings as characteristic of the scribe. The poet's rhyming practice appears to have been laxer than that of most of the texts in this volume, assonances in particular being so frequent as to guarantee their originality, and, in view of the repetitive, formulaic style of the poem, repeated rhyme-words within the stanza have not been emended merely on the grounds of the repetition.

Trounce dates the poem in the last quarter of the 14th century, but see notes on 49, 51, below.

1. Conclusion with a prayer is common in many 'minstrel-romances' (e.g. *SO*, *SMA*; cf. also *Hav.*) but opening with a prayer is especially found in tail-rhyme romances. *holy kyrke* (5) is more than a conventional variation, pointing as it does to a major lesson of the poem—the need to reverence the authority of the Church (in the person of Alryke).

1.8. *ffalsnesse* or 'untruth', the theme of so many late English romances (5 out of 8 in this book; cf. *Hav.* 1761 (C), etc.) means more than just 'disloyalty' but assumes the specific form of *False lesyngys* (7.11; cf. 70.6). It is thus not the breach of *trouþe* of a Godrich (*Hav.* 312–13) or an Ywain (*YG* 1626), but a positive act of treason like Mordred's false report of Arthur's death (*SMA* 373. 1–4). 'Þorwȝ wurd oure werk may sprynge' (8.3). Cf. 17 (C).

1.10. *weddyd*. The bond between the four men joined them as closely as *sybbe of kyn*. For a full discussion of sworn-brotherhood, an institution ultimately of Germanic origin but only a memory at this period, see T 11–14; for an ideal picture of it, see *Amis and Amiloun*, ed. McEdward Leach, *EETS*, Original Series 203 (1937), for a more 'realistic' one, in which love over-rules the bond between two knights who are sworn brothers as well as 'sybbe of kyn', see Chaucer's *Knight's Tale*, especially A 1129ff. Though it is the basic *donnée* of *Ath.*, the importance of sworn-brotherhood is exaggerated by T (especially Introduction, p. 14). Thus (i) though Alryke pleads with Athelston on the basis of their sworn-brotherhood, the substance of his appeal is not that he spare his *weddyd broþer* (Egelan) but [*his*] *owne blood* (*sc.* Edyff), suggesting the greater importance of sib-kinship; (ii) Athelston is unwilling to reveal Wymound's name not because Wymound is his *weddyd broþer* but because he has sworn not to do so (on the binding force of a king's oaths, cf. *SO* 463–8 (C); (iii) Wymound does not show 'compunction' at 15.8–9, rather the same cunning trick used by Iago against Cassio when tempting Othello (*Othello* III.iii.476–8: 'My friend is dead;/'Tis done at your request', etc.) Wymound's intent is unambiguously plain (7.10–12).

1.11. Z's emendation of *go* to *gon* (=*gonnen*) and *wolden* to *wilen* 'formerly' (also in 2.2) avoids the problem of characters with English names apparently being foreigners; *cuntre* would then mean 'region, district (of England)'. But perhaps in a situation where one of the messengers is *þe kyngys cosyn dere* (3.3) too much verisimilitude should not be sought.

2.5. The relative clause with relative pronoun subject omitted is common in ME and evidently particularly typical of this text; for other examples see 5.8, 34.6, 71.11. Omission of a relative pronoun object is of course still standard English ('the man I met yesterday'). See Mustanoja, *Middle English Syntax* (Helsinki, 1960), pp. 203–6.

2.6. A favourite minstrel tag which, in such forms as 'light as leef on linde' also occurs in Chaucer (e.g. *Clerk's Tale*, D 1211) and Langland (*PP*, B, I, 156). The *l*-alliteration seems to have rendered the phrase quasi-formulaic, not any especial property of the lime tree (though its leaves are light).

3.2. Athelston is probably 'a typical king' (T) but the choice of name may be due to the fame of the historical Athelstan. Grandson of King Alfred and king in succession to Edward the Elder (925) he defeated the Danes decisively at Brunanburh (937), an event celebrated in a poem included in the Anglo-Saxon Chronicle. He died in 939.

But why would the poet have wished to represent the great king in such terms?

4.4, 7. Dover's great castle made it a strategic port. Stone is near Dartford on the Canterbury road. Athelston enquires after Alryke and Egelan in the order in which Wymound would have visited them (9).

4.5. *covere* could also mean 'restore', 'relieve'; thus 'and so he (A.) relieved the poor man'.

4.11. *Edyff* is not a corruption of 'Edith' but from OE *Eadgifu*, a name borne by two sisters of the historical Athelstan.

5.4. MS. has the expected form *vacant*. This could assonate with *hand*, though the assonance would be unusual in that the final consonant is unvoiced and so should not assonate with a final voiced consonant (contrast *wonde* assonating with *wombe* in 26.10f.). The form *vacand*, however, is recorded only in Scotland. But it is not impossible that *vacant* has, for the sake of the rhyme, been assimilated to the form of a present participle of the type *levande* (40.9). This would be a typically Northern form, but extends as far as East Anglia, with which area Trounce (pp. 2, 34 note, 49ff.) tentatively connects the poem. A very similar formation *rampand* (cf. 'rampant') occurs as a variant in *SD* 370 (Egerton MS., of Suffolk provenance).

5.6. *wyke* may be < OE *wīc* 'town' but if it is < OE *wīce* 'office, function' we get even better sense, since *stede* in 5.7 ceases to be redundant ('Cauntyrbury' in 5.4 is plainly the archbishopric rather than the place).

5.9, 12. The forms *lyke*, *ryke* for MS. *lyche*, *ryche* are suggested not only by the rhyme-words in 5.3, 6, but also by 32.5. There the scribe writes *bysschopryke* 'bishopric', having failed to understand the adjective *ryke* in his exemplar. Here, he alters to the more familiar (Southern) form.

7.8. Trounce may be correct in attributing to *wyttyrlye* the sense 'that is to say'. But it is likely to be a mere rhyme-filler. Only the initial remains of the first word of the line, with spaces for two letters after it. It seems possible that the scribe wrote *þat* for *þe*, quickly blotted out the incorrect reading and subsequently failed to add the remaining letter. T suggests that the name 'Wymound' may have had overtones of treacherousness (p. 28).

11.2. *tylle* 'to' is redundant after *to* at the beginning of the line; perhaps we should read *þi chaumbyr . . .*, though there is no good reason for the corruption. Trounce suggests a more drastic emendation, reading as the couplet, '*Sere kyng', he sayde, 'ȝif þi wille be*/*To chaumbyr þat þou wolde te . . .*'; he postulates a northerly reviser followed by a Southern copyist, which is perhaps too ingenious.

11.4. There is no need to emend *a swete* to *unswete* as Trounce proposes; nor need *swete* be sarcastic. Wymound pretends to bring good news in such terms that the king suspects the contrary (11.7f.). Athelston's character is represented as so capricious and volatile that his subsequent readiness to believe the slander need occasion no surprise.

12.3ff. Either *lyff*/*þryff* or *lyve*/*fyve* should probably be emended to produce a correct rhyme; Trounce suggests the latter course.

12.9. Zupitza brings up a substantial battery of instances of *on* in the sense of *of* and replacing it in phrases such as this, and so keeps *on lyve*, followed by Trounce. But in this particular phrase *on* gives the exactly opposite sense to what is required, and in the circumstances the parallels cannot stand. *On* may be taken as a scribal slip.

13.1. The common asseveration 'so may I prosper' is here transferred into the second person: 'tell me, as you hope to prosper'. Cf. 20.4.

13.12. With this and similar interjections (15.12) cf. *Hav.* 328–37 (C). The author loses no chance to hammer home the moral that treachery is diabolically wicked. Likewise, 6.3 made explicit the *trewþe* ('fidelity') of Egelan (with which cf. the closely parallel *Hav.* 1761 (C)).

14.3. *counsayl* has a special significance: it was the king's sharing of his *counsayl* with Egelan that chiefly caused Wymound's envy (7.6), hence the appropriateness of Wymound's insistence on imparting his *counsayl* to Athelston.

15.1. For the tautological expression *be cros and roode*, see *SMA* 96.6 (C) in Part Two. Emendation would be possible here too.

15.2. Oaths were often backed by a refusal to eat or drink till they were accomplished, as a sign of urgency and determination; but 14.10f. gives also, perhaps, a practical reason for it.

15.12. The MS. is not clear and might read *schames dede*, which would perhaps give a more satisfactory sense, 'shameful death'.

16.2. The messenger proves to play an important role in the poem. His bearing the king's name, which may have some obscure connection with the latter's having been a messenger himself (cf. Orfeo's favouring of minstrels, *SO* 25–8), and his foundling-status, may suggest he has been brought up in the king's household and is especially trusted (cf. 18–19 (C) below).

17. Athelston is forced into *lesyng* himself, so that 'Þorwʒ word *his* werk may sprynge'.

18.5. *Take* in ME sometimes has the sense 'give' (*OED s.v.* IX, 60). Its ambiguity (cf. 'let'='hinder') led to its disappearance.

18.7–19.6. An awkward passage. A messenger would not be expected to know what the letter he carries says (but cf. 16.2 (C) above). It may be that to tell the audience its contents the poet has resorted to direct speech from the messenger, thereby (a) overlooking the problem of confidentiality, (b) rendering a *letter* strictly unnecessary (would a recognised king's messenger need the royal seal to authenticate so straightforward a summons as this?), (c) repeating what we already know from 17.1ff. At 34.7ff. he avoids the awkwardness; it is not clear whether 67.7ff. give the words of the messenger or of the letter, but the latter is possible.

21. Edyff's imprudent haste to ride to London though she is approaching her confinement (19.8) may be explained by the fact that the king's offer to knight his nephews is a great honour, one which should strengthen still further the already close bond between a man and his sister's son(s) (cf. 14.1, and in *SMA*, Lancelot's reverence for Arthur, who made him knight (2142–5) and the bond between Arthur and Gawain, e.g. 3142). The stratagem for luring Egelan's sons will therefore seem all the more odious—but so, if it were true, would their treachery.

22.3. *London* in the MS. ends with a very pronounced curl, which Z, against T, seems justified in taking as a contraction for -e.

24.4. An unrealistic but dramatically effective image (cf. 26.1f., 34.12, also *SO* 578, *SMA* st. 393.6, etc.). The violent and impulsive gestures prominent in romances are due partly to the heightened and stylized mode (see Pamela Gradon, *Form and Style in Early English Literature*, ch. 4, especially pp. 252ff.) and partly, it would seem, to the actual manners of the age. (Cf. *SMA*, 23.7 (C).)

24.8. The queen's offering herself, pregnant with the king's heir, as a formal suppliant at his feet, renders his act at 26.10f. all the more inhuman. The scene strongly calls to mind Shakespeare's *The Winter's Tale*, as does the King-Queen-Friend situation generally.

24.12. Something is evidently wrong with the rhyme: the corruption may be associated with the loss in 25.2ff. (see next note).

25.2ff. The break in sense and rhyme makes it clear that some lines have been lost here; as *Athelston* contains both six- and twelve-line stanzas, four or ten may have gone. Any explanation for the loss appears to have been lost with the lines themselves.

25.11f. Athelston's clear determination not to give Egelan and Edyff a fair trial renders his prayer at 39.5–12 pure hypocrisy. The request for divine intervention, however insincere, is nonetheless granted.

26.9. *abyyd* is for *aby* 'pay for'; the two words, however, became confused (see Trounce), and this appears to be an early instance of the confusion.

27.4–9. Some of the finest lines in the poem. The conventional phraseology of 6–7, reminiscent of 6.10ff., and of 'minstrel-style' generally (cf.*SMA* st. 23.3–4) is exquisitely brought to life in the context.

27.12. I.e. Wymound was put to death, while Athelston lost his heir.

28.11. T sees this as expressing the superiority of wedbrotherhood-ties over wedlock-ties in the poem (p. 13); but Athelston's preparedness to kill Egelan and his violent outburst against Alryke weaken his reading. More likely, the queen is recognising the *sacra potestas* wielded by the Archbishop (see also the invocation of divine wrath to back up ecclesiastical authority at 46.7–12), for it is this that Athelston in point of fact submits to (50.7–12).

29.1. The queen's Spanish earldom may have been suggested by the poet's awareness that John of Gaunt's second wife, Constance, was heiress to the kingdom of Castile. In 1381 Gaunt set out on an expedition to claim the crown in his wife's right.

29.7. A *more-geve* ('morning-gift') was given by a husband to his wife the *morning* after the consummation of the marriage. The term comes also to be inaccurately used to mean a dowry. Here the exact sense is unclear; the implication, however, is that the queen holds the land in her own right and is free to dispose of it.

30.4–8. The monastic rule divided the day into canonical 'Hours', of which the name of the first had passed into common speech (cf. *Canterbury Tales*, B, 1278, 4387). It is quite realistic for the messenger to have ridden since, say, 5 a.m. at about $5\frac{1}{2}$ mph. The 55 miles from London to Canterbury would take 7–8 hours and he has not yet had the first meal of the day (dinner, taken between 9 and 10 a.m.). As he sets off at once and returns with Alryke to London, his expectation in 11–12 is not unreasonable. (At 70.12, as T points out, the poet wrongly gives 40 for 50 as the distance from Dover to Gravesend.)

30.4. This overloaded line might be improved by the omission of the initial *And*, which may be an anticipation of *An* in the following line.

31.4–33.6. From the Royal Palace the messenger travels east to cross the Thames and then takes the famous pilgrim-route. In 31.6, *hors* is presumably pronounced *hos*. In 10, *Steppyngbourne* could be a scribal error caused by preceding *Stone* (i.e. he thought of '*stepping-stone*'): Sittingbourne would be a familiar name to one who knew this route. In 12 *mos* has its OE meaning 'fen, marsh'; it retains this sense in place names in north-west England.

31.6. See T for the rhyme.

31.8. *Ou* in the MS. has a blurred mark above the *u* which may well represent the contraction for *-er*. *Over* certainly gives better sense than *on*.

33.2. *bysschopryke* as one word makes no sense; as two, it agrees with 5.12, q.v.

33.3. *non er* is noted by Trounce as a possible East Anglian phrase, on the strength of its occurrence in the *Paston Letters*, 4.172: 'I received the box . . . on Friday last and non er' (1465). It appears to be a genuine if rare expression.

35.1. On *palfray* see *SD* 413 (C). The Archbishop uses nine of these in succession, the messenger a single steed which, having completed the return journey also at a gallop, quite understandably expires.

35.8. *ffynde* rhymed with *ende* is puzzling. Trounce cites some similar rhymes, but offers no clear phonological explanation. We should note, however, that *e* before *ng* was regularly raised to *i* before 1500 (Dobson, *English Pronunciation 1500–1700* (Oxford, 1968), §77) and Dobson further cites some 16th-century evidence that this happened before *n*+other consonants, including an instance of this same rhyme. The pronunciation 'ind' for *ende* may therefore have been available to poets in trouble with their rhymes as early as our text.

36.3. This phrase, used widely especially in tail-rhyme poems, is merely a handy filler, not serious evidence for a French original; the poet might have used it simply to lend authority to his tale. *romaunce* probably lacks also the generic overtone it seems to possess in *Amis and Amiloun* 157 (not a tail-line), where the *gest* of the Auchinleck MS. is replaced by *romance* in Egerton. (On both terms, see *Hav.* 2332–4 (C) and headnote.)

37.1f. The assonance is odd (cf. on 5.4) but evidently traditional (cf. 40.7f., etc.).

37.10f. Trounce resonably explains this difficult passage as meaning that the reward will be sufficient even if the messenger lives to be a hundred; MS. *and* at the beginning of 10 may well be an anticipation of the same word in 11. It is possible that Alryke is expressing the wish 'may God have granted you long life', but 12 gains point if it is a reply to 36.11, which Alryke's grandiose *hundryd* makes it seem (cf. Athelston's *or none* (43.5) replying to Alryke's *or none* at 42.5).

39.2. The rood was a large cross placed over the screen dividing the nave from the chancel. Westminster Abbey, which may be the *kyrke* of 1, still has its screen and would have had a rood at this period. At 40.2 Athelston looks through the pierced stonework of the screen into the choir, the part of the chancel immediately beyond it.

39.7. The scribe seems to have had trouble with this line, and first to have written *Gyltles men þat þay ne be. ȝiff* has been added above *þat*, which has a thin stroke through it, probably by mistake and *ne* is cancelled with a heavy stroke and three dots. Our reading attempts to represent the scribe's probable intention, and agrees with that of T.

39.8. Trounce rightly rejects French and Hale's rendering of *presoun ffree* as 'parole' on the grounds of inconsistency with 23.2 and 39.9. *MED* gives the alternatives of 'custody without torture' or 'prison under the jurisdiction of an incorporated city'. The second is inappropriate; the first makes sense, but lacks point. It may be that we have an extension of the sense 'noble' to 'great', 'powerful'. Trounce suggests 'strong prison'. For a similar loose use of *fre* in rhyming-position, cf. *Hav.* 2881 (C). It is conceivable that Athelston's *fre* (=noble) really applies to himself and is awkwardly transferred to the prison, producing the paradoxical reading.

41.9ff. The omission of the end of one stanza and the beginning of the next is probably due to the coincidence of the rhyme of 41.7f. and the tail-rhyme of the following stanza.

44.7–45.6. Alryke submits to Athelston's ejecting him from his see, but knows the king cannot impugn his spiritual authority. He accordingly interdicts the clergy from performing any services, including baptism (11), an extreme measure never actually implemented even during the great interdict of King John's reign. Churches must bar their doors and windows with thorn branches (T gives an example of this having occurred) and be allowed to become overgrown. The king when he dies will be treated like the heretics, who were not buried in consecrated ground but in cross-roads and ditches. (45.4 *dyke*, here a *ditch* rather than an embankment; the two words are etymologically the same, referring as they do to different results of the same process. *Dyke* 'ditch' survives in literary English as late as Dryden, and in local use to the present day (cf. 'February fill-dyke'); *ditch* 'embankment' survives only in dialect.) There are echoes in Alryke's action of militant archbishops like Becket and Stephen Langton, but the historical Athelstan had no quarrel with the Church. (On the ecclesiastical matter generally, see T, pp. 31–8.) The passage breathes a partisanship for the Church (as opposed to religious feeling simply) unusual in a romance.

46. The rhymes in this stanza are unusually repetitive even for this poet; yet the sense is reasonable and gives no indication of corruption. Repetition of lines, couplets and even stanzas, with or without variation, is characteristic of minstrel poetry, of which *Ath.*, if not a genuine example, is at least an assiduous imitation; but there is little point to it here.

46.1. The expression here is loose: it should not be assumed that the poet regarded absolution after death as a possibility. *þat I may see* has the force of 'for anything I can do', 'as far as I have anything to do with it'; for the usage, see *OED s.v. see* v. 10d.

46.12. Note the single instance of *borwe* in the modern sense 'borrow'.

48.4. *cursyd* is no mere abuse: Athelston has been excommunicated and it is now necessary formally to absolve the whole land from the sin of contumely against the Church committed by its king (51.11f.).

49.2. Cf. Chaucer, *Canterbury Tales*, B, 1185, and the expressions 'anybody, somebody', also 'body' used substantively in Modern Scots, 'Gin a body . . .'

49. The militant stance of the barons towards the king may echo the struggles of the anti-court party against Richard II which culminated in the king's deposition in 1399.

51.4. T shows that the Broken Cross, near St Paul's, was known as a place of assembly. It was not so called till about 1370 and was removed in 1390. But while this gives us a lower limit for dating the poem, it does not necessarily give an upper, for *Ath.* could have been written during or after the deposition crisis of 1399 and still have referred to a famous landmark removed a mere ten years or so previously.

52.8ff. The custom of trial by ordeal had died out by the 13th century and been replaced by trial at arms (cf. *SMA*, stanzas 198–205). T detects an apparent confusion in *Ath.* between the legal ordeal of walking over nine red-hot ploughshares and the legendary one of walking through a fire nine plough-lengths long. But it seems satisfactory to read the poet's account as one of the purely legendary type of ordeal. (See T, pp. 14–20, 54.10 (C), 60.4 (C).)

53.6. It seems peculiarly inept to compare fire to itself (also 73.6); the phrase was however a set formula. If the poet *is* really thinking of red-hot ploughshares, the comparison is, of course, appropriate enough. For an oddly effective use of platitude, contrast 65.6.

54.4, etc. On *scarlet* cf. *SD* 92 (C), *YG* 1103.

54.10. *hand* need not indicate a confused echo of the form of ordeal in which red-hot metal was carried; the phrase simply signifies 'all of him'.

55.3. The power of St Paul('s high altar) is apparently his/its sanctity, but the line may be padding and not deserve translating. The immense cathedral of Old St Paul's, destroyed in the Great Fire, was near the Broken Cross and so an appropriate place to go to. Presentation in church as an act of thanksgiving for a miracle dates back to Biblical times and no specific source for the practice is necessary (cf. T *ad loc.*).

56.2f. The trial of the children, who are presumably not involved in the plot, implies the idea of hereditary attainder. (If Egelan became king, his sons would become heirs to the throne.) On the whole ordeal-scene, see Introduction, p. 16. The repetitive style (56.4–6, 57.3–6, 58.1–2) enhances the ritual quality of the action (cf. also 73).

58.2. Both Z and T omit *þat*, leaving the line identical with 55.2. But the MS. reading makes sense and is a defensible variation of the formula.

58.3. Most probably 'disclosed, declared, manifested', so that it could be made known to the people at large (St Paul's being a centre from which news spread all over London).

59.7f. The prayer is fulfilled: the king's foe escapes alive only because he is pulled out.

59, 60. Trounce takes both these stanzas as having nine lines only, though the rest of the poem is all in stanzas of six or twelve, and each of these two shows signs of loss. We need a prayer after 59.9 to account for 60.1, and, whereas Trounce admits to being unable to understand 60.9 (while properly rejecting Zupitza's bizarre rendering 'it came to pass that she sighed'), there is no difficulty if we assume that 60.10–12 described what 'befell for all to see'.

60.4. Edyff walks through the fire a third of the way along (=three plough-lengths); T finds an echo in *prydde* of another type of ordeal (p. 17).

61.8. Men were presumably not permitted to be present at child-birth.

61.11. It is not clear if this is the famous St Edmund of East Anglia, king and martyr, killed by the Danes in 869. The historical Athelstan's successor was his brother Edmund, and that may be the ultimate source of the confusion (see further T, p. 31).

62.2. *Plas* is perhaps the open space before St Paul's Cathedral.

62.3. The child is born 'whole and sound' (in *SD* the phrase is applied to the mother) just as its parents were 'unblemished'. The

death of Athelston's own child (27.4–9) was the result, of course, not of
the queen's but the king's sin. The power of evil in this poem to destroy
the innocent recalls the murder of the hero's sisters in *Hav.* (472–3).

62.9. 'Mark', a money of account, not a coin, simply serves to swell
the phrase.

63.7. Oaths by St Anne were common until Shakespeare's day (cf.
Twelfth Night, II.iii.111); but T notes the saint's special popularity
after 1378, when her feast was introduced. 13.11 does not mention her,
however, and it may be best to place a comma after *sworn*, making the
oath itself parenthetical. This makes more sense, since an oath by St
Anne would not have been especially solemn.

65.2. In agreeing to disclose under seal of confession the *counsayl* he
received under pledge of secrecy, Athelston is playing the hair-
splitting hypocrite, of course: though technically he has not made pub-
lic (a quibbling interpretation of *biwreyed*, 14.8) Wymound's name,
nothing prevents Alryke from acting on the knowledge gained from
Athelston.

68.11. Probably ironic: the messenger was doing 'Wymound's
business' inasmuch as his ride to and from Canterbury is to terminate
in the latter's death.

70.9. Trounce interprets 'I shall cause the king to be at hand',
though with some hesitation. The bantering tone of the exchange, however, suggests that the messenger is pretending to take the credit for
Wymound's new earldom and promising him the kingdom by and by.

71.4. The Great Hall of Westminster was the chief seat of justice of
the Kings of England.

71.7f. A hint at Wymound as a 'Judas' (the archetypal traitor); cf.
Hav. 319, 355 (C).

72.4. *has . . . tan*, a locution characteristic of the vividly dramatic
style of ballad-poetry, which *Ath.* undoubtedly anticipates in some
ways.

72.7–9. The Archbishop, as a man of God, is concerned that
Wymound should confess his sin and receive absolution, not submit
under torture and perhaps die unrepentant; but even warnings of hell-
fire do not avail.

72.12. Zupitza's assumption that the rhyme-tag *in dede* has been inadvertently substituted for original *wiþ alle* (understandably, in view
of the rhymes in the next stanza) is certainly justified.

75.5. T argues plausibly that 'the Elms' means Tyburn, rather than
the place at Smithfield with that name, and notes that elms were used
for hanging malefactors.

75.7f. Dying an unrepentant traitor, Wymound is to receive no
burial but rot on the gallows. For the fierce animus against traitors in
this final stanza, see also *Hav.* 2481–90 (C). There might be some confusion here with the punishment of tearing apart by means of horses
(why do we need more than one horse to drag him to the gallows?).

Sir Orfeo

Sir Orfeo is preserved in MS. Advocates' 19.2.1 in the National Library of Scotland (A, the Auchinleck MS.), MS. Harley 3810 in the British Library (H), and MS. Ashmole 61 in the Bodleian Library, Oxford (B). The two last present an inferior version of the text and have been little used in this edition except to supply the defective beginning of the Auchinleck text. Both of them belong to the fifteenth century, the Auchinleck to the early part of the fourteenth. The poem occupies ff. 300–303 (col. 1) in the latter; the first thirty-eight or so lines have been lost, evidently as the result of the excision of a leaf from the MS., of which they would probably have occupied one column. The leaf may have been cut out for the sake of an illumination which would have stood at the beginning of the poem.

The three texts of the poem have been admirably edited by A. J. Bliss, *Sir Orfeo*, Oxford, 1951; the Auchinleck text, with the beginning supplied from Harley, is also to be found in K. Sisam, *Fourteenth Century Verse and Prose*, Oxford, 1921, etc., no. ii.

1–38. These lines, missing from A (see above), appear in one form or another in H and B. The first twenty-four lines of what is clearly the same prologue appear, however, as the prologue to the romance *Lay le Freine* on f. 261 of A. It is not clear to which of the two the prologue was originally attached; if, as Bliss suggests, the two are in fact by the same author, the lines may have been intended as an all-purpose prologue for these texts and perhaps for others (Bliss, *op. cit.*, pp. xliv–xlvii; 'The Case Against Common Authorship of *Lay Le Freine* and *Sir Orfeo*' is argued by John B. Beston at some length in *MÆ* XLV (1976), 153–63). In any event the *Freine* prologue provides an earlier version of lines 1–24 than H or B, and must be considered in the reconstruction of the text. For lines 25–38 we have only evidence of the two later MSS. In attempting to restore the text we have followed the principles put forward by Bliss, '*Sir Orfeo*, lines 1–46', *English and Germanic Studies* v (1953), 7–14, though not invariably following his readings.

1–24. The *Prologue* was probably first composed for *SO* and used again for *Lai le Freine* (see G. Guillaume, 'The Prologues of the *Lay le Freine* and *Sir Orfeo*' (*MLN* xxvi (1921), 458–64) and Bliss xlv for supporting evidence). The fact that the lays were sung to the harp seems to make Orfeo a specially appropriate hero for one. Of the types of subject-matter outlined in ll. 5–12, *fairy* and *love* are illustrated in *SO* (for *wer* see *Sir Degarré*). The range covered by the genre seems very wide (from 'love' to *ribaudy*—though religious themes are not mentioned), but the main defining feature is *ferli*, a conclusion supported by *mervailles* at line 18. Many of the ideas in this Prologue can be found in the *Lais* of Marie de France, e.g. with 13–16 compare Marie's *Prologue*, 35–8; with 15, *Guigemar*, 24–6.

13–16. A has *In breteyne bi hold time/þis layes were wrouȝt so seiþ þis rime*; the following couplet is in HB only. But the lines may well be genuine, and A's couplet looks very much like a padded version of H's line 13, *In Brytayn þis layes arne y-wrytt*. Yet H's couplet, which continues *Furst y-founde and forþe y-gete*, violates the careful rhyming practice of the A text, and must be corrected from B, where the rhyme-words are *i-wrouȝt* and *brouȝht*; cf. line 14 in A. A's *were*, moreover, gives a better sense than H's *arne*.

23. *Lordinges þat beþ trewe* introduces the idea of *trewþe* that forms the poem's main theme (see Introduction, pp. 26–8). *fairi* here means 'fairyland', 'the land of the fays', or 'the fays' collectively (OF *fee*, which comes from Lat. *fata*, 'the Fates'). Ideas about fairyland in the Breton lays are drawn from the common stock of Celtic folklore. See the descriptions of the otherworld in the story of *Pwyll* in the *Mabinogion* (Everyman ed., translated by Gwyn Jones and Thomas Jones (London, 1945, repr. 1973)) and Marie de France's *lai* of *Yonec*, especially ll. 360–4 (in *Les Lais de Marie de France*, ed. J. Rychner, Paris, 1971). See further H. R. Patch, *The Other World* (Cambridge, Mass., 1950) and Theodore Spencer, 'Chaucer's Hell: a Study in Medieval Convention' (*Spec.* 2 (1927), 177–200). J. B. Friedman, in *Orpheus in the Middle Ages* (Cambridge, Mass., 1970), pp. 191–2, finds some influence from Bk. VI of Virgil's *Aeneid*, especially ll. 637ff.

23f. The *Freine* prologue, naturally enough, rhymes on *soþe to sayn* and *Lay le Freine* instead of *þat ben trewe* and *Sir Orphewe* as in H.

25–38. In these, as in the preceding lines, the spelling has been as far as possible adjusted to the practice of A. The text is based on lines 33–46 of H (which are preceded by eight lines corresponding to A 39–46), occasionally corrected from B.

29. *lerned* B is much preferable to *loved* H, since it makes an additional point rather than stating a commonplace, and gives meaning to *him-self*.

33. *al* from B gives a more idiomatic expression; but Bliss's rejection of *neuer* H in favour of *no* B seems unnecessary.

37. An allusion to the angelic harmony heard in Heaven. The reference, suitable to its subject Orfeo (see also 438 (C) and 527 (C) below) contrasts with the likening of the Fairy King's court to Paradise at 376, heavily ironic in view of the palace's grisly contents (391–404).

38. *joy* H is superfluous, besides upsetting the metre, and has presumably come in from the previous line.

39. Only after 15 lines on Orfeo as a harper do we learn he is a king (though this is implied in 17–20). The musician-king is part of epic tradition (Hroþgar in *Beowulf* may be an example) but Biblical influence may also be relevant, since David is often represented in medieval art as the master-musician (cf. also his playing the harp to calm Saul in I Sam. 16, 23); on the existence of a medieval Orpheus-David tradition in literature and MS. illustration see Friedman, *op.*

cit., especially pp. 148–55. Friedman mentions the account of David as patron and organiser of musicians in I Chron. 15, 16–25 (p. 148) and notes that the association with David may account for Orfeo's being made a king (p. 155).

40. *lording* is here an otiose rhyming-tag of the kind typical in popular romances (cf. 23 above, where it is flatteringly aimed at the audience). Chaucer satirised minstrel-style in his tale of *Sir Thopas*.

42. *Largesse* was a kingly quality much valued by minstrels. It is later displayed (along with courtesy) by the Fairy King in his readiness to hear Orfeo play (444) and reward him when pleased (451). Orfeo's miraculous success is made to reflect glory on the art of the 'povre menstrels'.

43–6. The author of *SO* was clearly no classical scholar, to judge by his making Jupiter's wife a king. We may therefore refrain from seeing significance in the 'King Pluto' who is Orfeo's paternal ancestor even though Pluto was the classical god of the underworld and is called by Chaucer in *The Merchant's Tale* 'Pluto, that is *king of Fayerye*' (E 2227), since there is no hint that the Fairy King of our poem is related to Orfeo. Although the 'classical' side of the poem is not developed, an elementary decorum is observed in excluding explicit Christianity—a fact which may have led Chaucer to do likewise in his experiment in the Breton-lay genre *The Franklin's Tale*.

47–50. If the English author took the name 'Traciens' from his OF source, he might have found himself forced, when he decided to set the story in 'Inglond' and make Orfeo's seat its old capital, to claim 'Traciens' as the ancient name of Winchester. (If the OF original had *li reis Traciens*, 'the Thracian king' (i.e. Orfeo), then the *SO* poet presumably misinterpreted it as 'the king of Traciens', taking Traciens as the name of a place.) Taken seriously, *withouten no* would imply an audience too ignorant to know otherwise, but again it is only a tag; cf. 40, also *Hav.* 158 (C).

57–72. The setting of the abduction in May seems to have no significance beyond the fact that this was a traditionally happy time. The orchard is important, however, for it is an ostensibly secure place (cf. January's secluded orchard in *The Merchant's Tale*), not like the obviously perilous forest of *Sir Degarré* where the Fairy Knight rapes the Princess. The meaning of the *ympe-tre* that replaces the chestnut or other forest tree is obscure. If it symbolises the 'entrance' of the fairy world into the human world, it is hard to see how the audience would have grasped this. But its re-appearance at 407 confirms its significance, mysterious as that may be.

75–6. Midday was a traditionally perilous time, perhaps because of the Biblical phrase 'the destruction that wasteth at noonday' in Psalm 91, 6 (Vulgate, xc, 6: *daemonio meridiano*), which implied a special potency of the powers of evil at this time, as well as at the conventional midnight. It is in 'hot undertides' (281–2) that Orfeo glimpses the fairy band in the wilderness (58 suggests that *hot* weather is somehow especially associated with supernatural occurrences). Friedman's suggestion (*op. cit.*, p. 190) that the Fairy King *is* the noonday devil (=Satan) is unconvincing.

78–82. Heurodis' symptoms suggest that what she has undergone in sleep was no mere dream; rather, the powers of the otherworld have invaded her psyche in a manner that recalls possession by devils as described in the Bible (e.g. Mark 9, 16–28).

90. *sexti* was often used in ME for an indefinitely large number (cf. 304). It seems unlikely that the 'hundred' damsels of 143–4 is meant to indicate a numerical superiority on the part of the fairy antagonists: Orfeo's *thousand* knights (183) prove impotent against them (cf. 291).

103. A delicately humanising touch. Heurodis's 'stillness' is again illustrated at 324 and in the tableau-scene of 407–9. After finishing her account at 174 Heurodis does not speak again.

105–13. In this exquisite speech the traditional terms of praise for the lady used in lyrics alternate with images depicting Heurodis's distraught condition. There may be some influence from the descriptions of Christ in Crucifixion lyrics, such as *Candet nudatum pectus* (in Carleton Brown's *Religious Lyrics of the 14th century* (Oxford, 1924 etc.), no. 1).

108. MS. could read *as wan* or *al wan*: Bliss prefers the latter.

126. Elliptical: Heurodis means 'Do your best to endure my loss' rather than 'Do your best to prevent it'. Cf. also the stark line 200.

134. The pathos of *our* is intensified by *owhen* at 163 (C) below.

150. *gold red:* gold alloyed with copper, which had a reddish hue (also at 362); cf. the *burnist gold* of 368, gold polished to a high lustre.

156. *palfray*, a small saddle-horse for riding, used especially by ladies, distinguished from the large heavy steed or war-horse. The Fairy in Marie's *Lanval* rides a '*blanc palefrei*' (551), 'a white palfrey comlye' (*Landevale*, 427).

163. The *owhen* poignantly expresses an unfulfillable wish: Heurodis has already said *Y mot go* (126). *owhen* conveys the intimacy of their relationship and hints at its fragility—and perhaps that of all earthly happiness (cf. a similar effect at 322, where *owhen* further emphasises their separateness, also 479, 485 below).

170–4. The reality of the Fairy King's threat is later confirmed by the sight Orfeo has of the dismembered figures in the fairy palace (388–404, especially 391–2). It is not stated explicitly that these were people who resisted being 'taken', but that meaning is suggested by 389–90 taken with 403–4. (Friedman, *op. cit.*, 193–4, makes this point also.) With the Fairy King's imperious behaviour, compare that of the Fairy Knight in *SD* 107–12, whose power seems less formidable inasmuch as his exploit is scarcely beyond a mortal's scope.

176–8. A fine effect of plaintiveness is achieved by the 'l'-alliteration of these lines.

179–80. The repetition of *man* adumbrates the futility of merely human effort at 183–94.

187. The OE *scyld-truma* was a defensive formation in which the soldiers locked their shields to form a wall and roof. The scene is patently non-realistic, being intended to suggest an immensely large protecting force which proves ineffective. The presentation of earthly chivalry impotent against supernatural forces anticipates the hero's encounter with an enchanted figure in *Sir Gawain and the Green Knight*.

193. The first appearance of this sinister word, the pleasant modern overtones of which are largely the creation of Shakespeare in *A Midsummer Night's Dream* (though Chaucer's *Wife of Bath's Tale* (D 857–81), written less than a century after *SO*, already treats fairies with an affectionate playfulness stemming from disbelief in their existence). The fairy world of *SO* is in deadly earnest.

194. An important line. There is no question of mounting a 'search' for Heurodis such as Lancelot undertakes for Guinevere in Chrétien's *Lancelot*, which seems to be a rationalised account of the abduction of a mortal woman by a fairy.

205. The term *steward* has lost dignity since the Middle Ages, when it corresponded to OF *seneschal*, a high official of the royal household who was usually a great noble of the realm, and thus able to act as deputy in the sovereign's absence. The poet may also have wished to exploit the associations the word had acquired from the Gospel story of the faithful steward (cf. 415–16 (C)), but stewards in romance were traditionally disloyal and villainous (cf. *Hav.* 666), a fact which justifies the steward's testing at the end.

213. Orfeo's words echo Heurodis's reporting the Fairy King at 167–8. His resolve is no mere impulsive gesture but faithfully fulfills (if only in a sadly symbolic way) the first part of his affirmation at 129–30 (the second has now become impossible).

225. *schal* has a sense of external obligation, destiny almost, and does not express wilfulness as in the Fairy King's warning at 167.

229. *kirtel*, a man's tunic usually worn with a shirt (230) under a mantle.

230. An extra *no* is necessary, if clumsy. The scribe's confusion is understandable. The abandonment of all possessions as well as the renunciation of women are Orfeo's way of making his lot resemble that of Heurodis as closely as possible. The *sclavin* and bare feet show his wish to suffer; the retention of the harp points the difference between voluntary self-denial and mere despair (contrast Ywain in *YG*, who keeps no memorial of his knightly past during the period of his madness in the wilderness and is recognised only by a scar, *YG* 1719–22).

238ff. See Introduction, pp. 24–5, for an analysis of this passage. Orfeo's régime is that of the most ascetic hermits (cf. Ywain, who is fed with bread by a somewhat less ascetic hermit, *YG* 1671–1708). The ten-year period of privation, which renders Orfeo unrecognisable to the Fairy King as well as to his steward, may be a distant echo of the wanderings of Homer's Odysseus. Heurodis's recognition of Orfeo at 323–7 testifies to her love. That Orfeo recognises *her* in the fairy world 'bi her cloþes' (408) suggests that she too has changed physically, even if they are the same clothes in which she was abducted and the static picture of her beneath the same *ympe-tre* implies changelessness. (Cf. the indefinite *bi al þing* at 321.)

283. *o* for *of* ought probably to be allowed to stand. But one of two consecutive *f*s could easily be lost.

285. The common ancestor of the readings in the other MSS. (H *dv(n)nyng*, B *dy(n)ne*) was probably *dune* or *dine*, 'din', 'noise'. The context would appear to imply noise rather than the opposite. On the other hand, the hunt is remote from this world to the extent that it catches nothing, so *dim* (quite apart from its romantic flavour) can be defended as a genuine 'harder reading' and so more likely to be of authorial than scribal origin; cf. Chaucer's *Knight's Tale*, *CT* A 2433.

288, 296. The echo of 194 reminds us of the mysteriousness of the fairy world, which nonetheless does have a location in space.

314. Orfeo's laugh is the first break in ten years' gloom. The phrase 'on a day' (303) sharply distinguishes this occasion from the many glimpses of the elusive fairy world recorded in 281–302, with the mocking simulacra of human hunting and dancing to which Orfeo cannot respond. The sixty ladies here are manifestly humans, and their falcons really kill their prey, whereas the fairy hunt 'no best . . . no nome' (287).

324–7. Bliss puts a stop after *heiȝe* (326) and a comma after *speke* (324), glossing this with an inexplicable note (*ed. cit.*, p. 53). But the failure of either to speak cannot be caused by the pity she feels for him. The punctuation here given makes it clear that Heurodis's pity is real enough but is manifested in her tears, not (how could it be?) in their joint silence. This is logically correct as well as emotionally fitting.

331–42. Perhaps the most moving lines in the poem, outstanding in ME romance for simple truthfulness of feeling and perfect sincerity of expression.

343–6. Only at this point does Orfeo, with pilgrim's cloak and harp on back, set out on a *search* for Heurodis (cf. Introduction, pp. 26–7), fulfilling his pledge at 129 ('Whider þou gost Ichil wiþ þe') now in a *literal* sense (cf. 231 (C) above).

351–76. Friedman aptly calls fairyland a 'counterworld' or 'parallel land' (*op. cit.*, pp. 190–1).

355. *launde* H ('clearing') could be defended as a less usual word than *londe* A, and so more likely to be corrupted than the other way about. No forest, however, has been mentioned. Castles might be expected to be found in clearings (cf. for example, *Sir Gawain and the Green Knight* 765) and *launde* may be a scribal 'improvement'.

361–4. A 'flying buttress'; the cheapness of 'red gold' in the otherworld is shown by its use for mere structural work, which explains why it was too mean to be used in the Fairy King's crown (150 and (C)). A 'voussoir' is properly one of the wedge-shaped stones making up an arch, a surprisingly technical term for an unlearned poet; here perhaps used loosely for 'vaulting'.

376. A pregnant line. The description does indeed bring to mind the Heavenly City of the Apocalypse (Rev. 21) and looks forward to such elaborated developments of the latter as that in the late 14th century poem *Pearl* (973ff.); but *proude* is an unexpected epithet— until we remember its appropriateness to the arrogant Fairy King. The only other use of 'Paradis' is in praising Orfeo's harping (37). The contrast could not be more telling; it exemplifies the *Orfeo*-poet's poetic conciseness at its height (cf. also 415–16 (C) below).

382–6. The porter's alacrity in admitting Orfeo (if *anon* is not just a vapid rhyme-word) suggests the popularity of visiting minstrels (but cf. 430–4). We should perhaps see the porter's action rather as fulfilling the desire of the minstrel-class to which the author belonged for enthusiastic receptions. On the medieval tradition of Orpheus the Minstrel, see Friedman (*op. cit.*, pp. 158–9).

387–404. This frightening description may have contributed to Chaucer's Temple of Mars in *The Knight's Tale* (A 1967–2041). Bruce Mitchell's suggestion ('The Faery World of *Sir Orfeo*', *Neophilologus* xlviii (1964), 155–9) that ll. 391–402 may be a scribal addition because they do not occur in MS. H is hard to credit. It does not weaken Dorena Allen's argument ('Orpheus and Orfeo: the Dead and the *Taken*', *MÆ* XXIII (1964), 102–11) that an ancient Celtic belief existed that some apparently dead people had really been 'taken' by the fairies (see ll. 389–90). However, the passage resists complete explanation. Line 400 states unequivocally that some *were* dead (presumably the headless, strangled, and so on) while others had been carried off sleeping or mad (Heurodis's own condition on waking in the orchard bore traces of madness). But the emotional effect of 'þis mervails alle' (409) is overwhelming and needs no rational exposition: the fairy world emerges as indisputably potent *and* malign.

415–16. Any suggestion of Christ's transfiguration (Matt. 17, 4; Luke 9, 33) that may be aroused by the use of *tabernacle* earlier at 412 (Vulgate: *faciamus . . . tabernacula*) must be wholly ironical (cf. 376 (C) above). Orfeo himself is faintly suggestive of Christ rescuing imprisoned humanity from the bonds of hell, and there was an ancient tradition of Orpheus-Christus (discussed by Friedman, *op. cit.*, ch. III), but the poem's symbolism works on a universal archetypal rather than a typological, Christian level. The arguments of Penelope Doob (*Nebuchadnezzar's Children* (New Haven and London, 1974) pp. 181–3) are unconvincing (cf. Friedman, *op. cit.*, p. 190).

430. Orfeo's untruth is a white lie, not a serious breach of fidelity (cf. also 536–40 (C) below and Introduction, pp. 27–8). The advantage

held by his fairy adversary justifies the stratagem (cf. Gawain's attempted use of a magical girdle against his supernatural challenger, the Green Knight).

438. *blisseful* is here used unironically, as again in 527 (cf. also 412 and 376 (C), 415–16 (C), and recalls the paradisal melody of 37–8.

439–41. The court recumbent at Orfeo's feet recalls the kneeling courtiers of 249–50. Orfeo's self-restoration is accomplished through his art, which triumphs over fairy power. His suffering and humility enable him to achieve as a 'povre menstrel' what he could not as a king with 'ten hundred knights'. The poem can stand an allegorical reading which would see harping as the symbol of a life of virtuous self-discipline leading to spiritual victory, with the taming of the animals easily recognisable as the subduing of the passions within a man: an interpretation found as early as Clement of Alexandria's *Protrepticon* (discussed by Friedman, *op. cit.*, pp. 58ff.), though Clement is unfavourably *contrasting* the song of Orpheus with the 'new song' of Christianity. Friedman also shows how 'David's curing of Saul by music was equated with Orpheus's taming of beasts' (*op. cit.*, p. 55, and see his references on p. 145).

457–62. The Fairy King judges by appearances, Heurodis with the eyes of love (323–7).

463–8. The observance of *troupe*, obligatory for all men, has been universally regarded as a specially sacred duty of kings and rulers (for famous Biblical examples, see in the OT Jephthah's vow (Judges 11, 30) and in the NT Herod's promise to Salome (Mark 6, 22–8, especially verse 26).

469–71. The irascible tone of the Fairy King's words is confirmed by the double *swipe* of 472, 474. The former's rhyme with *blipe* in 471 is especially effective (it recurs at 593–4 below). Orfeo and Heurodis make away before the Fairy King can have second thoughts.

475. It is tempting to reject *out of þat pede* as a dittography from 474 *out of þat lond* and emend to *into his owhen þede*. But H supports A with *out of þat stede*, and B's *out off þat palas* points back to a reading similar to that of H (through intermediate *plas* for *stede*?).

477ff. The whole disguise-episode recalls the return of Odysseus, the harp corresponding in some degree to Odysseus' bow.

479, 485. The word *owhen* now has acquired new resonance since it last appeared (see 163 (C) above).

497. The return at midday seems appropriate, since it reverses the defeat that took place ten years before at that time of day.

508. No doubt the wrinkled appearance of bark is intended, perhaps suggested by Orfeo's long hair and beard, which make him look like a tree.

521–3. The crowd of musicians proves that Orfeo's steward has kept up faithfully his master's patronage of good players (cf. 27–9).

522. *crouders* were players of the *crowd* (Welsh *crwth*), an ancient

Celtic instrument with six strings, four played with a bow and two twitched with the fingers.

527. *blissful notes;* cf. 33–8 and 438 (C) above. The suggestion of heavenly blessedness is faint but real, like a flower-smell at night.

530. The steward cannot have failed to recognise Orfeo's unique musicianship because he thinks Orfeo is already 'spent' (cf. 215 above): no new king has yet been elected. The reason is purely dramatic: a real test of his loyalty is impossible unless Orfeo can first succeed in making his steward believe he *is* dead.

536–40. Orfeo's justification in telling this untruth—his being killed by the animals is a charming piece of fiction!—is that as king he has the right to test his deputy's loyalty (cf. the behaviour of Shakespeare's Duke in *Measure for Measure*). It is not *untroupe* in the sense of breach of pledge; cf. 430 (C) above.

544–5. An echo of 333–4. The steward's loyalty to Orfeo parallels the latter's to Heurodis. The swooning at 549 (recalling Orfeo's swoon at 197) completes the parallel.

558–74. This long sentence with its eight conditional clauses is structurally reminiscent of lines 241–56 above (and see Introduction, p. 25).

578–9. A typically vivid 'behaviouristic' description (of the kind Chaucer uses in *The Clerk's Tale*, E 1100–1103). The authorial comment at 583 seems weak and gratuitous.

596. The steward's succession to the throne, necessitated by the theme of '*troupe* rewarded', varies the conventional romance ending— the begetting of a numerous progeny (cf. *Hav.* 2977–83).

591. The 'wepe and wo' of 195 have been turned into tears of 'joie', a reversal hinted in ll. 5–6 of the Prologue.

598–9. The author's assertion that Breton harpers turned this *mervaille* into a lay recalls ll. 18–20.

602. Possibly conventional; but a sung *lai* about Orfeo could have existed.

603–4. The usual minstrel-ending of a blessing on the audience is revitalised by the preceding story of a truly marvellous deliverance from 'care'.

Select Bibliography

Collections of Texts
French, W. H. and Hale, C. B., eds.: *Middle English Metrical Romances* (New York, 1930).
Mills, M., ed.: *Six Middle English Romances* (London, 1973).
Sands, D. B., ed.: *Middle English Verse Romances* (New York, 1966).

General Studies
Auerbach, Erich (tr. W. R. Trask): *Mimesis* (Princeton, 1953) (ch. 6).
Baugh, A. C.: 'The Authorship of the Middle English Romances', *Annual Bulletin of the Modern Humanities Research Association*, 22 (1950), 13–28.
——: 'Improvisation in the Middle English Romance', *Proceedings of the American Philosophical Society*, 103 (1959), 418–54.
——: 'The Middle English Romance: Some Questions of Creation, Presentation, and Preservation', *Speculum*, XLII (1967), 1–31.
Gradon, Pamela: *Form and Style in Early English Literature* (London, 1971) (Ch. 4).
Ker, W. P.: *Epic and Romance* (2nd edn. repr., New York, 1957).
Loomis, R. S.: *The Development of Arthurian Romance* (London, 1963).
Mehl, Dieter: *The Middle English Romances of the Thirteenth and Fourteenth Centuries* (London, 1968).
Pearsall, Derek: 'The Development of Middle English Romance', *Medieval Studies* 27 (1965), 91–117.
——: 'The English Romance in the Fifteenth Century', *Essays and Studies* (1976), 56–83.
Stevens, John: *Medieval Romance: Themes and Approaches* (London, 1973) rev. by A.V.C.S. in *Times Literary Supplement*, August 31, 1973, p. 1008).
Vinaver, Eugène: *The Rise of Romance* (Oxford, 1971).

Background
Dronke, Peter: *Medieval Latin and the Rise of the European Love-Lyric* (2 vols, Oxford 1965–6) (Vol. I is a re-valuation of 'Courtly Love').
Lewis, C. S.: *The Allegory of Love* (Oxford, 1936).
Painter, Sidney: *French Chivalry* (Baltimore, 1940).
Mathew, Gervase: *The Court of Richard II* (London, 1963).
Southern, R. W.: *The Making of the Middle Ages* (London, 1953).
There are good select bibliographies in Mehl and Stevens (see above) and the standard reference work on romance is Severs, J. B., ed.: *A Manual of Writings in Middle English* 1050–1500 (New Haven, 1967), I. An annual summary guide to work on romances is provided in the chapter of *The Year's Work in English Studies* on 'Middle English: Excluding Chaucer' (section on 'Romances').